The Sea
Was Our Village

Other Sailing Classics

Miles Smeeton

The Sea
Was Our Village

GRAFTON BOOKS

A Division of the Collins Publishing Group

LONDON GLASGOW
TORONTO SYDNEY AUCKLAND

To Pwe, who shared our life for 18 years

Grafton Books
A Division of the Collins Publishing Group
8 Grafton Street, London W1X 3LA

First published by Nautical Books 1973

This edition published by Grafton Books 1986

British Library Cataloguing in Publication Data

Smeeton, Miles
    The sea was our village.
    1. Voyages and travels   2. Yachts and yachting
    —North Atlantic Ocean   3. Yachts and yachting
    —Pacific Ocean
    I. Title
    910'.091631   G477

ISBN 0 246 12922 0

Printed in Great Britain by
Mackays of Chatham Ltd.

Contents

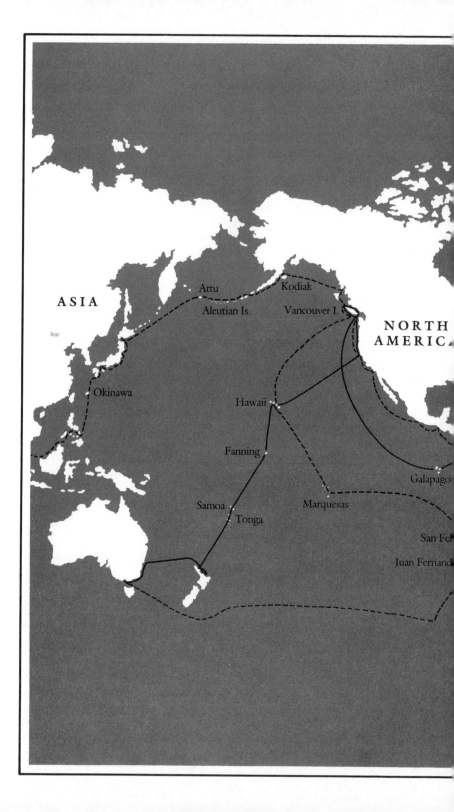

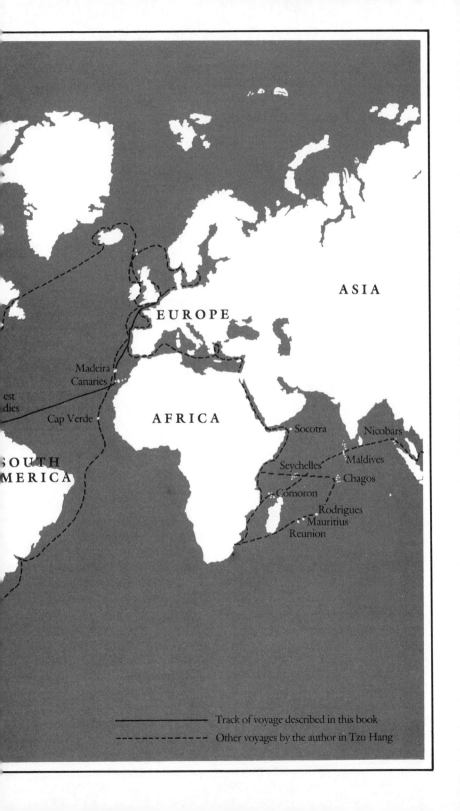

ASIA

EUROPE

Madeira
Canaries

est
dies

Cap Verde

AFRICA

Socotra   Nicobars

Seychelles   Maldives

Chagos

Comoron

SOUTH
AMERICA

Rodrigues
Mauritius
Reunion

——————— Track of voyage described in this book

- - - - - - - - Other voyages by the author in Tzu Hang

First Voyage

When Beryl and I, with Clio, aged nine, set off from Canada to buy a yacht in England and to sail it to British Columbia, even our staunchest friends would have had to admit that we had very little sailing experience to justify such an undertaking.

Neither of us had ever read a yachting magazine, unless while waiting at the dentist, and neither of us had ever been on a ship, excluding troopships and liners, longer than sixteen feet, which was the size of our small open motor-boat, that had so often carried us between Salt Spring Island and Vancouver Island, a few miles away.

Beryl is apt to say that the only time that she and I had ever been in a sailing boat was when—before we were married—I took her for a sail in a small yacht in Karachi, and sank it before we were out of the harbour. Like most wives' tales, there is a foundation of truth in this. We did sink, but we sailed back, with the hull and ourselves almost completely submerged, like midget submariners under jury rig—a prophetic journey. On the other hand, I had a little more experience than she gives me credit for. When a soldier in Egypt, I had sailed occasionally on Lake Timsah, particularly when the wind blew strongly, driving the sand before it like spindrift in a gale, and making other forms of sport ashore difficult or impossible. Once also I had sailed round Hong Kong Island, with a friend with a stiff leg to help me, who became so seasick on the seaward side of the island that he lay in the bottom of the boat with his stiff leg pointing skywards, so that I had to dip it every time we came about.

That was the limit of our experience. There was no superfluity of salt in our veins, no special unsatisfied longing to sail the seven seas, neither of us had been bred on the water, but since we had

9

come to live on the edge of the Pacific Ocean, and since one
boat leads to another, we had begun to think of owning something
rather larger than our small motor-boat, and of exploring the
sounds, inlets and islands of the lovely coast that had become
our home. The spur that pricked the sides of our intent was
economic. We were running short of money in Canada and,
owing to the financial restrictions then in force, were unable to
transfer money from England to the place where it was wanted—
our farm on Salt Spring Island. Perhaps it was just as well.
It might have gone down the drain. However, we decided to
buy a boat in England and to sail her out and sell her in Canada.
This decision was a turning point in our lives. From then on we
were first engaged, and later wedded, to the sea.

On arrival in England, and after leaving Clio under the stern
rule of a governess and the care of an aunt in Yorkshire, Beryl
and I set about looking for a ship. We had no very clear idea of
what we wanted. In those days there were not so many small
ships that had done long passages, nor were there so many
literate or partially literate adventurers from whom to gather
information. We had read *The Cruise of the* Spray, *Deep Water
and Shoal, The Cruise of the* Teddy, and *The Cruise of the* Idle
Hour. Then there was a book by Marin Marie, and Allcard's
story of his first voyage in *Temptress*, and that was about as far
as our reading had taken us. Now we grasped at anything on
sailing that we could find. We did not appreciate, since we knew
nothing, the ability of the small off-shore ocean racers then
making a name for themselves; yachts like *Cohoe* and *Samuel
Pepys*. The Vertue class we considered, and perhaps rightly,
too small for the sort of prolonged cruising that we wanted to
do on our way to Canada, and bigger, more modern yachts
would be beyond the reach of our pockets. We were thinking
more in terms of something about twenty tons, flush-decked,
strongly built, preferably a ketch, with not too large a sail area
for two people to handle, and perhaps of necessity rather old.
During our search for a yacht, our enthusiasms veered hither
and thither, and we had fleeting affairs first with one yacht and
then another, but slowly and inevitably we felt our way to our
one and only lasting love.

Our search took us all over England, and up to Scotland.
We saw a yacht in Essex, whose mast stood tall above the trees

in an inland field. She looked as if some tidal wave had washed her there, as indeed it had, and deposited her in a mud berth in a tiny creek, far from the river and further still from the sea. Round her the curlews piped the passing hours, until the sun should shine again, the yellow grass turn green, and men come on a spring tide to work her down to the river. In these surroundings the mast looked extremely tall and the hull too slender for Atlantic seas, but now I know that she would have been a good ship for what was then our intention, although not for the life that we were eventually to lead.

In Scotland we saw a massive double-ender, built to withstand all kinds of hardship and to outlast three generations, but always at a solemn pace. In Liverpool there was a steel yacht from Hamburg, war loot, covered with smuts outside and damp and sweaty within. In Lymington we saw a big ketch, built on National Lifeboat lines, with an inventory like a store catalogue and a great and highly polished diesel engine. "She'll never drown you. She may starve you," said the owner of the yard who was showing us round. If she didn't starve us we could have sold her for twice the price that was being asked because she was cheap and in splendid condition, but she looked too big and complicated for Beryl and me.

There were many others, but our nearest escape was in Dover, where there was a Colin Archer designed Norwegian double-ender for sale. The owner had offered her for service during the war, provided that he stayed on board. She had been used for running agents in and out of Norway, and for other duties related to the Resistance. Now that she had returned to more peaceful tasks, the owner and his family had continued to live on board, but the time had come to leave her. We had lunch on board and the owner told us long tales of her war-time and later adventures. She still had a bullet in her mast from one of her escapades, and this romantic touch decided Beryl and me that we must have her, in spite of her heavy gaff rig and ponderous size.

"But how can you bring yourself to sell her?" Beryl asked.

"Oh, my God," he said, suddenly realising that this was no longer a future possibility, but that this was, here and now, a sale. "I don't think I can." He buried his head in his hands. Then, suddenly looking up with a ray of hope in his eyes, he said, "Look here. Before you make any decisions, why don't you go and look at the Chinese yacht across the harbour? She'd do you splendidly, and I know that she's for sale."

"A Chinese yacht," said Beryl, her eyes lighting to match his, for she loves all things Chinese. "Come on. Let's go and see her."

We left the owner pouring himself another liqueur brandy, smuggled from France, no doubt, and something else perhaps that he would miss, should he finally make up his mind to sell his boat.

Across the other side of the harbour and secured to the wall we found *Tzu Hang*. She was all that we had pictured as the sort of ship that we should like to own, but it also looked unlikely that we would be able to afford to buy her. With her canoe stern and flush deck she appeared to our inexperienced eyes as the epitome of seaworthiness, and from the shape of her deck, seen from above, it seemed that she would be no sluggard. She had a jaunty look about her, as if she had called in for a moment, and was ready to leave if she did not like the harbour. The upward tilt of her short bowsprit, following the sheer of her deck, gave this look a touch of arrogance. "You'll never know until you sail her, whether you have bought a bitch or not," a sailor friend had told us in Canada, but there was nothing about our first impression of *Tzu Hang* that suggested bitchiness.

Up to now, most of the yachts that we had seen, because of the price limit up to which we were prepared to go, had been elderly, between twenty and fifty years old. Here was one which looked positively modern.

"We'll never be able to afford her," said Beryl.

"Her masts look rather thin," said I, out of the depth of my experience.

"But she's lovely, isn't she?"

"She's got a nice small doghouse, and a small cockpit," I continued, thinking that it would make little difference to her if it was filled with water, but never imagining that one day it might make all the difference between whether she sank or whether she swam.

"Well, let's go and ask about her anyway," said Beryl, the Norwegian double-ender already forgotten.

We hurried down the quay to a small boat yard where the manager told us that *Tzu Hang* was indeed for sale, but at double the price that we had set as our limit. He led us down a vertical iron ladder, from where for the first time we stepped on to *Tzu Hang*'s deck. She was absolutely motionless, and to our surprise did not appear to stir as we trod the edge of her deck. She felt strong and dependable, almost as if she was holding her breath as she summed us up; as if she knew already what we were beginning to suspect, that she would have as great an influence on our life as we would have on hers. We moved silently about her deck, not knowing what to say, but imagining all things, things yearned for, things beyond our reach.

Down below there was a clean smell of teak. She was well built and rather dark, with every locker and door solid and well-finished, as if weight had never been considered. Her floors were up and her bilges, newly painted with red lead, were absolutely dry. Although there was much to criticise in her layout, we knew so little and were so entranced by what we saw, that we never noticed it. We found that there was headroom for me, accommodation for the three of us, and that the galley was aft. The union was a mystical one. Two people groping in the dark had laid their hands on something that they knew, without knowledge, was good. We climbed the ladder again and said good-bye to the yard manager.

"I'm afraid that she's more than we can afford," I said.

"But she's lovely," said Beryl.

As we walked down the quay we paused to look back at her, the first of a thousand times.

"Too bad," I said, but *Tzu Hang* laughed.

"Thou sayest farewell, and lo," she said,
"I have thee by the hands,
And will not let thee go."

Although I did not know it, Beryl's mind was made up. We went on looking at yachts, but her heart was left in Dover, and sometimes she did not even bother to accompany me on my quest. I found a ketch called *Owl*, which I liked and whose name I thought would attract Beryl, but she seemed uninterested, so that ultimately we found ourselves in Southampton, negotiating with Charles Nicholson, who had *Tzu Hang* on his books. Rarely could two people have come to possess such a sizeable yacht, who knew so little about yachting. Charles Nicholson seemed to have got the same idea, for the next day we got a letter from him saying that he was extremely worried about two such inexperienced people setting out on such an ambitious cruise. He said that he had known so many great hopes founder on lack of knowledge, and that the upkeep of a ship of *Tzu Hang*'s size was usually far more than was expected. He suggested that as the sale was still in his hands, we might like to cancel it. He added that these fears were probably due to an attack of 'flu, from which he was suffering, and that we would probably tear up the letter and continue with our plans. If we were to continue, however, he strongly recommended that we should take with us an experienced crew. It was the letter of a kind and sensitive man, and, like much good advice, it received little attention, although I kept the letter for years.

Suddenly *Tzu Hang* was ours. Beryl and I moved on board. We only once caught a fleeting glimpse of the owner, disappearing down the quay, and it was not for many years that we met him and we became friends. At that time he could not bear to meet the people who had bought his ship, lest they should turn out to be unsuitable for her. He had had her built in Hong Kong just before the war, and she had been shipped home at its beginning. All through the war, the thought of sailing in *Tzu Hang* when it was over had buoyed his spirits and many were the cruises that he had planned for himself and his family. Some of them he had achieved, but not sufficient to soften the pain of parting with her.

It was the first day of March. A grey day with rain splattering and a wind that made us lean against the gusts as we walked down the wet quay. There were gale warnings for Sole, Plymouth, Portland and Wight. A yacht put in to Dover, over from Holland. Beryl and I watched her rolling at anchor in the outer harbour, and were appalled by the motion, as her mast swayed across the tattered sky and her bow lifted and fell to the swell. If a yacht behaved like this in harbour, what on earth was it going to be like at sea. During the next few days, while gale warnings persisted and our anxiety rose, we sometimes saw the skipper of this yacht, broad-shouldered, ruddy-cheeked, and young, striding confidently down the quay, or rowing out to his restless ship. He was our hero, while we, like two shrews, crept nervously round the harbour walls, on a daily trip to the telephone box, to consult the nearest weather station; anxious to break the cold chains of doubt that held us prisoner, yet fearing to go.

At last the forecast was favourable. We had arranged for Tucker Brown's yard, at Burnham on Crouch, on the north side of the Thames Estuary, to take *Tzu Hang* for fitting out. I came back from the telephone booth that evening with a new sense of purpose, but no great assurance that I could carry it out.

"They say that it's going to be fine weather tomorrow, with light north-east winds, so I think we ought to go," I told Beryl. "At least we can go under power to Ramsgate. We have the tide from ten o'clock."

"You know you wouldn't think anything of this if you were doing it in British Columbia," said Beryl, noticing my lack of assurance.

"I suppose I wouldn't, but somehow the sea seems different here. I don't want to make some awful bog. 'Inexperienced couple put yacht on sands.' I can just see the headlines."

"Well, I don't see why we should. If we go under power to Ramsgate, I don't see that it's any different from British Columbia."

"We'd better try the engine, then, and see that we are all ready to go." It was a Morris Navigator and started on petrol. As soon as the engine was warm it was switched to kerosene, which was a much cheaper fuel in England, and before stopping, the fuel was changed back to petrol, so that the carburettor was empty of kerosene for starting. The engine ran perfectly and I switched it off without turning it back to petrol.

"Well, that's all right, anyway," I said.

That night I slept badly, but eventually the day came, and the cold grey stones of the harbour wall moved slowly backwards and forwards across the porthole over my bunk. *Tzu Hang* pulled gently, first this way and then that, at her spring lines. There was little wind. After breakfast I walked over to tell the old seaman who looked after the gates that *Tzu Hang* would be moving out on the tide.

I felt a little heroic at setting off into the open sea so early in March. I hoped that he'd say something in appreciation of our devil-may-care nautical attitude, such as, "I wish you luck, but you wouldn't catch me going out at this time of year." Instead he growled through his woollen scarf, like an old bear that hasn't had his breakfast, "Ten o'clock. And don't be late." As I stepped

15

back on *Tzu Hang*, I noticed that the Dutchman had already left the outer harbour.

At ten minutes to ten I attempted to start the engine, but without success. Suddenly I remembered that I had not switched back to petrol the night before. I shouted to Beryl, sitting expectantly in the cockpit, that I had forgotten to change the fuel switches and would have to drain the carburettor. It didn't take long, but by the time I had finished I could hear the old bear grumbling that he couldn't keep the gates open all day. The engine started and we moved slowly away from the wharf and through the gates into the outer harbour. A tremendous experience this. *Tzu Hang* slid along making hardly a ripple as her engine burbled quietly, but when I advanced the throttle there was no change in its tone. *Tzu Hang* continued at the same speed. Perhaps that was what she was meant to do.

As soon as we were out of the harbour I went below to check our course, and called it up to Beryl at the helm. As I studied the chart and began to lay off courses and distances, which I might well have done before, I began to feel queasy.

"You'd better come up," Beryl called. "We seem to be heading straight for the White Cliffs of Dover. I'm not sure that I understand this bloody compass."

I came up and found that the white cliffs were ahead, but there was a destroyer in the Downs on the correct bearing, so I told her to steer on that, while I went below for a further study of the chart. Suddenly I realised that I was going to be seasick. I scrambled up on deck to find that *Tzu Hang*, with the tide behind her and in spite of her leisurely pace, was already approachin the destroyer. A number of officers were on the bridge, in duffle coats, for the north-east wind was cold. They levelled 8 × 80 magnification binoculars on this early yacht, appearing in the Downs like a crocus on a lawn.

"I'm going to be sick," I gasped.

"Oh, darling, not here," she said. "Not in front of the Navy."

I was overcome with the deepest sense of shame, but sick I had to be. I crawled behind the low doghouse on the side away from the destroyer, and was sick over the side. As soon as the paroxysm was over, I got to my knees and waved to them over the top of the doghouse, hoping that they'd think I'd been making some minor adjustment, which of course I had. They waved back, grinning like apes, I thought, and imagined that I heard their mocking laughter across the intervening water. Presently we left the destroyer behind and the fresh sea air embraced us, while the English coast, with its villages, spires, castles and watch towers, slipped past. One after another, the buoys appeared in their right colour and on the expected bearings. I began to feel happy and confident of our safe arrival.

All went well and in a few hours we were safely in the outer harbour at Ramsgate. Few passages could be easier than that from Dover to Ramsgate on a fine day, and within the shelter of the Goodwins, but for us it was a momentous occasion, and the sense of achievement rarely surpassed in all our other voyages. I was so pleased that as soon as one of the harbour men had caught our lines, which I had to throw up to him as the tide was now well down, I ran along the deck to Beryl and gave her a hug. The seaman on the wharf was the same brand as the one who had let us out at Dover.

"Come on, now," he shouted. "None of that there. Let's get moored up proper."

As soon as we were tied up, a uniformed officer from the Customs, or the Harbour Office, scrambled down the wet ladder, to ask where we were from and to collect harbour and light dues. The harbour dues gave us two weeks' stay and the light dues were for a year. No one minds paying light dues once a year and the harbour dues were not expensive, except that we were only stopping for a night and a remote relation of mine had built the harbour. Like most British officials connected with the sea, the officer was cheerful, smart and efficient.

We cast off with the tide next day, but to our surprise the engine, which ran with its customary lethargic purr, had no effect on the ship. We drifted on to a buoy and Beryl managed to hook the ring with a boathook, while I jumped on to the buoy and made fast with a line from the bow. We then went below to examine the engine and found that the propeller shaft had become disconnected from the drive, and that all the nuts and some of the bolts which formed the connection were somewhere ir-retrievable in the bilge. As we looked at this in dismay, there was the sound of a small motor-boat alongside, and our official of yesterday hopped on board.

"That'll be seven and sixpence for buoy dues," he said merrily.

17

"But we only hooked on because we were out of control. The shaft has become disconnected," I protested.

"Can't help that, sir. You have to pay if you use a buoy."

"But I don't want to use a buoy. I want to go back to the wall."

"Well, you have to pay, even for five minutes, and you'll be better off here while you get that fixed. You can use the dinghy to get ashore if you want to. Shall I send you a mechanic?"

I had no spare bolts and nuts for the prop shaft, and he promised to send me a mechanic right away.

Presently a man in overalls and carrying a tool bag whistled to us from the quay. Beryl and I had put the dinghy in the water. It weighed a ton, was made of teak, and had a bronze centreboard, and was hoisted out by wire lanyards that were attached to the main halyard. It was impossible for one man to launch the dinghy without serious damage either to himself, the dinghy, or the yacht's sides. Perhaps we never got the way of it. With two people, one to hoist and lower with one to fend off, the process usually went pretty well. I rowed it over to the quay. The tool bag was carefully lowered on a piece of string, and then the mechanic cautiously descended the ladder, stepped in his black leather nail-studded boots into the centre of the dinghy and seated himself on the after thwart. He was an elderly gloomy man. "Trouble?" he asked.

On arrival at *Tzu Hang* he climbed wheezily on board, nodded to Beryl, and found his way below. He clicked his tongue when he saw what had happened.

"Where did you say you were from?" he asked.

"From Dover. Actually we're over from Canada, but we got the yacht in Dover."

"From Canada," he said, and there was a long disapproving silence, so that we knew that in his opinion we had to be "outsiders" to have got into this position. "Well, you ought to look things over before you start," he went on disapprovingly. "Like as not you came up from Dover with only two bolts holding. They'd never drop off like that if they were all in. Don't look as if I could match them. I may have to cut you some more. Then we've got to get the shaft back to the drive. Get the two flanges together like. Might do that with a drawing tool or a clamp mebbe." He went on mumbling and peering down at the shaft. "Can't reach that nohow," I heard him say.

18

He turned to us. "So you're strangers from Canada," he said. "Well, you don't talk like Canadians. You ought to be careful. Where are you bound for?"

"For Burnham."

"Well, if I was you, I'd take a pilot. I wouldn't like to think of you people crossing the Thames Estuary by yourselves with all that traffic. You want a professional for that."

By this time Beryl and I found that our nerve was failing, and as he saw the effect of his homily on us, he brightened up and warmed to his task.

"Those foreign ships, they don't stop for no one. Don't see them perhaps, and there's many a good yacht come to grief on the sands between here and Burnham. If I was you, I'd get Captain Rogers to take you across. He lives by the garage up the road, and does a lot of these sort of jobs."

"What is he?"

"Well, he's a retired pilot like."

"What would he charge?"

"Oh, he wouldn't charge much. Do it for pleasure most likely, or a glass of beer. But you'll have to see him. I can't fix this in a day, you know."

After I had put him ashore, I rowed back to the ship. My few years in Canada had made me intolerant of this leisurely tempo. "Why the hell can't he fix it in a day," I said to Beryl. "He's only got to find a new nuts and bolts."

"Perhaps we ought to see this Captain Rogers," she said.

We found him living at the end of a row of cottages and we suspected that he was a neighbour of the mechanic. He was wearing a blue serge suit and a seaman's peaked cap without a badge and just about to set off down the road on a voyage. From his rosy colouring I guessed where the voyage would end. We told him what we wanted. He was non-committal and said that he'd like to see the yacht first. He came on board and looked round.

"When do you want to leave?" he asked.

"Tomorrow morning, if the shaft is fixed."

"Well, I could do that," he said.

"What would you charge?"

"That will be seven pounds and my fare home, of course. That won't be too much. Maybe fourteen shillings."

Beryl and I looked at each other and I could see that we both thought it too much.

"I think it's rather more than we can afford," I said. "May we think about it and let you know?"

"Aye. That will be all right. But let me know in good time so that we get the tide right."

We rowed him ashore and left the dinghy at the ladder, as we had some shopping to do. On the top of the quay he paused and looked back at *Tzu Hang*. "She's a nice ship," he said. "It would be a pity to let that one go on the sands. Or be run down," he added.

The starlings were singing, brilliant on the roof-tops, and the sparrows chirping busily in the pale sun. There had been a frost last night, but today there was promise of summer. The captain and the mechanic seemed to be piping much the same tune, and as he rolled away to his daily appointment, I felt annoyed and braver.

"I didn't like that last crack," I said. "I think we can do without him."

"Why don't we ring up Richard?" Beryl asked. Richard Orgill was a Sapper Colonel at Chatham. We had climbed with him in the Himalayas, and he was an ocean racing man, having sailed in the Royal Engineers' famous racing yacht *Ilex*. We rang him up and he said that he'd join us next day. Much relieved, we returned to *Tzu Hang*, but a few hours later received a message from the Harbour Master telling us to call Richard again. He had fallen off a ladder and broken his toe, but was sending two enthusiastic and inexperienced subalterns instead.

The two arrived next day, the one good-looking and assured, the other small and diffident, with eyes that peered through an enormous and precocious moustache, like a bird-watcher from a bush. We set off at about mid-day on the following morning, the shaft having been pulled together again and re-bolted. As soon as *Tzu Hang* was clear of the shoals near the entrance, we got up sail for the first time, and for the first time felt a yacht steady and lean to the wind.

> "Whither, O splendid ship, thy white sails crowding,
> Leaning across the bosom of the urgent west,
> That fears nor sea rising nor sky clouding,
> Whither away fair rover, and what thy quest?"

We were of rather different mettle; the sea was rising and the sky clouding, and beyond the foreland, as we approached it, I could see white horses galloping before a westerly wind, which was blowing out of the estuary. A fishing boat that had left Dover just before us put her head round the foreland and then turned back. The skipper may have found that he had forgotten his dog, but I took it that he preferred to wait until the wind had abated. If I do not like to confess to fear, I can admit to caution, and after all, this was the first time out with an inexperienced crew and the first time that we had put up sail. I was still, or at least partially, a motor-boat man, unaware of the power and the reliability of the wind on sails. I turned the ship round, and without switching off the motor, which we had kept running in order to help us catch the tide, hurried back to Ramsgate.

Turning back is always bad for morale, and lying in harbour when one ought to be out is worse. After a brief consultation with the weather office, who must have been getting to know my voice, we started again the same night. We left at about midnight, hoping to take the last of the ebb up to the Foreland, and then the flood up the Estuary until we cut across and took the ebb again up the coast. We seemed to be gluttons for new experience. It was with the thrill of real adventure that we lit our dim oil navigation lights, started the motor and headed for the entrance. There we stuck, climbing up and pitching down the steep little swell that the fresh wind was sending in. *Tzu Hang*'s motor seemed unable to send her out, and Beryl said that for minutes she watched one stone in the masonry of the pier that simply would not change its position in relation to the ship. Suddenly we forged ahead. We were out. The two buoys that we had checked in the morning appeared in their turn and soon we were able to alter course for the Foreland.

With a fresh wind on our beam, I thought that the Genoa would be all that we needed to take us up, but when we tried to set the sail, we found that it would not go up to the mast-head, but stuck half-way up; it filled like a balloon staysail with some of it still on the deck. We kept the motor going and *Tzu Hang* rushed off through the night in response to the sail while the motor chattered along behind, doing the best it could. As we rounded the Foreland, we stowed the sail, setting the motor to work in earnest now, for the wind of the morning was still blowing and as the tide turned it set up a steep short sea.

I made a list of the buoys in the order that they should be passed, and went below to lie down in my clothes, but not to sleep, leaving the wheel and the watch to Beryl and the small soldier. His friend had already succumbed to seasickness and possibly anxiety too, for which I would not blame him in the least; but Beryl's companion seemed to grow larger and to fit his moustache through the stresses of the night. I had not been below long before I heard Beryl calling.

"I think you'd better come up," she said. "You know that after the green buoy the next one is supposed to be flashing. Well, it isn't. We've passed the green and now here's another green one again."

I looked aft. The eyes of the soldier were glued to the compass, and at the same time he spun the wheel this way and that in pursuit of the swinging card. I climbed up the ladder and sat beside him in the cockpit. He had chased the compass card round the clock and was now on a reverse bearing. What with this delay, the steep sea and the head wind, and *Tzu Hang*'s ineffectual engine, which we found later was due to a maladjustment of the throttle so that she would only run at half-speed, we missed our tide.

Half-way through the night, a strange black object of great height appeared on our starboard hand. This dark colossus seemed to keep pace with us as *Tzu Hang* moved through the water. Like a handling machine of the Martians in the *War of the Worlds* it stalked beside us, menacing, silent, and unlit, with its feet splashing in the sea.

"What on earth is it?" asked Beryl for the twentieth time. "Are you sure you know where you are?"

"I can't imagine. There's nothing marked on the chart. It must be on the sands."

"But why don't we pass it? We seem to be going along quite well."

"It must be the tide holding us."

Gradually, as the tide slackened, we left it behind. Daylight came, showing brown water and sand banks exposed by the tide, leaning buoys to mark our course, and a low coast-line—a painting in sepia wash. The monster of the night appeared far behind us now as an anti-aircraft tower. It may have been marked in my chart as "sand tower" as I have seen it on others, but if it was I would never have linked it with that ominous figure that seemed to march beside us. Suddenly the engine stopped. Luckily all hands were on deck and we got the mainsail up in quick time for beginners, because small waves were breaking on the sands close to leeward, where it looked as if we would soon join them. With the main up, I took the wheel, while Beryl and the two soldiers got up the staysail. In the excitement of these moments I had shouted various instructions. Although no sailor as yet, I had all the right cries. I saw that we were making sternway towards the sands, while *Tzu Hang* stood in irons, her mainsail shaking. I did not realise that if I put the helm over she would answer to it because of her sternway, and that her head would fall off and she would begin to sail. Instead I called to Beryl to back the staysail.

I saw incomprehension if not mutiny in every outline of the small group huddled on the foredeck, whispering together.

"Back the staysail!" I roared.

They had had enough of my shouting. Beryl detached herself from the group and came down the deck. I could see that she was furious, and cared little whether we went aground or not, only that we should have this clear between us, that she would not be shouted at in a language she couldn't understand.

"What do you mean, 'Back the staysail'?" she asked. "For heaven's sake speak English."

"Like this," I said, jumping out of the cockpit, running forward and backing it myself, and then, after telling one of the soldiers to hold it there, running back to the wheel. *Tzu Hang*'s head fell off, her mainsail filled, and almost immediately she began to draw away from the sands. The staysail was allowed to go over, and we all stood staring at *Tzu Hang* in wonder; orders, counter-orders and confusion were forgotten. "She's sailing!" we cried in delight and astonishment as the sands receded, and as if this was not exactly what she had been designed to do. Soon jib and mizzen were up and we were spinning along. From then on, Beryl and I never fully trusted the engine again, although its only sin had been to run out of fuel. This was a conversion. A new light fell upon us. From then on we were sailors. Our trust and confidence were in the sails; but there had to be some wind too. Fortunately for sailors, periods of no wind are not usually periods of danger.

I took course over Foulness Sands. Beryl disapproved.

"Well, I wouldn't do it," she said. "You're just suffering from over-confidence as usual."

"But we've already got enough water, and the tide is rising," I pointed out.

"Well, Eric Hiscock went aground on them, so I don't see why you shouldn't."

Beryl has the faculty of remembering almost everything that she has ever read. Already Eric Hiscock had been quoted to me on every possible occasion; his book *Cruising Under Sail*, then newly-published, had become our text book. I was beginning to detest him, and did so until I met Eric and Susan a few weeks later. But his sayings have continued to haunt me, through the medium of his protagonist, for years. He is like a blue-water "Mao". It's all in his little blue book; a book which beginners should never be without.

We crossed the sands without touching them and found our way into the mouth of the river, up between low banks and marshy fields, until the trees and houses of Burnham appeared with a forest of masts in the river. The sails were down by then and *Tzu Hang* was speeding up-stream under her motor, for we had switched back to the other tank. "We had better just keep in the channel and hope to God that someone tells us what to do," I said. I need not have worried. Just as the jungle ahead appeared to be impenetrable, a small motor-boat with two men in yellow oilskins and sou'westers detached itself from the maze of hulls and masts, then came towards us.

"Is that *Tzu Hang*?" a deep voice boomed across the water.

"Yes," we chorused back.

"Well, follow me and no argy bargy."

We thankfully gave up control of the situation to someone who obviously knew what he was doing.

A few hours later, still under the euphoria of our first successful passage, a cocktail and a bottle of wine, having bathed and dined ashore, we made our way back to the dinghy. Beryl had changed back to her sea-going clothes, but I was still dressed for dining ashore except for sea boots. We found that the dinghy was now separated from the water by a hundred yards of mud; lured on by the dim flicker of our riding light and by the promise of a cold damp bed, we dragged the dinghy slipping and squelching in the dark, towards the water. Half-way there, I tripped over a mooring and measured my length in the slime. I was immolated in mud, and as I scrambled to my feet, I left a boot behind. It was as if the sea was determined to keep me in my place, the right place for a beginner, a newcomer to the domain.

CHAPTER TWO

Fitting Out and the First Cruise

The financial path that led to the purchase of *Tzu Hang* had been a winding one. As we had emigrated to Canada, we were subject to all sorts of financial restrictions, and when we wanted to sell shares in England in order to buy *Tzu Hang*, we found that we were unable to do so. This led to a visit to the Bank of England where we were conducted by a red-coated messenger to the office of a Mr. Plum, who had something to do with foreign accounts. There we were placed on two rather lower chairs than Mr. Plum's and from his superior altitude behind a large desk he placed the tips of his fingers together and regretted that he was unable to give us permission to sell securities to buy a yacht.

"But why not?" I asked. "We are selling English securities, to buy an English boat in England. No money is going out of the country."

"Ah," said Mr. Plum, "but the boat may."

By now the reason for coming to England, to buy a boat in order to sell it in Canada, had faded. We had already begun to realise that if we bought a boat we might not be so keen to sell it when we got back. The object at the moment was to buy a boat. I had been eighteen years in the Army and Beryl came from a family all of whom had been in the Army. We both had English passports. Now we were being told that we couldn't buy a boat in England with our money which was in England, because we had emigrated to Canada, instead of retiring to England and cluttering up the country as we waited for free medicine, possibly unemployment insurance, and ultimately the old age pension.

Suddenly all these petty restrictions boiled up in me. The

income tax that I paid in England on money that I was not allowed to touch, the money in our banks that we couldn't spend, the boat that we couldn't buy. I jumped to my feet and for the first time shook my fist at a man without striking him. "I'm going to bloody well buy a boat," I said.

Mr. Plum looked appalled, and Beryl showed her whole-hearted approval. "God help him," I thought, "if she turns on him."

There seemed to be a hush in the Bank of England. Mr. Plum shuffled his papers. Presently he cleared his throat. "Please sit down again," he said. "I should have explained that there is a way in which we may be able to accommodate you. We can give you permission to sell certain securities in order to buy Canadian securities at the free rate, and we will then purchase them from you at the approved exchange rate. It will of course involve quite a considerable loss to you on a paper transaction, but I'm afraid that is the only way that we can make the money available."

The loss amounted to about £1,000 and twist as we might, there was no way of avoiding it. Its eventual release involved further restrictions and freezing of funds so that we would be able to spend only this money and nothing else. Although from my upbringing I am naturally subject to discipline, Beryl is not, and the moment that the screw is turned too tight, nothing will prevent an evasion. Our own banks were already on our side. "We have no instructions from the Bank of England yet," said a friend in Beryl's bank, "and if you want to draw out all your money which is in your account, I can't stop you." Beryl cashed a cheque and so did I with mine. Loaded with pound notes, more money than I had ever carried except when drawing the regimental pay, and with Beryl marching behind me like a Securicor Guard, we made out way back to her brother's house, where we were staying.

"Good heavens, what's all this?" he asked. "Have you won a football pool?"

"No. We've been clearing out our accounts before the Bank of England freezes them," Beryl replied.

"You mean that it's hot money?" asked her delighted brother, three times wounded in England's wars.

"Yes. Can you put it in your safe?"

"Wait a minute," he replied. He put it in an envelope, after all it wasn't so very much, carefully labelled it "Hot Money", and put it in his safe.

"Now," said Beryl, "haven't we got some Post Office Savings certificates? And I have all those War Savings certificates without interest, that I bought during the war. As an ordinary English-woman in England, can't I just draw those out of the Post Office?"

"Do you think that the Bank of England has a check on them?" I asked.

"Well, if they have, it's going to be too late, and we'll be gone before they find out anyway."

It turned out that nothing could have been easier. We went to the Post Office and drew out our money. Not on that day, because it proved to be more than the local branch had available, but on the next. We returned to Beryl's brother with a guilty feeling of having outwitted the Bank of England. Another envelope marked "Even Hotter" was stowed away.

That evening, when we returned from spending some of our illegally-recovered money at Captain O. M. Watts' chandlery, we were met by Beryl's sister-in-law at the door. Anne's usually kind and merry face looked worried.

"The Bank of England have been on the phone," she said.

We felt as if the hounds of heaven, or rather of the Bank of England, were treading close behind us.

"They want you to ring up a Mr. Plum in the morning."

"Somehow I don't think Mr. Plum is dangerous," said Beryl.

I rang him up in the morning. "There are some papers," he said, "that I want you to sign. A formality only. I have sent them to your bank. I hope it will not be inconvenient for you to call there."

We had sufficient money now for fitting out and for the bare necessities of living, but we were under no illusions that there would be any to spare for clothes and shows and dining out. It was going to be quite a Spartan existence, but the last four years in Canada had been pretty Spartan too.

The morning after we arrived in Burnham, the Cole brothers, who ran Tucker Brown's yard, came on board; both tall upstand-ing men, speaking with a slight Essex burr, both, as one almost took for granted in men of this age and on this coast, having served in the Navy during the war. One complemented the other. One, the more immaculately dressed, ran the office, the sales, the yard and the public relations part of the firm; the other, more robustly built, more nautically attired, looked after the hauling out, the launchings, the moorings and all things and people afloat. Both of them on week-ends went dinghy racing in all kinds of weather.

"You can't live on board without a stove," said Sonny Cole. "I know you come from Canada, but that's carrying things a bit too far." One of the first things that we ordered therefore was a stove to heat the boat. It was called a "Little Nipper" and burnt anything that we put in, but it had no oven. Meanwhile Sonny lent us a hissing paraffin stove to keep the chill away. We went back to London to collect our treasure, and lodged it in the office safe in the little shack on the quay that answered as an office. "Here, what's this?" said one of them. "Hot money. Do you think we'd better touch it?"

"You bet we had," said the other as he started to count it, "it's the first time it's ever happened to us, a yachtsman paying in advance."

"It's not all for you," said Beryl quickly.

"You'd be surprised how much will be," said Sonny.

One day we went into the office, found it empty, the door of the safe open and our two packets of hot money fully exposed. But it was all right. "As safe as the Bank of England," said one of the brothers when he returned.

"The Bank of England!" exclaimed Beryl. "The biggest robbers of the lot."

While still looking for a yacht and before we had even seen *Tzu Hang*, we had been walking down a line of yachts moored in some Essex backwater, and had noticed a small bluish-green fishing smack with a long bowsprit and a short solid mast. A wisp of blue smoke curled up from her stove funnel or "Charlie Noble" and there were dim sounds of activity within. Her name was *Moonraker*, and we were to know her well, looking just like this, when a few years later she spent the winter with us in Canada, in the same cove as *Tzu Hang*.

As we came back, a small man, I should have guessed a few years older than us, with an alert, humorous and sensitive face, and rather pale and penetrating eyes, had just stepped off *Moonraker*, followed by a woman who in many ways matched his looks, so that one knew automatically that they were man and wife. They were Peter and Anne Pye, then perhaps the best-known cruising people on that coast, if not in England. Peter wore his old yachting cap and his darned blue jersey like a uniform, and it suited him exactly. As we got to know him, we found that he was sometimes apt to speak in capital letters like Nelson, when he said, "Sir Ed'ard, we must and shall beat the Northumberland. Make the Foudroyant fly." Now Peter, who had heard us talking about copper sheathing, said to us as we passed, "Are you going foreign?"

They asked us to tea in their cottage at Steeple, and we regarded them with great respect and admiration, very soon with affection too. We were still at the admiration stage when we moored up at Burnham. On the first week-end we saw *Moonraker* under sail, threading her way through the moored yachts on her way down river, guided by a helmsman whose skill we could never hope to equal. She tacked close by us and as she passed Peter shouted, "Is that your new ship?"

"Yes. How do you like her?" I replied.

"I don't like her freeboard," he answered as he drew away.

It was a dreadful blow. "But he's got none at all. Of course he won't like it," I said to Beryl to soften it.

It is generally recognised now that good freeboard makes a comfortable and dry ocean cruiser, although it can be overcome. It certainly has proved so with *Tzu Hang*, and I wouldn't sacrifice an inch of it now. Without it I should not be available to write this story, but at the time it was a disturbing comment, leaving us in doubt as to whether we had bought the right boat. When we next met him he did his best to correct the unhappy impression that he might have made; it was probably Anne, the more sensitive of the two, who realised that he might have created this doubt.

On return they asked us to go for a cruise with them the following week-end. Beryl and I were delighted, and it was not until the next Friday, when he came on board to make arrangements, that we realised he expected us to sail in our own boat. "I always tell anyone with whom we are cruising not to try to stay together, but we arrange where to meet. We'll meet here," he said, pointing to a spot on the chart a little up river from Harwich, "and if I was you I'd go through the Little Swin. You'll find that there is sand on one side and mud on the other, so just sound through and keep in the middle."

Our first venture in a yacht across the Thames Estuary had taxed our nerves more than we had realised. Since our arrival we had lived happily on its successful conclusion, and had not faced the fact that we would have to go out again. Now it was suddenly forced upon us. Saturday morning came in with a strong gusty wind from the west.

"He'll never go out on a day like this," I suggested hopefully to Beryl.

"I hope not," she said, "but we had better be ready."

I looked out at about the turn of the tide and saw *Moonraker* preparing to leave. "I'm afraid we've got to go," I told Beryl, and soon we were speeding down the river, our mainsail full and drawing with our bout of nerves gone. For a long time we continued to feel nervous before leaving harbour, whether on a short or long cruise; but ultimately that feeling disappeared. Perhaps that is the right time to give up sailing.

We had some gusty sailing in company with *Moonraker*, who immodestly showed us most of her bottom, while *Tzu Hang* primly kept hers in the water. We seemed to move at about the same speed, but then Peter carried every inch of sail that he could and got the best out of his ship. We were still feeling our way with ours, and had only the storm jib to set in front of the staysail, as the other two jibs were undergoing an overhaul. Peter had told us that if we were in doubt about finding our way up the river in the dark on the way home, we could always turn back for Brightlingsea, which was lit and easy to get into. We were ahead of *Moonraker* on our way back, but it was getting late and I decided to take his advice. We passed *Moonraker* just coming out of the Swin, swinging along, so assured and comfortable, and so appropriate to the waters that she knew so well. The two ships slid past each other for a moment, silent except for the calls of good night from their crews, and in a few more moments she was fading and gone. The Swin was lit and so was the entrance to Brightlingsea. We didn't go in, but anchored in shelter near a green buoy which turned out in the morning to be marking a wreck, to which we were uncomfortably close at low tide; but as Beryl was going up to London to meet Clio and bring her back to the boat, we left its jagged edges sticking out of the mud, and made our way into the harbour.

The boat seemed dead without Beryl's gay vitality and laughter.

Even when we were nervous, a bubbling spring of youth in her never ran dry, so that we soon forgot our anxiety in the excitement of shared adventure and in amusement at each other's doubts. In the evening I heard them chattering together as they came along the quay. It was the first time that Clio had seen *Tzu Hang*. She inspected everything with large solemn eyes which betrayed no secrets. We were desperately anxious that she should enjoy her first trip, and when we set off next morning did everything that we could to keep her interest going so that she should not be seasick. The sea was not rough, but it certainly was not smooth, and there was a cold wind. Just as we got into the river her face crumpled into tears and she was sick. "What have we condemned her to?" I wondered, but there was no going back now.

In fact Clio was too young then to find enough to do in the actual sailing of the boat, although within a year she was quite a useful hand. Still, things were not too bad. She was already a tremendous reader, she infinitely preferred being with us than away, and she was an enthusiastic traveller. She liked ports and foreign countries, but she missed the companionship of children of her own age.

During this time I had a letter from Kevin O'Riordan, who had recently crossed the Atlantic in *Vertue XXXV* with Humphrey Barton. They had been nearly overwhelmed in a severe storm, and the ship damaged, so that they had had to fight for their lives, half-flooded and in the dark.

He wrote that he had heard from a friend of my sister that we were going to buy a yacht and sail it back to Canada, and I guessed that my sister's account would not have passed lightly over our inadequacy. "As long as you have a buoyant ship, plenty of water, and do not mind being alone for days and days, you need have no worries," he said. This was the most heartening advice that I had ever received, and I was so thrilled with his letter that I wrote and asked him if he would like to join us on a cruise to Holland, so that we might benefit from his experience. He accepted, and since we did not plan to leave England until June, there was plenty of time for a cruise before Tucker Brown's started to fit out *Tzu Hang* for her long journey.

There was not so much to do. She needed two extra water tanks so that we would carry about 150 gallons of water, a new coat of bottom paint, some minor alterations to her rigging so that we could carry twin staysails for her Trade Wind passage, and some minor work below, such as the fitting of a chart table. She had too many doors and compartments, but we had not yet appreciated the advantages of an open layout with easy access fore and aft, nor the horror of doors that were liable to fly open and turn themselves into lethal weapons.

Kevin O'Riordan and his wife arrived two weeks after our return from Brightlingsea, he to join us for our trip to Holland, and she to see him on board and to have a word with Beryl. "You must tell your husband to excuse Kevin if he tries to take charge," she said. "He is just so enthusiastic. I told him before he left with Humphrey Barton, 'Now don't forget. It's Mister Barton's boat.' "

Kevin was a short, burly man, in his sixties. He had once been an international rugby football player, and he had been a fighter all his life. He had been Chief of Police in India, and in the ranks of the Great. He had white hair and a small white moustache, and mischievous blue eyes, which shone from a scarlet face. He was extremely well-read, had a memory that never failed, and a classical education, so that he was apt to make Latin or Greek quotations, especially if they put someone else at a disadvantage. A hard man at times, a gentle man, an exceedingly entertaining and humorous man, an exasperating and lovable man, an Irishman who'd spent all his life in the service of England, and the best sort of companion on a boat.

He arrived, having come through London dressed in an old blue reefer coat, a battered yachting cap, and wearing no socks. I was enthralled with this disregard for the niceties of dress. I was then forty-four years old and only four years out of the Army so still very much an Englishman and a newly-retired soldier.

"Don't you ever wear socks?" I asked him.

"No," he growled, "they give me colds."

All our money except for the bare necessities of life was being spent on *Tzu Hang* and on things to do with sailing her. Socks did not come into this category, not even into the bare necessities, although my heels were already bare. Beryl hates darning, and when she had so much on her hands I did not want to ask her to do them, nor was I prepared to darn them myself. Here

33

was the answer: rather than wear undarned socks, wear no socks at all.

Next day I had to go up to London. I was wearing a comparatively new and well-cut suit, in fact the last custom-made suit by a good tailor that I was ever able to afford, and my regimental tie—but no socks.

All went well until I sat down in the crowded London train. I then realised that it was almost impossible to conceal my bony ankles, pink with cold. I spent the rest of the journey standing up and a day of acute embarrassment followed, for I could not bring myself to go into a shop, buy a pair of socks and put them on. Kevin might have quoted to me that, "Poverty has no sharper pang than this, that it makes man ridiculous." The disastrous day culminated as I was crossing Pall Mall to go into Lloyds, when I heard a shout from down the street.

"Hello, Miles," I heard, and as I affected not to hear it, "Miles!" it cried, "Hi, there!"

I had to look, and there was Gerald Whitfield, a Brigadier who had once been my instructor at the Military College, and whom I had later known in India but hadn't seen since before the war. He had always been very well-dressed, and now I saw that he was wearing a bowler hat tilted forward on his forehead, showing a suggestion of grey curls above his ears. He was waving his tightly-rolled umbrella, and had on a short, rather loose-fitting overcoat, the first hint of returning men's fashions. Even from this distance I could see that his suit and his footwear—and no doubt his socks too—were all in the height of elegance.

"Oh, my God," I thought, "I can't speak to him without any socks," and contemplated a dash across the road, but the traffic would not allow it. I turned and faced him.

"Miles," he said, "how wonderful to see you. How is Beryl? Where is she?"

I explained what we were doing, bearing down on my trousers so that they fell over my shoes. I had long ago given up wearing a hat, and now I had never felt so undressed in my life. We had both reached the same rank in the Army, but I found myself reverting to the role of a cadet facing his instructor. "But how wonderful," he said. "You must have lunch with me at the club and tell me all about it. It's right here," he said, pointing to its doors.

Wild horses wouldn't drag me into the club, with all those

eagle-eyed admirals and generals, who had nothing to do but study ankles through the club windows as people passed. They would notice mine. I was certain also to meet someone else that I knew.

"I can't," I stammered. "I've got an appointment at the bank. Something to do with the exchange control. I'm late already."

"Well, another time," he said cheerfully, as I extricated myself, crossed the street with flashing pink heels, and dived into the bank. That was enough. I bought some socks, sat down blatantly in the shop, and pulled them on over exceedingly dirty feet.

If Beryl had been in such a position—although socks would be inapplicable—it would not have affected her in the same way. Once having decided on her furrow she ploughs on. Not for me this imperviousness to public opinion and the overt glance. Although I have changed with the years, I was then very much a creature of the herd, of my herd. But the change had started.

Next day we set off and as we prepared to leave, Kevin, in oilskins and yachting cap, took up a commanding position in the cockpit. "Now," he said, "we don't want to drift down on to the yachts below us, and it's rather crowded ahead, so the way we will do it is like this. If you cast off from the buoy, Miles . . ."

I saw that unless I did something then, Kevin was going to be the skipper, and I was going to be the crew. I already had the taste of commanding my own ship—that is, as far as anyone commands his ship with his joint owner and wife on board.

"Wait a minute, Kevin," I said. "I'm the skipper, and you must let me make my mistakes."

"Of course, of course," he cried. "I was just explaining how to do it. I'm the crew. Now, if you . . ."

He was extremely good and patient with me, letting me have my own way; but it must have been a great strain at times.

The first part of the journey went well enough, but as we made our way out of the channels, a north wind got up, giving us a choppy sea. At one point we tried to use the engine to clear the end of a bank without tacking, but found that a fuel-line had broken at its connection and needed soldering. My efforts at locating what was wrong made me seasick; Clio was already sick and had gone to sleep, while Beryl, gallantly cooking supper, became sick too. We never allowed seasickness to interfere with whatever we had to do, but Kevin must have wondered what on earth he had let himself in for. He must have wondered still more, a little later in the dead of the night. After taking in the jib, so that *Tzu Hang* would sail in a more leisurely fashion to make Harwich by daybreak, where we might have the fuel-line repaired, I tripped over a skylight. I put my hand on to the stay-sail boom to save myself and dislocated my shoulder.

It was a shoulder that was apt to go out, and I had dislocated it several times, but this was an awkward place to do it, on deck in the dark with a choppy sea and half a gale blowing. I lay between the shrouds and the skylight on my cabin, and Beryl bent over me and shouted, "What's the matter?"

"I've dislocated my shoulder again," I shouted back, sitting up.

"On, no," I heard her say. And I could imagine the instructions that she had got from the doctor in Canada spinning through her head. "Put him on his back like this," he had demonstrated. "Then very slowly pull the elbow across his chest like this. You can take ten minutes to do it. Then flick his hand outwards like this." Ten minutes! I began to pull by elbow slowly across my chest myself before she had time to get to work on me. Suddenly there was a resounding thump and the shoulder was back in place, and I got a trifle groggily to my feet. It was the only time that I ever managed to get my shoulder back into place by myself. Necessity knows no law.

We spent the week-end in Harwich, while the fuel-line was repaired and we had a good rest, so as to be much better pre-pared, except for a stiff shoulder, for the passage across the North Sea. Now we always make a point of sailing only a few miles to the nearest anchorage, if it is possible, to have a rest and tidy up before setting off. The last days in port are nearly always hectic and often anxious so this sort of break is often invaluable and adds greatly to the enjoyment of a voyage. On Monday we set off again.

I suppose I felt sick as I kept the last daylight watch, and the dark sea came rolling. It was still rough from the wind that we had had over the week-end, but there was only a pleasant breeze by then. We all had supper and none of us—Kevin was never sick—had actually been ill. There was no land or light in sight and for the first time I felt the thrill of the loneliness of the sea, the same thrill that I have had on a mountain in the cold evening, when there is no sound or man-made light; only the eternal rocks and the eternal snows, watching, waiting, while we pass. The solitude is the same, but the sea is different from the mountains in that it is a busy thing, even when at peace, always moving and always whispering and talking to itself. Both can be equally terrifying and equally lethal in storm, both warm and all-embracing in the sun.

An hour later I saw what at first I took to be lightning in the sky to eastward, and then all across the horizon a faint, double, or treble or single flick of light. The loom of coastwise lights telling us where we were and where we had to go. Navigation wasn't going to be so difficult after all. Morning came sneaking in under low clouds, and soon it was light enough to see around us. The flickering lights and the imagined shore had disappeared. We held on to our course for Ijmuiden, and it was not long before we saw chimneys and the roofs of warehouses poking up above the horizon. Our surroundings took on the colouring and the aspect of an old Dutch print, the same greenish-brown sea, the short waves, the low shore. The regular line of a sea wall appeared, although we could not yet make out the entrance to the harbour, but here was a buoy to mark the channel. As we took down the sails and started the engine, a Dutch yacht came out of the harbour, rolling and heaving in the short sea, and betraying the entrance as a bird that leaves its nest.

Tzu Hang entered the outer harbour and, still rolling leisurely, made her way towards the lock gates, which led to the inner harbour and the canal for Amsterdam. Once inside, we turned to starboard and moored up to the town wall in front of a row of barges. We had crossed our first sea, and made our first foreign port—soon Clio had made her first foreign friend. We came back to the boat, where we had left Clio while we went shopping. She met us round-eyed.

"Mummy, I've got a friend," she said, "and do you know what?"

"No, what?"

"She speaks Dutch."

On the morning that we decided to leave for Amsterdam, a fresh wind was blowing us on to the wall. Kevin suggested how we should leave, but I preferred to leave my way. I proposed to push the stern off from the wall, and then to go astern, past the row of barges that were moored two-deep behind us, as another ship in front of us restricted any movement ahead. I had not realised the effect of the wind on the foremast, the bow, and the shallow keel for'ard, while the deeper keel aft held the stern, as a pivot.

All went well to start with, and *Tzu Hang* moved astern, while Beryl, hanging on to the shrouds, fended off from the wall. We were already passing the first barges when the wind took charge, and *Tzu Hang*, paying no attention to the rudder, swung her bowsprit in towards the sea wall. It caught in the shrouds of the first barge, and then seemed to go twanging down a line of shrouds, like a guitar player's fingers on his strings. One after another they fell slack.

The crews of these barges, large sea-booted or wooden-clogged men, had been sitting on deck, or on the sea wall, smoking with their backs to the wind, for it was a holiday. Now they rushed to the weather rail, grabbing boathooks as they came. *Tzu Hang* was confronted by a row of waving boathooks and angry shouts of "Not good—bad!" It looked like the battle of the Texel once again, but fortunately they had no guns to rake us, and before they could board us, we had drawn clear.

"Did we carry away their shrouds?" I asked Beryl anxiously.

"No," she said. "They had a quick release, which they were letting go."

There was no sound from Kevin. I looked round for him. He was sitting on the deck and had pulled his old blue coat over his head to hide his yachting cap and the badge of his club.

We had an uneventful trip to Amsterdam, the bridges all opening obediently to our squeaky fog horn. In the city itself we passed a Dutch destroyer heading seawards. We lowered our ensign in salute and saw to our satisfaction a seaman clatter down from the bridge and run the whole length of the ship to the ensign staff. The great ensign then gave us a haughty nod of six inches and shot back into place, as if it was almost ashamed of this courtesy to so humble a visitor. Shortly afterwards we went into the yacht harbour and found a vacant place next to a magnificent motor yacht. Seamen materialised from everywhere to assist us and to prevent us from touching its glossy sides. It turned out to be the Queen's yacht, but even then I wondered whether news of our departure from Ijmuiden had not already reached Amsterdam.

We left Amsterdam on a week-end and found the lock that opened into the Ijsselmeer full of yachts. As a pilot I chose one much larger and beamier than ourselves, but unfortunately with less draft. Soon we were stationary, while all the others, some under sail and some under power, swept on. We set sail, so that *Tzu Hang* heeled, and soon ploughed our way back into the channel, but from then on, I took care to check the chart carefully and go my own way. Even then we had sundry minor groundings and not until we hauled out in Burnham did I discover that *Tzu Hang*'s draft was seven feet, and not the six feet that for some reason I had believed it to be. A few inches are apt to make quite a difference when cruising in Dutch waters.

We anchored for one night in a channel amongst tall reeds on the east side of the sea. A quiet place with wild duck flighting and the murmur of cyclists talking as they sped homeward over a road bridge a little further up the channel. Next day, with a calm sea and gentle wind, we sailed across to Enkhuizen, with distant windmills and church towers all around just showing on the horizon, almost as if they were themselves afloat. We had a problem at Enkhuizen because *Tzu Hang* was considerably lower than the top of the sea wall. Stolid Dutchmen sat on benches and watched Beryl clamber ashore by way of the shrouds and lightboards, so that we could throw lines up to her to make fast to the bollards. The streets were full of notices about emigration to Canada, so Beryl and I hoped that those who went would be a little more outgoing and helpful than the natives here.

The next day we sailed to the locks in the Aflutsdijk which contains the Ijsselmeer, and the following day passed through them bound for Terschelling. Much must have happened in Terschelling since we were there twenty years ago; the old town, clasping its harbour in its arms and sheltered by a cloak of low sand dunes and yellow grass, had turned its back to the north wind and the brown eroding sea. It seemed untouched by time, as if the slow pulse-beat of the great old lighthouse, built of bricks, that peered over the dunes from the very middle of the town, regulated all life in semi-hibernation.

Its rhythmic beat illuminated the windows of all the town besides the skylights of *Tzu Hang*. How many thousands of Terschellingers must have been conceived under its watchful and fleeting beam; how many must have seen its flash on window and wall as they entered into life; and how many as they quitted it. I felt that those who had spent their childhood under the light must show some sign of its effect on them when they grew up. A twitch perhaps, or a slow and ponderous walk, or a tendency to view things from all sides. How many Dutchmen, I wondered, far away in Indonesia, or in Japanese jails during the war, had been reminded by some passing light that momentarily illuminated a wall, of Terschelling, of ordered and reliable things, and had gained hope for the future. There was something about its timing, an insistence that it would never stop; or if it stopped, that it would do so only to give warning of some dire calamity, such as the dikes breaking, or the Mayor of Terschelling falling into the sea.

The narrow streets were lined by looking-glasses attached to sitting-room windows, so that eyes within could watch all that went on up and down the street without betraying vulgar curiosity. Should Dirk for one moment hold Maria's hand at the corner, fifty eyes could see, two hundred and fifty fingers stop their needlework, and twenty-five mouths start talking.

One afternoon in Terschelling, a small sailing craft sailed up to us, and failed to put about correctly, so that it made sternway and its mast became entangled in our shrouds. It was manned by two cadets from the Nautical School, both no doubt captains now. They came on board later to apologise, and before they knew what had happened they were entrapped by Kevin into a long and only partially understood lecture on sailing. A piece of paper was soon covered with wind arrows and hulls and sails.

"Now, this is where you should go about," he explained. "If you come too close you see, the wind is deflected and so you missed your tack."

"We are sorry," said the two earnest young men in unison, their fair heads bent over Kevin's drawing. "We drifted backwards."

"Then you should have thrown out the anchor," said Kevin severely.

"We have no anchor," they said, still in unison.

Next day we passed a yacht that had run on to a buoy and was being hauled out for repairs. "Now, let that be a lesson to you," Kevin said. "Never go too close to a buoy." It seemed a lesson hardly worth pointing out, and yet on occasions since then I have remembered it as I have seen the tide sweeping me towards a buoy that I was rounding.

We had intended to sail up the Friesische Islands, those

fabled islands of the *Riddle of the Sands*; but we broke a boom fitting rolling in a choppy sea with too little wind, so had to put back to Terschelling to have it repaired. By the time this was done, it was time for Kevin to return to England, as he had a date to honour aboard another yacht. We started in calm weather, sailing quietly down the coast; yet by next morning there was a fresh following wind and we came racing into the estuary, past sand banks and through deeps, where the Dutch and British guns had once thundered in desperate battle. Beryl, Clio, and I all felt seasick again and I best remember Kevin trying to keep Clio amused in the cockpit so that she would forget it.

He was wearing several jerseys under his blue jacket with oilskins on top. He had put his white cap cover on, as it was May 1, and fastened the whole thing on his head with a woollen scarf, tied under his chin. He was a rotund figure and now he burst into a Punjabi song, stretching both arms out level with his shoulders, one pointing over the weather rail and one across his chest. Then he rolled and waggled himself about in imitation of an Indian dancing girl, writhing his tubby, powerful fingers as he sang:

"Hamen lao pani-a nati-a se" (he sang).
"Bring me water from the well, from the well, from the well,"
"Bring me water from the well" (his voice rose to a quavering shriek).
"Bring me water from the well" (and then fell again)
"Bring me water from the well, from the well, from the well."

Nothing could possibly be more unlike the slim silver-belled figures that I remembered, or imagined I remembered; but it charmed Clio. Her laughter mingled with the gull's cry. Seasickness was forgotten. "Go on," I heard her cry, and Kevin went on asking for more water from the well. I watched the two figures, the one sere, stout and strangely wrapped, the other so young and slim, swooping up and down close together across the hurrying sky, until the sand banks gave us protection. Soon we were into the Crouch and moored up on our buoy, a cruising yacht returning from abroad. Had we enough money in our pockets, we could have leant against the bar and listened with condescension to humble little stories of coastal yachtsmen. Had I a yachting cap I might have grown a beard.

CHAPTER THREE

Down Channel

It was decided to put *Tzu Hang* on a mud berth against the town wall for fitting out. The two riggers came on board to move her, one a small neat sailor who worked aloft, the other his mate, a bulkier man, who hauled him up and spliced below. Both were salty characters.

"Now do you want me to take her?" asked Bert, the little man and the leader of the two. "There's a nasty tide running and we'll have to pop her in fast."

I was only too pleased to hand over to these sailors who were always handling yachts; putting them on buoys, on mud berths or on slips, as if they were accustomed to every idiosyncrasy that any yacht might display. He took her downstream and then lined her up for a newly-vacated berth in a row of yachts along the wall. The tide was carrying her down fast as he angled across the stream, and then at the last moment straightened her out.

"Damn it," he said, "I'll have to give her the gun or we'll be too low." He opened up the throttle which had now been adjusted. There was a surge of power and *Tzu Hang* ran smoothly into her berth, but she didn't stop there. She paid no attention to the engine hard astern, but climbed up the mud so that it looked as if she was going to run into the wall. Instead, she poked her bowsprit over the wall just as a cyclist came down the footpath, striking him as Sir Launcelot smote Sir Sagramour le Desirous, "so that horse and man fell both to the earth".

"What the bloody hell?" asked the cyclist as he picked himself up and peered angrily over the wall.

"You want to look where you're going," said Bert, unmoved, "and you shouldn't be on the footpath bicycling."

"And you don't want to be on it neither," shouted the furious cyclist.

May already, and soon we should be leaving. We bicycled over to Steeple to see the Pyes at Mizzen Cottage, and to absorb all the good advice that they could give us. Peter and Anne had already been across the Atlantic to the West Indies, so we based our timing on his advice, not to leave before June and not to start across the Atlantic before October. This was going to give us plenty of time to see something of Spain, to call at Puerto Santo, Madeira and the Canaries.

One day, bicycling back to Burnham in the dark, after leaving the Pyes much later than we had expected, and having no lamps on our cycles, I told Beryl that I would go ahead as a scout, and if I saw a policeman I'd whistle. As I went on ahead, all my military senses now on the alert, I could hear Beryl and Clio chattering away and a loud squeak from one of Clio's pedals. A light rain was falling, and although it was dark, it was not yet so dark that one could see nothing. The May evening still lingered and there was a sweet smell from the hedgerows of wet grass and flowers refreshed by rain. I came to a corner, dismounted and walked round. I have always had extremely good night sight, and now I saw something like a tree coming down the centre of the road. After a moment's hesitation, I recognised it as a policeman in his cape, wheeling a bicycle. By now Clio and Beryl were close behind me. I blew a piercing whistle on my fingers, and every sound that followed, the sudden scrape of feet, the crash of a bicycle on the ground, the whispers and the giggles, betrayed the sudden and urgent dismounting of my family. A moment later they appeared round the corner, rather out of breath. The large dark figure passed us in a haughty and suspicious silence, without the customary "Good night."

Peter had suggested that we should leave from Fowey in Cornwall, and he advised us to allow ten days for our trip down Channel, as head winds could make this a slow voyage; in the old days sailing ships sometimes anchored for weeks in the Downs between Dover and Ramsgate, awaiting a fair wind to take them down Channel.

Tzu Hang was taken from her mud berth and put on the hard to have her bottom painted with anti-fouling. She was then put back on her buoy, while other small tasks were completed.

We made various trips to London for charts and navigational books and instruments. Beryl got herself a small sextant, designed for use in lifeboats, and with this and Mary Blewitt's *Celestial Navigation for Yachtsmen*, she was soon able to take and work out a sight. She never really knew what she was doing, nor ever has, but like some fair witch she followed Mary Blewitt's formula, stirred her pot, and out came the right answer. My sextant was a much older model with a bone arc and vernier scale, but easy to read and lacking only a good telescope and a light for reading in bad light. The first time that I worked out a sight was on the buoy at Burnham, making a guess at the horizon, when to my surprise the position line came out correctly.

We left in the middle of June, making the French coast on the first night and then tacking back towards Dover. We were destined to have a head wind all the way, and on subsequent passages down Channel have never yet had a fair one. As we approached Dover, the wind strengthened and I discovered something wrong with the mizzen track which required repair. We decided to put in to Dover, but had just got outside the harbour entrance when the engine stopped. Beryl and I had to get up sail sharply, so called Clio to the wheel.

"Turn her this way, Clio, this way. No, not that way, turn the wheel the other way. Ha ha. That's right. You're doing fine." We neighed and gnashed our teeth in false smiles. It is difficult to conceal anxiety from a child and both Beryl and I were needlessly anxious, feeling too close to shallows and cliffs, with the tide setting strongly out of the harbour. As soon as we had the sails up and *Tzu Hang* on the right tack, I went aft to relieve the small figure who had been anxiously turning the wheel as her parents shouted instructions. I was all real smiles now. "Well done," I said, but it was too late. Her parents obviously had feet of clay and she dived below in tears.

The next half-hour I spent making my self seasick on paraffin as I cleared a fuel stoppage. The engine started again, but by now the tide had taken us some way from Dover, so we switched it off and tacked slowly up against the tide towards the entrance. A powerful Colin Archer-designed double-ender beat past us, while we tacked slowly up under short sail, just holding our own against the tide. Presently we saw them take down their sails.

"There you are," said Beryl. "I bet they are going in to Dover too. I don't see why we have to flog about like this."

"Because I want to be near the entrance when the tide changes."

"But Eric Hiscock says that we should not get tired and that we should have a warm meal. And you're tired and we haven't had a warm meal." By now the yacht was drifting past us with no one on deck. "There you are, you see. I bet that's what they are doing. Having a rest and a warm meal, all snug below."

A couple of hours later they were almost on the Goodwin sands, approaching a forest of masts of wrecked ships, most of them remains of war-time disasters. "They are getting mighty close to the sands," I said. "I wonder if they are all right."

"Of course they are," Beryl affirmed.

At about the turn of the tide we were near the entrance to the harbour again and I started the engine without taking down the sails; but before we went in, the other yacht passed us, its sails stowed and its engine exhaust burbling happily.

"They really know what they are doing," said Beryl.

Life with her had been one of laughter, and sometimes I wonder how she could have put up with me for so long, and I marvel at the luck that led me to her; but there have been rare occasions when I have felt just the opposite. This was one of them. We had, after all, after various vicissitudes, arrived in Dover harbour. Beryl's complaint, if she had voiced it, would have been that we had bumbled our way in six hours later than we should have done, unlike these other efficient yachtsmen, who, finding the tide against them, rested and fed below until it was time to go in. We shouted to them to come over for tea, which they did. One was an Englishman and one was an American, both experienced yachtsmen, who were delivering their ship to Spain.

"For God's sake, did you see us?" asked the American. "We bust our backstay."

"Had to take sail down as we thought the mast would go. Then the engine wouldn't start. Full of water."

"We had to mop it out and then fill it with gas and set it on fire to dry it," said the American. "Charles was standing over it with the fire extinguisher."

"Never thought we'd get it going. We were almost on the Goodwins. Thank goodness it started in time."

45

The rest of our passage down Channel was made in sunny or hazy weather, with one day of fog, when some tired and lost pigeons flew round us. They wouldn't settle on *Tzu Hang*, but kept attempting to land on the sea. We were often in sight of the English coast, continually surprised at the ground that we hadn't made with the tide against us, and relieved at the distance that we made good when it was with us. As the sea was calm we would have done better to have "tided" down Channel, as ships used to do, anchoring for the contrary tide, but we wanted the experience of staying at sea, of keeping watches and of keeping going.

Nothing is nicer than sailing down the English coast in fine weather, seeing all the cliffs and headlands so steeped in history. Nothing makes my pride in English origin greater than to see her shore like this, when I do not have to suffer the penitence of spreading towns and overburdened roads. A week after leaving Burnham we saw the white cones of the china clay quarries on the green Cornish slopes and sailed into Fowey to anchor in the harbour.

Next morning a man rowed out to us from the yacht club steps and asked if he could come on board. Beryl and I were surprised at such an out-going display of friendliness, but it turned out that he was an Australian on a holiday to see something of the Old Country; he had his own yacht in Australia and was a great enthusiast for stainless steel rigging, which was then still suspect in conservative yachting circles. He brought us an invitation from the club to make use of its facilities, which were not very extensive as far as women were concerned, but after this glimpse through a window of kindliness, the curtain of club reserve fell back into place. During our stay in Fowey, Clio was the only person who met a yachtsman, and he was an elderly one, sunning himself on a bench on the club lawn. She was already showing some of her mother's sense of humour, with a good feeling of the ridiculous.

"What were you talking about?" asked Beryl.

"Oh, he was asking me where we were going, and things like that."

"And what did you say?"

"I told him that we were sailing to Canada. He said that we were lucky because we could get something to eat there. And do you know what?" she added, her eyes sparkling. "He said that the Government was keeping the meat rationing on in England, because if they didn't there'd be a revolution. He said he noticed it with his dogs. They never fought when they didn't get meat."

While we were in Fowey we heard from a friend that a young man who had just finished engineering college would like to do a trip with us before he started work, and was prepared to tutor Clio.

"I think that we ought to see him first, before we come to any decision."

Bill Ellingworth arrived next day. He was carrying an enormous suitcase which he put on board *Tzu Hang*. It was obvious that he had already decided that he was coming with us, and one look at him decided us too. He was half Australian, like Beryl, so they got on well together. He was tall, with a merry freckled face and a pleasant self-assurance. Although he had been educated in England, that great open sunburnt country Australia had left its mark on him, something intangible but good. He couldn't join us then, but we arranged for him to do so in Corunna.

The last rite before leaving port is almost invariably that of taking on water. For this we went up the harbour and tied on to a pier from which china clay was loaded on to small cargo vessels, and from which white dust drifted down on to *Tzu Hang*'s deck and through the skylight into the cabin. A three-inch fire-hose was lowered from the pier head and taken through a skylight to fill the two forward tanks which had no deck fittings. They were sited under the forward bunks, and it was necessary to remove bedding and drawers to get at them. The cocks which controlled the water were at the other end of the pier, a hundred yards away. The pier watchman stationed himself at the water cock, Beryl at the head of the pier and myself in the cabin. We explained that we only wanted a quarter of a turn, but fire-hoses know no moderation.

"All ready!" I shouted up to Beryl and heard her repeat it down the pier. Suddenly the pipe swelled and writhed as water thundered into the tank. In a matter of seconds, it was over-flowing. "Too fast!" I yelled, pulling the nozzle out to plunge it in the other tank, as water sprayed over the bedding and into the drawers, and before there was any diminution in the stream, that tank too was overflowing. "Stop!" I yelled, my voice shrill

47

with anxiety lest *Tzu Hang* should sink before we got the water turned off. I pulled the nozzle out and doubled it back, pushing it through the skylight and spraying the deckhead and myself as I did so. In the end, the excess water didn't amount to so very much, and we finished off watering through the deck fittings, then washed down the decks before making our way back to the anchorage.

We spent the night at anchor, now complete with water, fuel, food and charts. *Tzu Hang* felt replete, so replete that the waterline had risen an inch along her side. We felt excited and eager to go. Now we were on our own, and in Peter Pye's words, were going foreign—Clio, Beryl, myself, and a hamster; but we did not feel nearly as nervous as we had done when we first set off from Dover.

I have not mentioned the hamster before, possibly because it was one of the most devilish creatures that we ever had on board. We gave it to Clio soon after our arrival in England, thinking that it would be a convenient little pet for her to have on board. When she went to Yorkshire, my sister, who is also my twin, was adamant about the hamster. She would not have it. Beryl and I were landed with it and its nasty habit of eating anything thrown down near its cage, but Clio loved it dearly, so we had to look after it. One morning we found it dead, probably from a glut of yellow oilskin; we decided to replace it without telling Clio, but had the greatest difficulty in matching it with anything that would fool a grown-up, let alone a child. We looked at thousands of hamsters but there was always something wrong in colour, size or expression. Eventually we settled on one which was a poor substitute, but in every bad respect exactly duplicated the other, especially in its sly and destructive eating habits.

When Clio rejoined us she recognised immediately that it was not hers. However, for better or for worse, it was now part of the ship's company, and "Oh, that bloody hamster!" became a common cry on board. It was apparently determined that we were bound for the Arctic, for it was possessed with the idea of laying in a store of wool, at the expense of our clothes and bedding.

We sailed next morning. Past the Dodman and past the Lizard that night. Next morning we were off the Runnelstone when the *Mauretania* overtook us on her way to New York. Past the distant black and white pillar of Wolf Rock lighthouse, all in gentle summer weather, until on our second morning at sea we had the low outline of the Scillies behind us as we headed south with the intention of giving Ushant a berth of forty miles.

Three times have we crossed the Bay and each has been uneventful, but on this run we had the worst weather, beating down towards Finisterre. It was rough and wet so we were soaked, lying in wet clothes on wet bunks, and wondering whether we were experiencing a gale or not. This is what we imagined ocean passages were like anyway. It was not until another yachts-man homeward bound from Portugal wrote of a Force 8 following gale and gave the date and position, close to us, that we promoted our experience beyond "getting a bit wet", as we thought Eric Hiscock and Peter Pye would refer to it. Since *Tzu Hang* was going to windward on long tacks, she sailed herself under short sail. We kept our watches, usually in the cockpit, but sometimes under the shelter of the doghouse.

One day, while *Tzu Hang* was sailing herself and I was sitting in the hatch-way, a cargo ship approached and altered course to have a closer look at us. We had tied a large blue teddy bear of Clio's to the wheel; it was wearing oilskins and a sou'wester, sitting on the cockpit seat, with a paw lashed to a spoke. I slipped down and called to Clio and Beryl to come and watch. It was a rough wild day, and as the freighter rolled ponderously past, I saw the Captain come out of his cabin, in shirt-sleeves and braces, and look down on us. Then he ran back and returned with a pair of binoculars which he fixed on "Blue Bear" until we had drawn apart. We remained well hidden below until they were out of sight.

It took us a week to make our landfall, and on the day before doing so, the weather having moderated, we hove to for a good sleep and a dry out. Clio and the hamster were as lively as ever. We were both dead tired, but after a few hours' sleep, much re-freshed and ready to go again. Though my sights had corres-ponded with my dead reckoning, I had as yet no proof that either was correct, nor during that last night did we see any trace of a light; but according to my calculations we should have been approaching the coast about ten miles west of Corunna.

Daylight came, and with what hope I scanned the horizon; but there was no sign of land. It was not until breakfast time that I saw it, at first grey and indistinct, but higher than I had expected, and almost part of the cloud that shrouded it. Then it took on more solid shape; colour began to show, and here and there the small white square of a cottage on the hill.

Presently we could recognise Cape Ortegal away to port, and the Isla Sikargas to starboard, both dim and distant, so we turned east for Corunna. *Tzu Hang* sailed past a fishing boat in the bay, where a fisherman was pulling in lobster pots. "Dondé estamos?" Beryl shouted to my shame, for by now I had seen the Pillar of Hercules at Corunna.

There was still a rough sea, and I thought that we would find better shelter in Ferrol, so into the narrow channel we sailed, through the passage that the Spaniards used to block with chains against Drake's ships, to anchor in the harbour off the village of La Lusada. We celebrated our arrival with lobsters and a bottle of wine ashore, and never have lobsters and wine tasted so good. back on the boat we slept as if drugged, and it was a day or two before we caught up on the rest that was missing.

CHAPTER FOUR

In Spain

We spent a week in Ferrol, and during this time had gusty winds and rain, so there was little chance to dry out our clothes and bedding. We walked on the cliffs by the sea, where there was gorse and heather shaken by the wind, wet with rain, sparkling for brief moments to fleeting sunshine, while showers filled the valleys and hid the hills behind. If I had fallen asleep and opened my eyes without knowing where I was, I should have guessed that it was the west coast of Scotland. Bill Ellingworth was not due for a week or more, so we had time to fill in, and every day the sound of rockets popping in the sky showed that some village near was holding a fiesta, rain of fine.

Three naval officers from a Spanish cruiser sailed over to *Tzu Hang* one evening in a grey whaler; they came on board, a Lieutenant-Commander and two Lieutenants. Soon the two younger officers had discovered Clio's small rubber elephant, which squirted water from its trunk, and were busily engaged in soaking her and each other. The Commander spoke French, which we spoke after a fashion; Beryl could get along in Spanish, which she had picked up in South America during her travels there, including the long ride that she had made up the Western Cordillera from Magallanes, but I spoke no Spanish at all. They insisted that we should come to supper with them on the cruiser, so we and the elephant embarked in the whaler. The elephant was soon dropped overboard and, being fully charged, sank to the bottom of Ferrol harbour. Clio was dismayed.

At this moment we were passing under the stern of the beautiful three-masted Spanish training vessel, the *Galatea*. The settling sun had momentarily illuminated her mast-heads, as the rest of the ship was in shade, when a bugle call rang out, and her ensign was lowered. The Commander let his sheet fly and brought the whaler into the wind. The three officers stood up at the salute as the ensign, and the ensigns of other ships in the bay, came down.

"What are they doing, Mummy?" asked Clio as the notes of the bugle died.

The Commander, still at the salute, bent towards her. "Pour le pauvre éléphant," he told her solemnly.

Soon after the loss of the elephant, we sailed over to Corunna and tied up near the yacht club in oily water. *Tzu Hang* has never enjoyed the atmosphere of big ports and rarely that of yacht clubs, although she owes much to their hospitality, so no sooner were we there than we began to think of leaving a message for Bill Ellingworth to join us in Camarinos Bay, a few miles down the coast.

While cashing a cheque in the bank, a young Englishman, Joe Mitchell, hearing my problem with the language, came up to me and asked if he could be of any assistance. He had been in the Royal Artillery during the war, and after his demobilisation had gone to Australia. He and Joy, his partner in a photographic business, were on a holiday in Spain for the first time, but before coming they had both learned to speak Spanish fluently. He was an eager but as yet deprived yachtsman, and he jumped at the offer to sail to Camarinos with us, leaving Joy to find her way by road. It was his first time on a yacht and he was desperately seasick. Too sick to go below, and after a time too weak to use the rail as a head. We seated him on a bucket by the shrouds to which he clung, sitting on one receptacle, with an alternative readily available, and making use of both at the same time. Since those days, Joe has risen from strength to strength, and is not only a very successful businessman, but has owned his own cruising yacht, and is a very experienced racing helmsman. He had to be tough and dedicated to go on with it after that initiation. We put in to the small village of Corme, in a bay exposed to the west, and there had a meal in a restaurant on stilts overlooking the anchorage, and later exchanged two old shirts for two magnificent cooked lobsters which we brought on board. Next day we came to Camarinos, a lovely bay, although it offered little protection from the south-west, where we anchored outside the small fishing harbour and its impoverished village.

Here we met a tall Spaniard, an engineer on holiday from Madrid, who spoke English. He came to Camarinos every year and was known by everyone. One day, while having a drink with him in a village bar, he was answering questions put to him by the local fishermen.

"What were they saying?" I asked him later.

"I was telling them about you and about where you were going," he replied. "They said that if God had been so good to you as to give you so much wealth that you can own a boat like that, then you should stay ashore and enjoy it. They said that it is absolutely wrong to risk the danger and discomfort of an Atlantic passage in so small a ship, when there is obviously no need to."

In those days, only a few years after the war, there were obvious signs of poverty, particularly in the larger ports; there were beggars and thin, pinch-faced children with large eyes. In the country and in the small fishing ports it was different. There were bread and olives and cheese, sufficient for all, fish when the boats came in, and always wine to be drunk and time to be wasted in the warm sunlight, or at a fiesta over the hill. There was also an easy relationship between the rich who came to spend their holidays here and the poor who lived here, an equality in the sight of God. Perhaps those who came to spend their holidays in a fishing village rather than in more sumptuous hotels were good and sympathetic people anyway.

Memory holds the door open on sunshine, but there were clouds too. Our chief problem was financial. We had not much left over from the money that we had been allowed to take out of England to maintain the ship for a long voyage, and to feed ourselves. Our days in port were often spent in long trudges in search of some article of ship's equipment which turned out to be unavailable in Spain, where there was only fishing boat tackle, heavy blocks, black iron and sisal rope. Inevitably, beginners ourselves and with our first boat, the voyage showed all sorts of things which had to be done although they should have been done before we started. Then there was the problem of stores with daily marketing and long, overloaded trudges back to the boat. Cruising sometimes seemed remarkably hard work.

One day in Vigo, a British yacht came in and made fast off the yacht club, and very soon the well-dressed crew were ashore and off to the club for a cocktail before lunch. That is what I felt we ought to be doing as I remembered the two cases of whale meat (canned in the Antarctic) that looked as if they were going to be our staple diet at sea. The other crew didn't seem to have a care in the world and at times we felt overburdened with them. It was largely due to inexperience and shortage of cash. As the voyage progressed and the sun shone brighter, so did our confidence and enjoyment increase. Whale meat turned out to be our favourite dish, and when we finally got back to Salt Spring Island, we gave our American neighbours a deep-sea dinner on *Tzu Hang* of whale meat washed down with the Barbados rum that had replaced the Scotch with which we had left England, both, of course duty free. I don't know whether it was the rum, the whale meat, the novelty or their good manners, but they voted it the dinner of a lifetime.

Because of the inevitable shopping and chores that took up so much time in the bigger ports, we enjoyed particularly those anchorages where there was only a village or nothing at all. Camarinos was one of these.

Bill arrived by bus from Corunna after a crowded third-class journey across France, when he had had to stand in the corridor all the way. At Corunna a guide had offered to find him a hotel, but it was the day of the big bull-fight and all the hotels were full. Finally the guide offered to give Bill a bed in his own house and Bill, tottering with exhaustion, accepted. They went up long flights of steps to a small flat, where the guide opened a bedroom door. Several children were asleep in one bed. "Out," ordered the guide, and they scurried away into the darkness as if they were used to this sort of nocturnal disturbance. "There is your bed," said the guide. "I hope that you will sleep well." Bill did not mind where he slept as long as he got his feet up.

He was looking flushed when he arrived, and soon confessed that he wasn't feeling very well. Beryl took his temperature in the same way as she was accustomed to testing Clio's, by putting her lips to his forehead. "You've got a temperature," she said.

"I've got a rash," he said.

"Take your shirt off and let's have a look at it," Beryl ordered.

Bill had already told us of his night in Corunna, so it did not take the veteran of third-class accommodation, caravanserais and camps long to diagnose his complaint.

"Those are bites," said Beryl. "Bed bugs. You must have

slept with thousands." Next day Bill was recovering but Clio was bitten, and we began to wonder how many Bill had brought on board with him, and how we would get rid of them in a wooden boat. The following morning for the hundredth time I imagined something walking over me. Inspection showed that something was. A large bed bug was caught and killed and proved to be the only adventurer who had accompanied Bill from Corunna.

We left Camarinos with the friendly engineer and his son and sailed to Corcubión, and on the next day, giving Corrubedo Bay and its hidden rocks a wide berth, we sailed into Muros Bay. A thick blanket of cloud was capping the mountains beyond Muros as we headed for the harbour. Beryl called my attention to the glass, which had dropped an inch in a very short time, but it never occurred to me that in a short time we would not be safe in harbour. A line of white water to windward gave us only a moment's notice before the squall hit us. *Tzu Hang* heeled far over and then surged forward. In a moment the bay seemed to shrink to half its size, and, as the sailing marks disappeared in driving rain, it seemed fraught with danger. Bill had only made one short passage with us and did not yet know his way about the halyards. In the rush to get off sail, he was letting go anything that came to hand, so that we soon had a halyard streaming to leeward and another with its shackle at the mast-head; but at least we got sail off, and with only stay-sail and mizzen set, continued to rush across the bay. On our placid way up I had noticed several fishing boats get up their anchors and make for the lighthouse behind us, so as we put about and came back on a reverse bearing we saw a congregation of boats, including some of our size and larger, huddled close under the light in a patch of sheltered water. We could make the same place on our tack, and as we came astern of the larger boats, every fisherman throughout the congregation of craft made the gesture of throwing overboard the anchor. This we did as *Tzu Hang* turned into the wind and soon she was lying securely while we set about tidying up the halyards.

The violent wind passed as quickly as it had arrived and suddenly all was calm and sunshine again. "The tornado is over!" shouted the fishermen as they got up anchor and made off for the harbour. The skipper of the nearest and largest signalled to us to follow him, which we did, and anchored near him. He called us over to a meal of fresh sardines cooked in a large open pan on deck and eaten with the fingers.

Next morning, following Peter Pye's instructions, we sailed further up the bay to Punta Capitan, and there Emilio Borraz rowed out in a small dinghy to make us welcome, and took us in immediately to a picnic on the point, where we drank white wine and ate oysters that an old servant pried off the rocks. Emilio is the oldest brother of the three Borraz men, who make their home with their mother at Punta Capitan and whose family have lived there for generations. Emilio is the sailor and usually at sea, while the other two brothers run the farm and look after some of the mussel rigs which now fill the bay but which were then non-existent. Of all the hundreds of happy days that we have spent in *Tzu Hang*, those at Punta Capitan have been among the happiest. There is a permanence about the old farm-house with the Borraz crest over the gate, that contrasted with our own gypsy life. There is a permanence about the old grey walls and the ivy that grows on them, about the apple trees in the orchard, and the courtyard with a trellis of vines under which we ate.

The three Borraz men must be three of the most energetic men in Spain, as they never appear to need sleep and consequently always seem to have time for leisure. Time to talk, time for a song, time to drink a glass of wine or set off on an expedition. In summer there are visitors from Madrid who have summer houses in the village, and the most distinguished of these was Señora Recoy. We went to a party at her house and Bill, demonstrating a waltz with Beryl, cut his head on a glass chandelier in the centre of the room, which was not rigged for men of his or my height.

Señora Recoy was most distressed, and as she was enquiring after his small hurt, I noticed that Bill had taken one of the Señora's table napkins out of his pocket and was mopping the cut with it.

"I do apologise for him," I said to the Señora. "Of course he is absent-minded and took it by mistake. What a dreadful thing to have done."

Meanwhile Beryl put her hand into my breast pocket and took out another of Señora Recoy's napkins, which she returned with a laugh, leaving me to apologise on my own account.

"How did you know?" I asked her afterwards.

"I didn't," she replied, "but I know you."

Our stay ended with an expedition to Villagarçía, where the fisherman who had fed us sardines at Muros had explained that there lived the most beautiful women in Spain, at the same time making a wineglass shape with his hands. By the time that we started on the expedition, we had a platoon of Borraz men and women and their friends on board. One of them was an elderly grey-haired man of extreme gentility, who sat in the cockpit wearing a grey felt hat and resting both hands on the top of a gold-knobbed cane. He had been an enthusiastic amateur bull-fighter in his youth, and in moments of excitement was apt to snap his fingers and call, "Ha—Toro, toro." Unable to retain his seat while Beryl, who was steering, got up to change to the weather side as she put the ship about, he always leapt to his feet and bowed, but unfortunately he usually bowed too late, so the boom caught his head as it came over.

We had agreed to the expedition only on the condition that we returned to Punta Capitan before dark; but the platoon went ashore like an assault landing and were soon dispersed throughout the town. It was long after dark by the time that we had rounded them up again, and without a detailed chart, I had little idea of where we were or where we were going. Fortunately Emilio, the sailor, fortified by "el (duty free) Scotch", was at the helm. "Me and the Capitan, we navigate very well," he shouted as each successive danger was avoided, assisted by the shouts of one brother to steer to starboard and the other to steer to port. The dangers proved usually to be small fishing vessels with the crews frantically striking matches to show where they were. A skin of wine and "el duty free Scotch" had circulated freely and everyone agreed that it was a stupendous party, but in Spain very little is needed to make a party a success. I was glad enough to have them all safely home at the anchorage, but still had not even seen the beautiful wingelass-shaped women of Villagarçía.

From Punta Capitan we sailed to Pontevedra Bay and from there to Vigo. The yacht club there was magnificent but there were few yachts, and none to match it, while the basin was the dirtiest that we have ever been in, full of oil and indescribable refuse.

We were going anyway, as *Tzu Hang* had been persuaded to

take part in her one and only race, an annual affair organised by the Yacht Club of Vigo to Bayona. It was a day of no wind so the start found *Tzu Hang* facing in the wrong direction and unable to turn round. When this was accomplished she was last by some distance, while *Lightnings and Stars* quickly enlarged the gap. The only other yacht in *Tzu Hang*'s class conceded the race and went off fishing, so that *Tzu Hang* became the winner in her class—winner of the slowest race in history. *Tzu Hang*'s performance was not enhanced by her sails, as before leaving Burnham we had had a set of flax sails made with vertical seams, having been persuaded that this was the only material for a long passage. They were disastrous sails, heavy and stiff when new, and hanging like flour bags as sun and weather softened and stretched them. They only set well when reefed or soaking wet, but nevertheless they gave us great service.

In addition to her heavy flax sails, *Tzu Hang*'s halyards were all of hemp and these needed constant attention, setting bar-taut in rain and slackening in sunshine. Now in the days of dacron and terylene, the trials and tribulations of the old-fashioned materials are forgotten, and as far as *Tzu Hang* is concerned, the work in both sailing her and in her upkeep have been halved. Yet there was something honest and traditional about the old materials and I am glad that we used them.

As well as the extra work, we gave ourselves a great amount of unnecessary discomfort due largely to inexperience. The cockpit coaming had water escape holes to let the water out, but they let the water in with equal efficiency, and we had no slatted seats to keep us out of it. Our skylights could never keep out solid water, even with canvas covers, so that in bad weather *Tzu Hang* was not only dark below, but dank as well. All this Beryl and I thought was an inevitable part of the game, and it was not until we had some years of sailing behind us that we were able to make a trade wind passage to windward and keep a dry boat.

The happy and ultimate arrival of all the yachts in Bayona was celebrated by a dance at the country club. Bill represented *Tzu Hang* and noticed a particularly lovely and aristocratic-looking girl, in great demand and obviously enjoying herself. He wondered how he could get an introduction, but before he had made any headway in this direction there was a screech of tyres in the drive outside and an elegant, equally aristocratic, and obviously furious man, came bounding up the long curve of stone steps, burst into the ballroom, seized the girl by the arm and dragged her away from her astonished and alarmed partner.

The band stopped. The dancers, headed by Bill, surged to the porch to watch the end of the drama. The dark-clad man and the girl, wearing a white dress and dragging behind, cascaded down the steps to a black Hispano Suiza. He pulled the door open and flung her in across the driver's seat, and as he followed her in and shut the door behind him, the one on the far side opened as the girl attempted to escape. She did not get far. Like Eurydice she was snatched back into darkness and to who knows what passionate climax, as the tyres screeched again and the car roared off into the night.

A sigh of pride and some envy rose from the watching dancers on the top of the steps. "Ah," they said. "That is the nobility for you."

At Bayona we had the good fortune to meet a Dr. Fernandez, a specialist from Madrid who, with his wife and sister-in-law, was spending a holiday at Bayona, living in a flat that they owned at the top of one of the waterfront houses. His father, before the war, had been for many years the Spanish Consul in Glasgow and the children had been educated in England. One brother, born in England, had become completely English, and was in the Royal Army Medical Corps.

Dr. Fernandez asked us to a meal at a restaurant on the water-front one night, and it was arranged that he and his family should first come on board *Tzu Hang* for a drink. As a result we did not get ashore until about eleven thirty, when the night appeared to be just beginning for Dr. Fernandez. We had just sat down and started ordering our food, when Dr. Fernandez spotted his brother and his English wife, who were also on holiday in Bayona, about to leave. He called them over and introduced us.

The English Dr. Fernandez, dressed in such orthodox English clothes that no one could mistake him for anything but an Englishman, came over rather reluctantly. The Spanish Dr. Fernandez was on the top of his form. "Sit down and join us. The night is young. What will you have?"

"No. Really. Thank you very much. We had our supper ages ago. We've got to go."

"Impossible," said his brother. "Go where?"

"To bed," said the English Dr. Fernandez.

Another evening we had a meal with them in their flat and after dinner they all sang songs, the cook and the maid joining in and accompanying themselves with a spoon and fork held in one hand and clicked together like castanets. It was the happiest of evenings and yet so little was needed to make it so. The flat was sparsely furnished, there were no pictures, the meal was of the simplest, but there was wine, warm hospitality and a gaiety which is typically Spanish. As we were leaving, Beryl noticed two old brass candlesticks on a dresser. They looked as if they had come from a sailing ship.

"Aren't they lovely?" she said.

Dr. Fernandez seized them in both hands and thrust them at her. "Take them," he said. "I insist. To remember this evening by."

They were about the only ornaments in the flat, but we were not permitted to refuse them, and we have them still. Perhaps we were guilty of some breach of etiquette, or perhaps one should never admire anything in Spain.

Dr. Fernandez told us of a yacht which a few years before had sailed from Norway for the Galapagos where the Norwegian family who owned the yacht had a house and intended to settle. It had been wrecked on the coast near Bayona during a storm and the whole crew had been lost except for the daughter, who was about the same age as Clio. She was found on a rock, like the little mermaid at Copenhagen, but suffering from shock and cold, and unable to speak any word to her rescuers except Norwegian. When someone who could speak Norwegian came to see her in hospital, she was able to explain that a sailor, one of the crew, had managed to get her on to the rock, but had been washed away himself. She had gone back to her relations in Norway.

"It's the Costa del Muerte," explained Dr. Fernandez.

On the day that we were due to leave Bayona, a fog hung over the clean little bay, the water dead calm. We decided that we would wait for the fog to clear. Soon after breakfast Dr. Fernandez appeared in a small rowing boat. "Come along," he said. "The octopus are in. It is the first time we have had them this year. You've got to come into the restaurant and have them. In this calm water they can spear them. Absolutely fresh."

We went in and had our meal while the word went around

that we were leaving for Canada. All the occupants came out to see us off and as we got into the dinghy they waded out with us, singing the song of farewell as we rowed away. They stood watching us. The fog was still there but beginning to show signs of lifting. In spite of the Costa del Muerte, fog or no fog, we had to sail now. Bill and I turned to the anchor.

Our first port in Portugal was Leixois, only about seventy miles down the coast from Vigo, and five miles north-west of Oporto; we made it comfortably after a night's run. It has a long, artificial breakwater extending south with a lighthouse at the end and is easy of access but has nothing very attractive about it. We were lucky in having an introduction to friends of Peter Pye, who came on board, bringing an excellent bottle of port, as soon as we were tied up. They drove us across the Douro, over Eiffel's iron bridge, which spans the river in one long arch. A hundred and fifty years before, the Duke of Wellington, marching up from the south to chase Marshal Soult out of Oporto, had heard a loud explosion and discovered that the previous bridge had been destroyed. On learning that some wine barges, over-looked by the French, had been discovered on the far bank and ferried over to his side, he gave the laconic order, "Let the men cross," surely the shortest order for a river crossing ever given. The Duke and his men were welcomed with port—like *Tzu Hang*—by the members of the British factory there, and it is said that the Duke also had the pleasure of eating Marshal Soult's lunch, which was left on the table.

Our friends took us back to dinner in their low-ceilinged, whitewashed house, and when the children were brought in to see us, they said something that made the others laugh. "They said that you were only Rosbifs," they explained, a term which had perhaps been handed down from the days of the Duke of Wellington.

61

CHAPTER FIVE

Lisbon and the Canaries

We sailed from Leixois at midnight, quietly down the inside of the breakwater, hearing the waves thundering on the other side. *Tzu Hang* was like a racehorse walking out of the paddock, about to turn and canter past the stands. She slipped along, silent and attentive, and as she rounded the lighthouse her hull lifted to the scend of the sea, and she set off, straining eagerly for the south. It was a wild rollicking sail and daylight came with grey following seas behind and grey hurrying clouds above. In the afternoon the Islas Berlengas appeared out of the haze to port without any sight of the land behind, a welcome check on our position. It was after dark when we headed in for Cascais and found the navigation lights difficult to pick up among all the lights of the cafes and cinemas ashore.

On our first day in Cascais we had a visit from the British Consul. He had been a regular officer in the Indian Army, like me, and after leaving the Army had taken the necessary exams and was now happily embarked in a new career.

"Is there anything that I can do for you—apart from baths, of course?" he asked.

"Yes," said Beryl. "We want a mouth organ. Could you help us to get one?"

The mouth organ was not for ourselves, but for Emilio Borraz, who had told us that the one thing he wanted was a mouth organ. We had promised to try to find one. Consuls are asked for financial assistance, for legal protection, for passports, for passages to England, but rarely for mouth organs. This one took the request in his stride. "Of course," he said. "Let's go and get one tomorrow. I know of an excellent shop in Lisbon."

Next morning he drove us in his car to Lisbon, to a shop full of mouth organs of all sizes. A selection was put out for us on the counter. "I know absolutely nothing about mouth organs," I said. "Do you?"

"A little," he replied. "They are all good makes. Let's try one." He picked up a mouth organ at least a foot long, moistened his lips and began to play. Never had we heard a mouth organ played like that, nor, obviously, had anyone in the shop, nor a few people passing outside. The Pied Piper had come to Lisbon. He put the instrument back on the counter with reluctance.

"But you are wonderful," said Beryl. "What were you playing?"

"Oh, a little thing by Bach," he said. "Actually I've always been fond of mouth organs, but perhaps that one is a little sophisticated for your friend."

In the end we bought one only six inches long, but extraordinarily expensive. Years later we met Emilio again and asked him how the mouth organ was going. He confessed that he had never been able to play it, but that he had a friend who played it very well.

After a few days in Cascais, another friend of Peter Pye's, and of many yachtsmen who have visited Lisbon, came down to pilot us up the river to Barreiro, across the river from Lisbon, and a quiet and safe anchorage. This was Tony Reynolds, from one of the old English families that have been in the wine or the cork business since the end of the Peninsular War.

Here we enjoyed the hospitality of what seemed to be a small village of Reynolds between the river and the country, bathed in sun, scented with flowers, and bright with children. There was a communal swimming bath and a communal tennis court and they seemed to link both countries with something of the best of both.

From this anchorage we set off one sunny morning down the river and bound for Porto Santo and Madeira, five-hundred-odd miles away. We crossed the busy shipping lane off Cabo Rocas by daylight, and soon had the sea to ourselves. As if to balance the rough weather in the bay and the boisterous Portuguese trades down the coast, we now had only light winds and much sunshine. It was five days before the fairy-tale little hills and jagged points of Porto Santo showed dark above the sea one early morning. The voyage was not completely uneventful. The hamster, after eating its way through Bill's duffle-coat and a camel-hair coat of mine, turned its face to the wall and died.

In order to assuage Clio's grief, we gave it a formal burial at sea, committing the body to the deep in a most punctilious manner. It was only after the funeral that Clio discovered in one of her books on animals that hamsters sometimes went into a coma, from which they recovered in due course. An awful doubt was born in her mind, but her mother promised her a Siamese cat if we could find one in Madeira, and her worries disappeared.

During one of the comparatively short periods when we were completely becalmed, Bill discovered a troop of fish, who, in well-dressed line, marched up and down the shady side of *Tzu Hang*'s hull. "About turn!" roared Bill as they reached the end of their beat, and to his great amusement the fish invariably complied, until *Tzu Hang* began to move, when they broke formation but continued to accompany her.

On arrival at Porto Santo we anchored off the pier in a sandy bay, where there was good swimming, and we made our pilgrimage to Christopher Columbus' house, where it is said that he spent six months without ever seeing Madeira, which is only forty-five miles away. We sailed from Porto Santo at night and presently were able to make out the dark outline of Madeira, first betrayed by lights on the hills, showing like faint strange stars in the southern sky. Morning came with a bustling northeast wind which sent us spinning along until we were a few miles from Funchal, where it dropped us dead and left us becalmed. We started the motor and carried on for the habour; the crew, all on deck in happy anticipation of going ashore, watched the terraced town take shape—the white houses, the red roofs, the patches of colour from garden and trees, the sunshine and the shade. We were met by the pilot boat whose captain showed us where to anchor and called out "two shackles" as he left us—left us wondering what on earth he meant by that.

For Clio, arrival in Madeira meant a Siamese cat for her very own, but although there was a Siamese cat, no kittens were expected just then, and the Siamese cat was not for sale. Instead, Clio discovered a black puppy tied to a vegetable barrow in the market. The owner tried every heartrending wile to induce us to buy it, but we had no intention of having a dog on board and managed to escape without it. We escaped, but not without word going round that there was a girl on the yacht that wanted a puppy and that some weakness had been detected in the parents.

For the next few days we were besieged by bumboats who brought every foundling dog that they could capture in the streets, young or old, large or small, hairy or hairless.

In the end, of course, we got one. Clio had been given her pocket money and with this she bought a small brown puppy only a few weeks old. Its face was pinched, its ribs were sticking out, and its stomach was swollen, a balloon puppy with cardboard legs. By the time we realised what had happened, the puppy was in Clio's arms and the bumboat making off as fast as possible for the shore. The bumboat men had easily discovered the amount of money available and Clio had happily handed it over. I tried to explain the principles of bargaining, but for her, and for them, the whole transaction was absolutely satisfactory.

While we were in Funchal, we decided to make a trip over to the Islas Desertas, making for an anchorage on the lee side of Isla Grande, where a scree falls into the sea, giving the effect of a small pier. Here a yacht can anchor close inshore, with various lines attached to the rocks. I do not think that I would have attempted it if there had not been a fishing boat already there, with men to direct us and take our lines. The north-east wind, blowing over the ridge of the island, leaps over the anchorage before thundering down in gusty down-draughts. It leaves a surprisingly narrow gap of sheltered water, so that a ship coming in is rolled and buffeted by the wind until it seems that she is nearly ashore. Once she is securely tied up, the sheltered water looks considerably larger than it did during the approach, when backed by steep cliffs. Close to this anchorage there are caves at the foot of the cliffs with blue grottoes, and into one of which we were able to row the dinghy.

The Islas Desertas themselves are a fascinating backbone of treeless rock only a few hours' sail from Funchal. We clambered up steps cut in the rock to a lookout in the ridge summit, where a watch was kept for whales, with a radio to inform Funchal of their sighting. Similar stations were maintained at other high points in the Islands. Back at Funchal on the following morning, after a glorious fast sail, we were told that we could go out on one of the tugs that towed the whale-boats on the next chase. We hadn't too long a wait before there was a loud explosion in the town, as a maroon was fired to warn the whale-boat crews that a school had been sighted.

Then there was such excitement in the town as if the enemy was at its gates, and as in Belgium's capital, "there was mounting in hot haste" of bicycles and boats and anything that could get the whaler crews out to their crafts. The bumboat men dropped their lace napkins and seized their oars, the butcher and baker and candlestick-maker threw away aprons and ran wiping their hands on their trousers. All was excitement and shouting as the tugs got under way, each towing three whale-boats, but in all the excitement, the skipper of the smaller tug remembered to come alongside on his way out, to take us with him.

Although we were directed by radio from the mountain-tops, and the whale-boats were towed out by tugs, everything else was in the real Moby Dick tradition. The narrow whale-boats with the harpoon line running down the centre of the boat and coiled in tubs, the long iron throwing harpoon with bamboos lashed round the shaft, the helmsman with a steering oar, the harpooner in the bow when the time arrived. As we made our way towards the east point, it was discovered that one of our three boats was a man short, and that they were signalling that they wanted Bill to replace him. It made me realise that I was getting older, in that they wanted young Bill. However, Bill had not been backward in telling us that he was quite an oar; he had, in fact, rowed for his school and his college, so that we felt that at least he would be a credit to *Tzu Hang*, even if he had never handled such heavy sweeps as those in the whale-boats.

As we rounded the end of the island, excitement mounted. The course that the whales were taking was more or less traditional, and from their last sighting it was possible to assess approximately where they would blow again. The old method of whaling was still used, rather than the harpoon gun, as they thought its noise might cause the whales to avoid the islands altogether.

Presently the boats were cast off and rowed out into a line; almost as soon as they were in position, a whale spouted, but off to a flank. The two end boats set off after it, rowing not exactly like university crews at Barnes Bridge, but with equal energy. One of them was Bill's, and he seemed to be holding his own at number two. The whale continued on its way, rolling lazily up to blow every minute or so before sounding for another long period under water. The men on the tug were counting the blows

66

as the two crews drew near. "That's the last!" they shouted. "That's it! They won't get him now." Soon we could see that the crews were resting on their oars. The tough Portuguese pulling out cigarettes, shouting across to each other, laughing. But number two in the leading boat was not laughing and talking; his head was on his knees in obvious exhaustion.

We saw two whales killed and fortunately Bill had no more long races, but he was not in the boat that made the kill, although if time enriches his memory as perhaps it does mine, he may be in that boat by now. The first whale gave the most gory and brutal battle when, after towing a whale-boat for some time, it was forced to come up and struggle on the surface while the other boats drew near and tried to get their harpoons into some vital place. Eventually, with the sea around red with blood, it was taken over by the tug still alive, while the men on the tug tried to finish it off with a long lance. It was getting late, and to our relief we left the tug and headed homewards, but another whale was sighted and was soon blowing close to the tug and not very far away from one of the boats, so that we were able to see every detail of a short and exciting chase.

In a very short time the boat was alongside the whale and the harpooner drove in his harpoon at a range that could not have been closer. Almost immediately there was a great flurry on the surface. The head raised up and then plunged down as a spout of blood and foam shot from the blow-hole, then up came the tail, towering into the air and smashing down with tremendous force. It caught the stern of the boat, knocking off the sternpost, and throwing the steering oar high into the air. The boat was upset and the crew tipped out into the water. The whale, however, was dead, killed in a few moments by that one fatal harpoon. Another whaler was already picking up the crew when we arrived and took them and the smashed boat on board. Meanwhile, the big tug steamed up and was soon on its way with two whales to the station at the end of the Island.

I think that it was Marin Marie, perhaps with more imagination than truth, who described the toredos at Funchal tapping at his hull as they endeavoured to get in, but he was able to sleep soundly because of his copper sheathing. Toredos are woodworms armed with a drill head like the head of the drill on an oil rig. They are drillers, not tappers, and enter unprotected wood in

67

tropical waters, making a minute entry hole, and in the case of a ship's planking, working along the plank as far as the butt and then turning round and coming back again, growing all the time until their burrows leave only paper-thin wood outside. Copper paint or any anti-fouling paint with enough copper in it is an adequate protection, provided the boat is regularly hauled out and painted.

On our first night in Funchal, as soon as we had turned in, I was aware of a steady tick, tick, ticking sound round the hull of the boat.

"Do you hear that?" I asked Beryl.

"Yes," she replied. "What is it?"

"I hope it's not those bloody toredos."

"You mean the noise Marin Marie heard?"

We imagined them crawling round, tapping away, searching for some unprotected place, and felt as if we were besieged. It was a noise that bedevilled our nights at anchor in certain places until we hauled out several months later and found no trace of toredos. We did not discover that the noise was made by the snapping shrimp until we read Rachel Carson's book, *The Sea Around Us*, some years later. The snapping shrimp is the most common noise-maker, but there are various fish that can be heard in a boat through the hull. We have heard fish that made a croaking noise like a frog, another that makes a drumming noise, and the high-pitched whistle or squeak of porpoises.

As the puppy grew up, it was obvious that he could hear noises that we could not. He always heard porpoises or whales from below, and if we were all below, long before we knew that they were there.

We sailed soon afterwards for Tenerife, about three hundred miles away, which we made in three days; but we were close to the island before we could see it, owing to the haze which hangs about the Canaries. Meanwhile, we had pricked the balloon puppy with a worm pill. It was a Spanish worm pill, the only pill that was any good, we were told, for Spanish worms. Its action was violent, almost immediate, and astounding, and the puppy soon began to assume a normal puppy shape. It was also given a name.

Moored next to us in Madeira had been a Portuguese yacht whose sailor had a small dog on board. As he washed the decks each morning, he ordered the dog "a popa" or "a proa" in order to have it out of the way, and the dog always obeyed. We called the puppy "Popa" which soon degenerated to "Poopa". One night a strong wind got up and the Portuguese boat began to drag. Beryl and I went an board and let out some more chain when, to our relief, the anchor took hold again. The owner was so grateful that he made a small mat for us out of hemp-line so that we got a mat and a dog's name out of the Portuguese yacht. The dog died in Rhodesia at the age of twelve, after an adventurous life. We heard the other day that a cactus that we planted over his grave has grown to a large tree. The mat is still with us and in use today.

After the worm pill, Poopa's eyes grew bright and his coat began to shine. His appetite was enormous and he gnawed everything that he could get hold of. His house-training was started immediately and he was made to use a coir mat which was attached to the mast on deck, but could be towed overboard for cleaning. There were times, however, when we sat on the lee rail and put our feet in the cleansing water, wishing it was the hamster and not the puppy that was with us.

At Santa Cruz de Tenerife the harbour is an artificial and an oily one. *Tzu Hang* soon had a black waterline where the small waves had lapped her white paint, and the dinghy, which we had left in the water, a black bottom. We received an invitation from the Club Real Nautico addressed to the "Tzu Vancouver Hang", which made us sound rather more important than we were. The Club Real Nautico also provided a watchman for us, to spend the night on *Tzu Hang*, while we went off to climb Monte Teide.

Monte Teide is 12,180 feet high, but half of it can be climbed in a taxi, leaving about 7,000 feet of rocky footpath. We asked at the Tourist Bureau if there was a rest house where we could spend the night. "But of course," explained a neatly-dressed and well-groomed Spaniard, who looked as if he might never have strayed outside the town precincts. "There is a Refugio within 500 metres of the top."

"Not finished yet," interjected a more down-to-earth colleague.

"Surely it is finished," said the other. "It was to have been finished a year ago."

"Can we sleep there? Are there beds? Do we need bedding rolls? Can we get food there?" I asked.

"But of course. Everything. Beds, food, coffee, showers, dancing. Whatever you wish," said the first, letting his imagination run riot.

Beryl, however, was cautious. She had not travelled in Latin America without learning something of an optimism that is apt to be misleading, that bounds lightly from what is to what may one day be. "I think we'd better take blankets and some food," she said, and arranged through the Agency for a mule driver and a mule to meet us at the foot of the path, where it could carry our small amount of baggage and be a mount for Clio if necessary.

Next day, a taxi drove us up out of the semi-tropical vegetation of the lower slopes, out of the oranges and the bananas and into a ruder country of thorn, yellow grass, cactus and rock, where thin cows and fat donkeys were tethered. At the bottom of the footpath that led up the hot stony flanks of the mountain, there was a long wait, while our taxi driver went off in search of the mule man. When we set off, the rocks seemed to have gathered the heat of the day as we passed like fire-walkers over them. Up we went, the mule with its light load lagging behind, and soon the sea spread out below us, disappearing far below what should have been its horizon, into the soft heat haze of the late afternoon. Higher still we got into light cloud and it was cooler, but the air was thinner, and ship-softened leg muscles began to feel the strain. The thought of the Refugio—and coffee—kept us going. The idea of relaxing in cane chairs in the cool evening, breathing the mountain air in great wine-sweet draughts spurred me on. What was I thinking of? Perhaps of the Officers' Mess at Newcastle in Jamaica, high above Kingston, when on some evenings we could look down and see the buoys in the harbour twenty miles away; when the air was heavy with the scent of flowers and the sound of men kicking a football came from the square below; and when the Major would put his eyeglass in his eye as he settled in a chair on the mess verandah. "Ah, time for a gin, I think," he'd say.

"Do you think that's the Refugio?" I heard Beryl ask, and looking up saw part of a stone house showing above the shoulder of the hill.

"It has rather an unfinished look," said Bill.

When we arrived, we found that it was very unfinished and that the workmen were just quitting. They were lodging in what was one day to be the kitchen but the caretaker had a bed, his wife and two children, in a large central room which had a roof and a wooden floor. The floor was covered with cement powder, empty cement sacks, and the refuse from the workers' meals. There was an improvised fireplace, but no chimney. A large black kettle was on a wood fire and the room was filled with smoke. That was the end of the tourist facilities. If we had known that the Refugio was so unprepared for the reception of its first guests, we would have come better equipped for a night in the open, but since the caretaker, with true Spanish hospitality, pressed us to share the large room with him, explaining that it was sure to rain during the night, and that the only other room with a roof and a floor was the kitchen occupied by the workers, we accepted.

"Don't leave any food about, for the rats will get it," warned the caretaker. As darkness came to the mountain and the clouds sank lower to envelope the Refugio and to extinguish the lights that showed in some places far below, we lay down beneath a haze of smoke that drifted from the wood fire to wrap the caretaker with his wife and children in their wooden double bed.

"Anyone want a pillow?" asked Bill, and receiving no answer pulled the rucksack under his head. The action went unnoticed by me.

I awoke cold and rather damp, for the fire was out and the mist crept in through the open spaces where the windows were to be installed. I could hear a mouse gnawing away close to my head, and presently realised that it was gnawing at the rucksack after the food.

I raised myself on an elbow. The gnawing stopped. It was pitch dark. I waited and the gnawing started again. Taking careful aim, I smashed my hand down on it. Rarely could a mouse have viewed such a miscarriage of an attack aimed at itself. There was a bellow or rage and pain from Bill, who started up ready to beat off an attacker, there was an anxious shout of, "Qué pasa, qué pasa?" from the caretaker and a gabble from his wife. I could hear Beryl enquiring sleepily as to what was going on. Fortunately, Bill was more annoyed than hurt, for the blow had been a glancing one on cheek and ear.

The next morning we climbed the remaining 2,000 feet to the top of the mountain, but Clio became mountain sick and

Beryl took her down while Bill and I went on. At the edge of the crater at the top, some sulphurous fumes drifted out to mingle with the mist that enveloped it. There was nothing to see. Just the top of a mountain with its slopes fading into cloud, stones and rubble and sparse grass. Something I have seen many times, and, because of its isolation and silence, the thin fresh air, the feel of the wind, and the mist drifting past, it is something I have always loved.

We hurried down to find Clio quite recovered. "Ten thousand seems to be the height," said Beryl. "Directly she got over ten thousand she got sick, but she recovered as soon as we got down below it. I'll go up now. I won't be long." Off she went with her easy stride, and I knew that she would not stop till she got to the top. When she returned we hurried down the footpath and by a miracle of organisation the car was waiting for us when we got to the bottom. That evening we were back on *Tzu Hang*.

Next morning a gaff-rigged cutter appeared outside the harbour and put in to anchor beside us. She was flying the Belgian flag and was the *Omoo of Ghent*, with a crew of three, Louis and Annie Van der Wiele and Fred. They had just come up from Las Palmas, filling in time before starting across the Atlantic. Fred had stayed in Las Palmas, and we watched Louis and Annie, both dressed in track suits, handle their ship with the efficiency of a well-matched team, each knowing exactly what was required without the necessity of a word. They were at the beginning of a circumnavigation which was to produce one of the best cruising stories ever—written by Annie—and called *The West in my Eyes*.

Annie is small and vigorous; ever since we have known her she has always looked ten years younger than she should. Louis is tall and dark, with a long, gloomy face, and a sense of humour which can quickly prick the bubble of any conceit. He is a marine architect and *Omoo* was his own design. They were as unlike Beryl and I as two married couples, each undertaking a long voyage, could be. Their voyage, their ship, and everything that they did was the result of long and careful planning, and of practical experience. They had already made a passage to the South Seas in a friend's yacht to gain experience, and they were both dedicated sailors—Louis to yachts and to the design of the ideal cruising ship and the completion of a good passage, but Annie to the sea itself, a veritable mermaid in her natural element. In our love for travel and adventure, however, we were the same. It was the question of organisation and disorganisation, yet somehow our disorganisation produced results too.

We decided to sail together to Las Palmas. *Omoo* was off first and, holding rather a freer course, gradually drew away from us. I was beside myself with my competitive spirit fully aroused; Clio supported me while Beryl was entirely unmoved. Towards evening, *Omoo* closed the Gran Canaria shore, leaving a long windward leg, while *Tzu Hang*, pointing for the weather end of the island, was some miles behind.

I could see *Omoo* making up the shore and was at first in an agony of doubt that he had discovered some favourable wind, until I saw the headsails come down and realised that he had resorted to his motor.

"Well, I'm damned," I said. "I do believe he's motoring."

"He's going to be in long before we are," said Beryl.

As far as I was concerned, the Belgians could motor, but the British would sail. As a result we were eventually becalmed about a mile off the entrance to La Luz in the most filthy sea which rolled us all over the place. We then started the motor and arrived well after dark.

Next morning, we awoke to a great splashing and yapping and looked out to find that the various island schooners round about us were giving their dogs a morning bath by dipping them over the side. Every schooner, of which there were several in port, seemed to have a dog, and each morning they were dipped in the sea. Poopa was growing fast, but was still considered rather young for such vigorous treatment.

We had been warned that the thieves in the harbour at La Luz were incredibly skilful, and would filch things off the deck, or through a port-hole, using a hook on the end of a stick. Perhaps that was the reason that each schooner had a dog. *Omoo* had a dog, too, a black Scottish terrier called Tallow, who would undoubtedly protect his ship; but ours was far too young.

One evening, after a dinner on *Omoo*, we got back late to *Tzu Hang*. Before turning in, I put my head out of the hatch to see that all was well. I noticed a small rowing boat rowing quietly past our stern as if trying to make as little noise as possible as it disappeared in the direction of *Omoo*. Presently it came back from amongst the one or two yachts that were anchored further up the harbour, and again rowed quietly past our stern. "Oh, ho," I thought, "so you are a thief waiting until all is quiet." As he rowed away, I got a short heavy stick that we used for knocking fish on the head. I then concealed myself in the small cockpit, in an extremely cramped position. Presently I could hear the dip of oars again, as the boat once more approached *Tzu Hang*, the sound stopped. I thought that in a moment I would hear the thief's hand on the rail. I could hear my heart beating as I grasped my truncheon and waited, ready for violent action. Then I heard the dip of oars again, and looked up cautiously to see the small boat disappearing into the darkness.

I waited for an hour, during which time the boat once more approached *Tzu Hang*, while my heart beat as if I were sitting up for a tiger. Again it passed by. My desire for bed and the discomfort of the cockpit made me decide that the thief was not going to pay *Tzu Hang* a visit that night, and I turned in. In the morning I went to the yacht club to report the midnight prowler. "Oh, yes," they said. "That is the club watchman, Antonio, keeping an eye on your ship."

La Luz was a dirty port, and I understand it still is. Las Palmas, which we reached by bus and where we did most of our shopping, was only flooded by tourists on the days that a tourist ship came in. To begin with, *Omoo* was the only yacht in the harbour other than the prestige yachts and the small sailing yachts at the yacht club, but presently we were joined by a small steel yacht from Holland bound for New Zealand. It was sailed by Dirk Tober, a tall Dutch ex-naval officer with a weather-vane nose.

Dirk was young and a typical single-hander, self-reliant and efficient. He seemed to live largely on potatoes, and was assured that once his anchor was down he would stay approximately in the same place by keeping another six in reserve. One of these was of such gigantic proportions that it seemed to me that at least two large men would be needed to get it up from the cabin floor where it was lashed.

There was one other yacht there in which two Americans were hoping to sail to Texas; but which had been detained by the police owing to some phoney salvage claim made by a Spanish tug. The day before we sailed, another steel yacht from Holland arrived, sailed by two brothers also on their way to Houston.

74

CHAPTER SIX

Across the Atlantic

Being in all ways ready for the passage, and having rigged our twin staysails, we put Bill on *Omoo* to await the coming of the *Highland Princess*, a passenger ship that would take him back to England; then we set off on October 11, the first of the small trans-Atlantic fleet. We had seven months' concentrated experience with *Tzu Hang* and were at least beginning to know something about sailing.

We would have liked Bill to stay with us, but he had to go back to England to work. I do not think that he had taught Clio very much, but he had been the best of companions. We might equally well have remained to see him off, for after three days Hierro was still in sight. Then the trade wind came, bursting on us with its usual enthusiasm after a lull, blowing for a week and gradually fading as it shifted from north-east to east; then it left us almost becalmed and fretting for a day, before it blew once more with renewed vigour from the north-east. This was the pattern that it maintained during the twenty-three days of our passage, interrupted at times by thunder and squalls. It was our first long passage and at times it seemed to me, as our noon positions crept slowly across the chart of the North Atlantic, that it would never end. Day followed day, each different yet essentially the same, and at times I felt desperately bored with the limitations of our immediate surroundings.

Tzu Hang's twin staysail sheets led aft to the tiller, so that if she slewed away from her course one sail spilled the wind, slackening the sheet while the other pulled harder, bringing her back on to her course. The staysail booms were fitted with goosenecks which dropped into a fitting clamped on to a double forestay. The inward thrust on the ends of the booms was strong,

75

and unless a tackle was rigged on each end of the fitting, bracing it to the deck, the pressure capsized it, so that the two forestays tended to cross, and at the same time were subjected to lateral strains. It was not a good arrangement and the sails were too small to get the best out of *Tzu Hang* except in strong trade winds, the only advantage being that they were so far forward that she virtually had to sail herself. A far better arrangement and the one almost universally adopted now, if twins are used at all, is for the poles to be set on the mast in the normal manner for spinnaker poles. With the advent of steering vanes, almost any rig—conventional spinnaker, or main and staysail boomed out on the opposite side—can be used. With a short-handed crew and strong following winds there is nothing that feels so safe and secure as twin headsails, especially if the booms are rigged with lifts and preventer guys. Then one sail can be dropped, or both, with the booms left out, or brought in. The sails are always under control, and can easily be lashed on to the booms, or they can be set half-way up the stay in a strong wind.

I would never dream of undertaking a long passage before prevailing winds without them, in spite of the most efficient vane steering devices.

Tzu Hang's heavy teak dinghy was stowed on chocks amid-ships, right way up, with a canvas cover. In this way it was in the best position for launching; but it was a bad arrangement. The dinghy was too tempting a stowage place for fenders and ropes which were always chucked into it, and the canvas cover was discarded. In heavy rain it became full of water. Only on one occasion were we grateful for it; we were all on deck with a fresh trade wind blowing, absorbed in changing a block on the deck through which the sheet leading to the tiller passed. I had brought the forward preventer guys aft and fastened them to cleats to act as a sheet, while we released the sheet and passed it through a new block. For a short time, therefore, the self-steering was not working, nor had we taken sufficient pains to see that *Tzu Hang* was still balanced. She ran off, came broadside to the sea—in fact, she broached to.

"Hang on!" I shouted, but Beryl yelled, "The dog, the dog!" and Clio just had time to snatch him up and throw him into the dinghy before a wave swept us. *Tzu Hang* quickly came back

76

before the wind with no damage or loss other than to my own esteem.

Before the trade wind, *Tzu Hang*'s mast swung like a pendulum across the sky, and continued to swing almost the whole way across the Atlantic. Our first day or two was spent in getting accustomed to the motion and in trying to stop all the clinking and the rattling that it induced. We gave up keeping watch and spent the night in our bunks, although we kept the period of our watches so that the ship was someone's responsibility and if some strange noise started, we knew whose turn it was to see to it.

We were half-way across when suddenly the days seemed to go quicker and we began to realise that there would soon be an end to the journey. A few days from Barbados we were becalmed. The glass fell more than it should do in those latitudes, and I began to worry about a late hurricane, to read about dangerous semi-circles, to study storm tracks, and even to screw the slatted teak covers on to the doghouse windows. There followed a night of thunder rumbling in the distance and of lightning all across the western sky. Next morning brought torrential rain hissing down upon us and flattening the sea, while *Tzu Hang*, under her main and jib, with twins stowed, sailed as she had never sailed before. Below, the speed of her passage made an urgent roar, and on deck the helmsman in bathing dress and oilskins was soon shaking with cold. The front passed, the sun shone again, and soon the trade wind returned to speed us on our way.

We were twenty-four days out, or rather twenty-three and twenty hours, with the sun shining, blue sky, flat-bottomed cotton wool clouds, and a deep blue sea, when Barbados should have been on the horizon. I climbed the rigging and there it was, low and already green—right ahead. A few hours later we sailed round a low point and up to anchor off the Aquatic Club, close to the Royal Barbados Yacht Club.

That night the ship rolled at her anchor and the cups clinked in exactly the same way as it had done for the last twenty-four days. Sometime after midnight I awoke, thinking that we were still at sea. Sleepily I rolled out of my bunk and made my way aft to look out of the hatch and check how we were sailing. Right ahead of us and not two hundred yards away was land, and lights, the outline of a building. With a startled shout to awake Beryl, I sprang out and flew into the cockpit, pushing the tiller hard over. Beryl appeared at the hatch. "What on earth's the matter?" she asked.

"We're nearly aground."

"But we're anchored," she said.

I gazed stupidly at the land. So we were. The passage was over, and we were lying to a land breeze, and rolling in the swell. We were not sailing.

"I thought that we were still at sea," I said, as I made my way back to my bunk.

"Do you want some tea?" Beryl asked, her invariable recipe for those in shock.

"No. It's O.K." She kissed me goodnight again. I wondered before I fell asleep if I had not been more worried by this passage than I liked to admit to myself or to anyone else.

Next morning we were sitting on deck much refreshed after a long sleep and a good breakfast, watching the flying fish boats skimming home with their foresails in the water, when a small sailing boat, a Lightning, sailed up. The owner was an Englishman and in business in Barbados. "Where are you from?" he hailed us. We told him and asked him on board. He had always wanted to sail the Atlantic, he told us. We showed him over *Tzu Hang* and he discovered Clio reading below.

"Hello," he said. "How lucky you are. Did you enjoy the passage?"

"Yes," said Clio, in a non-committal manner.

"Didn't you find it a wonderful experience?" he asked.

"But I have so many experiences," replied Clio. It sounded intolerably smug, but it was not so. For a ten-year-old she really had had a lot of experiences, and an Atlantic crossing was just another. It was one that she had enjoyed, but it did not seem anything to get excited about. He turned to me. "Would you like to come for a sail?" he asked. I had just been sailing for twenty-four days and it was not the thing that I wanted to do at the moment. In the face of such enthusiasm, with less truth than that shown by Clio, I feigned eagerness, and off we went.

Back on board, a rowboat came out to us, bringing a black reporter from the local paper. Beryl and I had never been interviewed before on board *Tzu Hang*. We made some more coffee while we told him of our voyage. "It will all be in tomorrow's paper," he promised.

The following morning I said to Beryl, "I wonder what time the paper comes out. Shall I row in and get it?"

"If you like, but why not wait till we all go in?"

I waited impatiently until I could read what he had written, and after a successful surf ride in the dinghy on to the club beach, found the paper in the reading room. "Yesterday," the report said, "the first trans-Atlantic yacht of the season arrived in Carlisle Bay and is now anchored off the Aquatic Club. It was sailed by Brigadier Miles Smeeton, his wife Beryl, their daughter Clio, and a small dog. Miles, who looks rather more than his forty-four years, says the voyage was completed without incident."

"Well, for heaven's sake," I said, but Beryl was delighted. We are the same age and she likes me to look older than she is.

"I think that he ought to have said something more about Poopa," added Clio.

Poopa was already in trouble with the police. The Chief of Police had been in Jamaica as a young police officer when I joined my regiment there, and on our first trip ashore we had paid him a visit. Poopa had learnt his lesson about the coir mat on board ship but was unable to find one ashore. It was not until he discovered one in the house of the Chief of Police, with "Welcome" on it, that with a sense of great relief and right-doing he let fly with all he had.

My hurt at what I felt was rather an insulting reference to my looks was put right later in the same day. I went into a small Bata's shoe shop in Bridgetown, where a large negress was sitting fanning herself on a stool, and yawning like a hippopotamus on a river bank.

"Have you got a pair of gym shoes?" I asked her.

"You help yo'self, Honey," she said. "I'se too hot to move."

I searched the shelves and meanwhile a negro came in and sat beside her.

"Who's dat man dar?" I heard him ask.

"Dat man dar?" she replied. "Dat's Gary Cooper."

The Chief of Police lent me two ponies for a game of polo. I had not played since before the war, but in those days, especially in my Indian Cavalry days, I had played a lot. It sometimes happens that one can leave a game for a long time, and the first time that it is taken up again, it can be played with the old skill;

but the second time is another story. I found that I was hitting the ball all over the place and all round and under my horse. I don't think I touched their legs and I scored several goals. As I rode off at the end of the last chukka I heard a man, whose nose may have been slightly out of joint, say, "Anyone can see that son of a bitch has been used to playing on horses only worth a few dollars."

"What used to be your handicap?" asked someone respectfully after the game.

"Oh, I was only a 3," I said, increasing it a little in order not to disappoint him, or perhaps as is one's habit with increasing age.

I should have left it at that, but was unwise enough to play again after two days, when I was so stiff that I could barely ride, let alone hit the ball. My moment of repute as a polo player (who should at least have been a 4) was gone forever.

An elderly man, obviously of great authority in the island, a member of the Governor's Council, and Commodore of the Yacht Club, with the innate hospitality of the islanders, took us for a long drive to show us the north and east coast. We got out of the car and walked along a low rocky shore. It was quite different from Bridgetown. The trade wind clouds hurried low over the beach and the waves came piling and rumbling in. The rocks were backed by sand, coarse grass and stagnant pools. I could have imagined that I was on another coast forty degrees further north.

"Do you get any duck here?" I asked.

"Not so much duck," he replied in the slightly sing-song accent of those who have spent much of their life in the West Indies, "but we get the kaloo."

"A kaloo?" I repeated. "What sort of bird is that?"

"We get two kinds of kaloo. The crook-billed kaloo and the straight-billed kaloo."

I wondered about this bird, but did not like to pursue the subject. However, the wild surroundings reminded me of another and its haunting cry.

"Do you get the curlew here?" I asked innocently.

"Why, you foolish bitch, man," he exploded. "Isn't that what I'm telling you?" In the West Indies you can be associated with a bitch for almost anything without offence, for bitches are dear to an Englishman's heart.

Omoo arrived, having made a faster passage than we had done by three days. We swam round her as they came up to anchor near us, comparing notes on the voyage. *Omoo* had steered herself comfortably all the way under twins, but with the sheets lashed. Fred was eager to get ashore and experience the delights of Bridgetown, and as soon as all the work was finished he was off. Next morning Annie was on board when I saw Fred tottering home. "What on earth has Fred been doing?" I asked Annie.

"The usual," she said. She said it with slight disdain, but with affection and compassion too. "In search of something new, I suppose," she added.

A few days later Dirk arrived, having made the passage in twenty-five days. He also anchored near us, and by the time that he was cleared by the Customs and Health, Annie was rowing out from the club beach with her day's purchases. I was on board *Omoo*, giving Louis and Fred a hand with their charging engine which they were repairing. With Louis and Fred, "giving a hand" implies sitting and watching for me, for they were both quite capable mechanics.

Annie rowed up to Dirk's boat, *Onrust*, which looked well-named from an English point of view after his passage. They started talking. Presently Annie climbed on board. She had not been over the boat and Dirk showed her below. There they stayed for a long time, lost in each other's account of the voyage. Louis began to look anxious. Then gave a stentorian shout of "Annie!" There was no response. Louis' eyes kept turning towards the Dutch boat. "Annie!" he shouted again. There was still no answer. Louis stood up and roared. Annie looked out of the hatch, then climbed into her boat and rowed over. Louis spoke to her angrily in Flemish, which I could not understand, and she disappeared below, not without a word or two on her part. Later she came on board *Tzu Hang*. "Louis is ridiculous," she said. "He was angry because I went below with Dirk. 'With a Dutchman of all people', he said. 'What will the English think of you'?"

I didn't tell her what we thought, but we thought that they were a wonderfully well-matched couple, and lucky in each other.

CHAPTER SEVEN

In the West Indies

Dirk was travelling like all of us on a limited budget, but perhaps his was a little more limited than ours. He was never at a loss for the companionship of a girl in port, and was often to be seen rowing ashore to take one out for dinner.

"But Dirk," Beryl asked in her direct way, "how on earth do you afford it?"

"Well," he replied solemnly, "I only stand them one drink. After that they have to pay for everything. That is my rule."

One day, when Dirk was on *Tzu Hang* showing me how to splice a wire rope, I noticed a girl swimming round and round his yacht. "I think someone wants you," I told him.

He looked up from his splice and recognised her. "She can wait," he said, and left the girl swimming for another twenty minutes while he concluded the instruction. She was a Canadian girl on holiday in Barbados and Dirk offered to take her on a cruise along the coast. He came on board to borrow a chart. "How long are you going for?" I asked him, wondering whether we would not be gone by the time he returned.

"For as long as the food lasts," he replied, his eyes glittering.

I met the girl the same evening, ruffled and indignant. "Hello," I said, "I thought that you were off on a cruise with Dirk."

"I started off with him," she said, "and we sailed to that beach up the coast, but he wouldn't take me ashore; he never told me that there wasn't a 'john' on board, and we had nothing but potatoes to eat, which he expected me to cook. I jumped ship, swam ashore, and got the bus back." Dirk's approach on this occasion seemed to have lacked his customary finesse.

In the early mornings, soon after the light through skylights and ports had awakened us, when the cocks ashore were crowing and the sea was resting as it murmured lazily on the beach, there sounded a splashing and a blowing near us; it was as if a school of whales had arrived. This is a time in the West Indies when one should be up and doing something, before the sun gets too hot, and preferably something on a horse; it is a good time for a swim also, when everything is fresh and still, waiting for the day. So lucky is the person who can combine the horse and the swim. The noise turned out to be the local trainer exercising his not-so-sound horses in the sea. He himself was in a rowing boat, but his stable lads were swimming, hanging on to mane or tail, and guiding their horses by splashing them.

Louis was worried about *Omoo*'s underwater paint, which had come off in one or two small places. He worried more about his ship's bottom and rust than we did about ours and toredos. *Tzu Hang* was beginning to show signs of growing weed so we arranged to haul out with *Omoo* in the dry dock at Bridgetown, where two yachts could be taken out at once, thereby halving the cost of using the dock. We hauled out over the week-end so that we could do the work ourselves; but there was still a lot of work to be done by the dock labourers in the actual docking and the shoring up of the hulls as the water went out, so that we could stand in safety.

Enthusiasm for work was at its lowest ebb, and in the West Indies that means a nadir of unwillingness, for England was playing the West Indies in a cricket match in Jamaica and everyone wanted to listen to the radio commentary on the game.

Those working at the docking of *Tzu Hang* moved like men in a trance. Their minds were far away on the sun-baked cricket ground of Kingston, their ears were stretched towards a radio set on the dock side. Suddenly they dropped the baulks of timber so essential to our stability, and performed little individual dances, splashing about in the water that still remained in the dock. An English wicket had fallen. "Man," cried one in joy and excitement, "that fellow bowl so fast no man can see his ball. Bim bong, like that, into wicket keeper's glove."

"That finish the match, man," cried another with typical optimism. "We win for sure."

Throughout the long afternoon, while we sweated and covered ourselves with paint, they and all of Bridgetown sat in the shade, murmuring and laughing and listening to the cricket.

83

We sailed from Barbados one evening and next morning had St. Vincent ahead of us. After entering Kingstown harbour and duly paying our respects to Captain Bligh's breadfruit trees in the Botanical Gardens, a friend took us to a sheltered bay a short sail away, where we anchored in bright blue water behind a small island, guarded by old guns in the crumbling ruins of a fort. Here was a wooden jetty from which fishermen sailed, but they were not the cheerful black fishermen that I had known in Jamaica, with tombstone teeth and faces corrugated by wind and weather to the texture of a lava flow. These were more subdued, with pale dead skin, like the skin of all white men who have stayed away too long from colder latitudes. These were the "Red Legs", descendants of the thousand Englishmen who had been shipped as slaves to the plantations after Monmouth's Rebellion in 1685. Their sentence had been visited on their children and their children's children, and Judge Jeffries should lie uncomfortably in his grave at the thought of them, for they are outcast from black and white society, a forgotten debris of a people, marked by pale skin, often with fair hair and blue eyes.

Tzu Hang, in all the years that we have owned her, has never been locked up. It has seemed pointless to do so, since she has had no adequate defence against a screw-driver. Only twice has she been boarded and had something stolen. The first time was in this quiet bay while we were out to dinner. When we got back we found that a locker had been opened and that a tin of sardines had been stolen; they were sardines that had been sold at a reduced rate and Beryl had bought them for the dog, so that the thief could not have selected anything that we would miss less and there were all kinds of other tins. Had the puppy barked and frightened him, or had he just come on board to allay his hunger? We gave Poopa the credit for protecting the boat.

From St. Vincent we sailed north to St. Lucia. The chain of islands from the Grenadines north to Dominica are known as the Windward Islands; their eastern coasts are gnarled and battered, while the wind is boisterous in the passages between them, particularly in the afternoon when the trade wind blows strongest; then a yacht is all sunshine and dark shadow, wet decks and flying spray. Passages are quickly made and quietest at night. We sailed to St. Lucia by night, arriving in the morning at the dreary little town of Castries, which had been destroyed a few years before by fire, and showed no signs of recovering from the scars.

Dirk, who was anchored in a little bay just across from the main harbour, told us that we should move over there. I asked him about the way in.

"No problem," he said. "I'll pilot you in, so just follow close behind."

We followed close behind and ran smack on a reef. Only when you have no chart should a yachtsman ever accept the guidance of an amateur pilot, and then only in his home waters, when there is every indication that he knows them well. We had a chart of the entrance to Castries, and if I had navigated myself I would not have run aground. It was the only time, among the few occasions that we have touched bottom, that there has been any damage. We found that we had pulled a piece of copper sheathing from the deadwood just aft of the lead under the keel. The copper sheathing was covering a place that could not be painted when *Tzu Hang* was on the beach, so we decided that we would have to get it nailed back if we wanted to avoid the danger of getting worms into the wood. A Canadian had a diving business there and was doing odd jobs round the harbour; he brought his boat alongside *Tzu Hang*, which was moored by the bow to a rickety jetty and had a stern anchor out. His partner, an Englishman, went down, while two West Indians worked the pump to his breathing apparatus and watched his line.

Although *Tzu Hang* was well tied up, she insisted on moving, and a volley of oaths kept sounding from the Tannoy equipment, as she drifted away from the diver just as he was preparing to knock a nail into the copper, but in the end he made a good job that was to last us for many years. Meanwhile a thunderstorm had moved over the harbour, a black cloud rested on the hills and the rain pelted down, hitting the water like falling shot.

"All finished," squawked the Tannoy loudspeaker in the diving boat. "I'm coming up now."

"No boss, no sah!" shouted the boys from under the tin roof which covered the pump and the stern of the diving boat. "You can't come up now."

"Why the hell can't I?" asked the diver.

"Because it's raining, Boss."

Poopa had an annoying habit, when we wanted to catch him

and put him in the dinghy for a trip ashore, of running up and down the deck, barking hysterically and grimacing, but keeping just out of range of whoever was trying to reach him from the dinghy. One of us on deck that afternoon caught him and dropped him into the dinghy. He fell awkwardly, catching a hind leg across the centre-board and suffering a green-stick fracture just above the hind foot. Clio and I took him ashore in search of a vet and eventually found one who had just returned from the University of Toronto. Poopa must have been his first case, but he set it as best he could and wrapped it up in plaster and tape. As soon as we were back on board Poopa set to work to remove the plaster, and after several days of continuous effort, punctuated by groans and cries, and assisted by occasional dollops of salt water, he was successful. As a result, the leg set slightly crooked, and for the rest of his days he was dot and carry one, except when hunting or excited.

As soon as Poopa was patched up we sailed for Martinique. St. Lucia has changed hands several times between the French and English, and as a result the country seems to have an ill-defined character and the inhabitants use the most unintelligible patois; but Martinique, which was only captured once by the English and returned shortly afterwards, has remained entirely French in character, and to visit it from one of the British West Indian Islands is like crossing from Dover to Calais. Martinique was captured during the Seven Years' War. The port is one of the best in the West Indies and was well-defended by forts and fortifications from any attack by sea. A landing was made on the coast and Admiral Rodney's sailors hauled their guns across country to subdue the defences, just as later they were to haul their guns to the summit of Diamond Rock, a perpendicular rock sticking out of the sea off the south-west coast. Diamond Rock, which overlooked the southern approach to Fort de France, or Fort Royal as it was then called, was commissioned as a sloop, and when Admiral Villeneuve hurried across the Atlantic commanding the French and Spanish fleet, with instructions to cause as much trouble as he could in the West Indies, all he effected before the arrival of Nelson was the surrender of H.M.S. *Diamond Rock*.

At Martinique we soon had a French visitor who came out to see us. He took us to a meal ashore and a drive in his car to Saint Pierre, which was destroyed by the great eruption of Mont

Pelee in 1902. A gloomy place, with the great volcano brooding above, the few inhabitants of Saint Pierre behave as if their inevitable destruction in another cataclysm is only a matter of days away, yet they draw a certain macabre satisfaction from their unenviable position. On return to the boat we found that our friend had an ulterior motive in his approach to us; he wanted a yacht from which to sell perfumes off-shore to private agents throughout the islands. We were not sure whether he wanted us to share in his smuggling or whether his object was to buy *Tzu Hang* as a scent smuggler, but anyway we had to turn his offer down. We really had to get back to Canada in spite of the attraction of a new and perhaps a profitable life.

From Martinique we sailed for Dominica, seeing Roseau, the capital, only from a distance as we headed up for Portsmouth, a well-sheltered bay in the north-west of the Island. It was a good anchorage, but there was a long row in the dinghy from the ship to the shore, to a scruffy little village, which, since it was Christmas, smelled strongly of rum.

In Barbados we had met the owner of a big plantation near Portsmouth, with his brother-in-law and their wives. They asked us to come to Portsmouth for Christmas since there was a child of about Clio's age. They had a comfortable house and a great deal of hospitality to offer us, and carried us off on a wet night along red muddy roads to a fancy-dress dance at a neighbour's house. Time seemed to have stood still and, hearing the sound of frogs and crickets outside, and the music inside, I could have imagined that I was back in my subaltern days in Jamaica. Time seemed to have stood still at the plantation too, for the brother-in-law, who was recently retired from the Army, was managing the estate. The marks of his activities were everywhere, shown by neat painted notices which directed you to the "Allemein Plantation", or along the "Trigh el Abd". I felt sure that if the owner's patience and the gallant colonel's enthusiasm persisted, there would be rows of white stones along the paths, and banana trees would be ordered into stiffer lines. My own enthusiasm for whitewash, which I had once so much admired, had evaporated in Canada, where we had to do all the work ourselves.

On this voyage we had all suffered for the first and only time from an affliction of boils, which started as pimples and developed into running sores. Beryl is very rarely ill or out of sorts, but when she is she goes in for it in a big way. Now she had developed a regular carbuncle on her leg and I was able at last to persuade her to show it to the Portsmouth doctor. It was Christmas Eve and Beryl left Clio and me in charge of a cake that was cooking in the oven.

"You will remember to take it out at five o'clock, if I'm not back, won't you?" she told me. "Clio—you'll remember, even if Daddy doesn't," she added. We both assured her that we would remember but we were then the last people to leave in charge of a cake in the oven. With passing years Clio has developed a responsibility in these sort of things, but I was even then well set in forgetful ways and have continued to slip down-hill.

At six o'clock, Clio and I, having wrapped our presents and listened on the radio to Christmas carols and broadcasts from other parts of the world, began to worry about Beryl's return. At least, I began to worry, and Clio to speculate when it would be. A violent wind was blowing off-shore, making *Tzu Hang* pluck at her anchor and veer with the gusts, while the rain poured down as if the heavens were determined to give Portsmouth its annual quota in a few hours. The wind was so strong that I doubted if Beryl would be able to pull back to the boat if she overshot in the dark that was now falling. Seven o'clock and still no signs of her. Clio and I put on oilskins, sat in the cockpit and hung up a light.

Suddenly I saw her, bearing down under full sail, for she was standing in the dinghy and paddling with one oar. "Throw me a line!" she cried, as she found herself a slave of the wind, which was rapidly carrying her off to sea when she tried to turn the dinghy and head in to our side. I threw her the coil of the main sheet, which was nearest to hand, and which fortunately landed across the boat.

"What on earth have you been doing?" I asked, as she came along. "And where is your other oar?"

"The doctor walked back with me to the pier," she explained, "and we found the dinghy gone. With his help we discovered that two negroes had taken it. They are all drunk and singing in the rain. Some of them started shouting into the night and presently two drunks appeared in our dinghy, having lost one of the oars. They were quite nice but too far gone to know what had happened to it. So I started off with one oar, hoping I'd hit

Tzu Hang. I didn't realise quite how hard it was blowing till I got further out."

"You would never have made it with one oar if you'd missed us," I said, and started to wonder how long it would have taken us to get off in pursuit in the dark, and of the faint and imagined cries that we would have heard, and of what a ghastly Christmas Eve it would have been.

My thoughts were soon interrupted. "What is this dreadful smell of burning?" I heard Beryl say as she stepped below. Clio and I looked at each other in dismay.

From Dominica we sailed for Antigua, past Guadeloupe, and in the channel between it and Dominica past the Isles des Saintes, which gave their name to Admiral Rodney's victory over Admiral De Grasse and the French fleet. It was a battle with more ships engaged than at Trafalgar, and fighting under De Grasse were also two famous French explorers, Bourgainville and La Perouse. La Perouse had a few years earlier named an island off the New Zealand coast the Isle Percé, because of the wave-washed hole through one of its cliffs. Captain Cook, unaware that La Perouse had already been there and named it, called the same island by a strange coincidence "Percy Island" after a First Lord of the Admiralty; we were to see it, too, a few years later.

In the battle of the Saints, the British fleet, unable to cross the "T" of the enemy, and at the same time gain the weather gauge, were forced at the last moment to turn down the enemy's line to leeward; so that they sailed close past each other in opposite directions, the French close-hauled and the British with the wind free. It was then that the wind shifted and caught aback two French ships in different parts of their line where two gaps were temporarily formed. Rodney, with the wind on his quarter, led through the first gap, and by chance Captain Affleck of the *Bedford* found the other, and was followed through by Hood's squadron. As each ship followed the others through, they were able with both broadsides to rake from bow to stern the ships on each side of the gap, while the French could barely reply. It was this fluke in the wind that gave the British an overpowering tactical advantage.

During the critical time of the breakthrough, Rodney is said to have walked from the quarterdeck into his cabin, and look through the stern windows to see whether the next ship had been able to follow in the confusion of smoke and battle. As he walked through his cabin he noticed a midshipman whom he had told to get him a drink, mixing a lemon squash with his dirk. "That may be all right for the midshipman's mess but not for the Admiral's cabin," said the Admiral. "Call my steward." The story has a ring of truth about it.

In this action also the *Formidable*'s hencoops were smashed and a bantam cock is said to have flown up on to the bulwark, crowing and flapping its wings at every broadside. Thereafter, on the Admiral's order, it became the ship's mascot and probably died from over-feeding.

CHAPTER EIGHT

Antigua to Panama

As we entered the narrow channel that leads into English Harbour, I began to have the usual beginner's doubts as to whether it could be safely accomplished under sail. Of course the harbour could be entered under sail and it had been done a hundred thousand times. The question was whether it could be done by me under sail without some appalling mistake when under the eyes of that experienced yachtsman and sailor, Commander Nicholson. He was then living with his wife and family in the old paymaster's office, with a notice still on the wall about rates of pay, dating from Nelson's time, and was then at the very beginning of his great yacht charter business based on English Harbour. I felt sure that he would be keeping as critical an eye open on the entrance as ever Admirals Rodney or Nelson did.

Just in case of trouble, I decided to test the engine, leaving this decision until the wind in the channel faltered, to remind me that I ought to be prepared to use power if necessary. The engine would not start. Our sails flapped listlessly as the wind fluked. I let go the anchor and we brought down the sails. *Tzu Hang* lay peacefully, head on to a renewed wind, while I went below to clean up the magneto points. She was on the edge of the channel, not very far away from some rocks, and I hoped that she was well out of sight of the paymaster's office.

Her hull was, but not her masts. Presently I heard the noise of a small outboard motor, and then a great voice that must once have made the hair of midshipmen stand on end, asking if we were aground.

"Oh, no," Beryl replied. "We're just fixing up the engine before coming in."

"I saw your masts," I heard the Commander say, "and I

couldn't make out why you weren't moving. Thought that you must be aground. I've never seen a yacht anchor there before."

When the engine started we motored into the harbour and tied up to the quay, with its old careening anchors still in place. There were only two yachts there; one was a large steel yacht just being prepared for charter work, as the first of the Nicholson fleet, and also *Tern III*, once the famous yacht of Claude Worth. She was still in good condition and well looked after, but swarming with cockroaches, with whom the lively and attractive owners, the Ciccemaras, carried on a perpetual but unsuccessful war. Commander Nicholson's own yacht, *Mollyhawk*, was out on charter.

We had heard that Roach Hives, small cardboard cylinders about the size of a 35 mm. film case, with poison inside, were fatal for cockroaches, and we were able to get them later in Panama. We placed them in strategic positions round the ship, and occasionally found a dead cockroach thereafter, but saw no live ones. Years later, in the Indian Ocean, we found that we had cockroaches on board, and with great difficulty got more Roach Hives from New York. To every man his own poison. The Indian cockroaches thrived on American Roach Hives, but disappeared as soon as we got north into a colder climate, or perhaps because they showed a partiality for some other pesticide.

Tzu Hang sailed in the New Year for Cristobal, having spent only a few days at English Harbour. They were extremely good days, and almost at the end of the first leg of our journey. The weather was perfect, and Clio found a companion in Mrs. Nicholson, who is one of those happy people with the faculty of making herself one with a child. They went off together on long expeditions looking for shells on the beach and both apparently unaware of time. Like a remnant of humanity after Armageddon, we camped amongst the ruins of the old harbour and, except for a few noticeboards, there was no evidence that anyone had ever cared for it since the last wooden ship, with creaking yards and rush of bare feet on the deck, had loosed her sails to the trade wind and glided silently away.

Much has been done since then and the harbour is always bright with yachts; but when we were there we had the place almost untouched, to ourselves, the Nicholsons and the Ciccemaras.

At night I could imagine the harbour peopled with ghosts of

sailors and the quays with masts and rigging like a wood on the water's edge. Ghosts loading shot and powder, salt beef and pork, files of ghosts to draw their pay, elegant ghosts strolling in blue coats, silk stockings and white breeches, or perhaps in shirts and cotton trousers, since they were not having their portraits painted. But in the early morning, if I went on deck and saw the light coming in the eastern sky, the ghosts had gone, warned away, not by the rumble of traffic and the sound of feet hurrying along a pavement, but by the softening of their wind, the land breeze, and by the first notes of the birds. It was a peaceful, secret place, and one day when a party of tourists arrived, wandering round the ruins, peering and photographing, the women over-decorated, the men hung about with coats and cameras, we felt as the Caribs must have felt with the coming of Columbus.

From Antigua to Cristobal, usually about a week's passage for a yacht of *Tzu Hang*'s size, the trade wind blows fair and often more from the east than the north-east. Although the weather chart shows no gales in this pocket of the Caribbean, the trade wind can blow strongly, and even up to force seven for short periods. We soon found ourselves flying along and for part of a night we ran under storm jib alone. This storm jib, or spitfire, was a handkerchief of a sail, of old-fashioned tanned canvas, and we found that *Tzu Hang* would hold her course under this sail alone with the wind on the quarter. It was not necessary to sail like this, but I was still much of a novice, unused to strong winds and uncertain how much sail *Tzu Hang* could safely carry.

Towards the end of the passage, we lay a-hull for a few hours to avoid arriving at Cristobal during the night. I was much impressed then by the way *Tzu Hang* behaved; I suppose the seas were running about ten feet high and the wind was force seven, for we had sailed with a strong trade for three days. *Tzu Hang*, with her helm lashed down and sailing at about half-a-knot from the pressure of the wind on her masts and rigging, tried to head up into the wind, but then fell away, so that she pursued a slow and wavering course on each side of a line at right angles to the wind. Meanwhile she drifted to leeward at about the same speed, leaving a short slick to windward, caused by the water boiling up under her keel. It is said that this slick will help protect a vessel from breaking crests, and it may do so with a big ship, but I failed to see then how the few feet of smooth water left by a small yacht could provide the least protection if the waves were bigger. However, it seemed to me a good way of riding out a storm, an impression for which we were to pay dearly in due course. The motion without any canvas set was horrible, and no doubt it was a strain on a ship even of *Tzu Hang*'s strength; but having rolled our way across the Atlantic, we were almost inured to any motion.

In the evening, when the wind slackened, being assured that we would not arrive until daylight, we continued on our way. We had ample time to check our position, and our evening sight showed that we had strayed only a few miles from our noon position. Long before daylight the glow from the lights at the Panama Canal entrance showed that our course was right. Soon after breakfast we could make out the breakwater and found our way inside.

A launch came up to us and we were hailed:

"Where are you from?"

"Antigua."

"Right. Follow me and I will show you to an anchorage. Remain there until you have been boarded. Customs, Immigration and the Port Doctor will be alongside shortly."

We were soon anchored and were cleaning up below when we heard a launch hailing us. It was the Customs officer.

"Have you a table to write on below there?"

"Yes," said Beryl, indignantly.

"All right, we're coming alongside."

We soon had them down below and round the table, for the launch brought the two other officials.

"Who's the captain?" asked the doctor.

"I am," I said.

"Ah ha," he replied. "I have a yacht. Show me the captain in a matrimonial boat. I know."

I might have quoted Longfellow if I had been more apt:

> "As unto the bow the cord is
> So unto the man is woman;
> Though she bends him she obeys him,
> Though she draws him yet she follows;
> Useless each without the other!"

but it would not have been strictly true.

We had lost our vaccination certificates, although we had only recently been vaccinated. Beryl assured the doctor that we never "took". "I'll soon fix that," he promised and he did, in such a way that in a day or two we all had extremely sore arms.

All the normal formalities were quickly over and we were told that we might take down our quarantine flag and move to the visitors' berth at the yacht club. I leaned on the life-line as the launch left, to see how the ship was lying to her anchor, and suddenly the line parted at a place where it passed through a galvanised post and had rusted. I was waving my arms in a frantic and futile attempt to regain my balance, when Beryl caught me by the shirt and just saved me from plunging ignominiously into the sea.

Like Tom Worth in *Beyond*, we had been dreading the passage of the Canal, thinking of it as a huge mangle into which vessels were drawn and then squeezed out on the other side. The officials were light-hearted, efficient and courteous while the arrangements were soon done; they included a visit by the Canal Company's admeasurer who assessed *Tzu Hang*'s size in their own inimitable way, and at a charge of 72 cents a ton we had to pay a few dollars which included the services of a pilot.

"Come through any time," they said, "now that we have you on our books. Just report at the office." It sounded as if they expected us to flit backwards and forwards, but when we came through again, it was sixteen years later. Then they pulled out a file and it only took a few minutes, and the same number of dollars, to arrange our transit.

For the time being we were only thinking of getting through once without damage or shame. We had heard stories of disturbance in the locks as the water came in, which whirled small ships about, of lines that had to be flung and caught, of numerous fenders that had to be used, of broken cross-trees, and of a current that jettisoned you out on the Pacific side as the salt water came in under the Gatun Lake fresh water in the locks. We heard that the only safe way of effecting a transit was tied to one of the small banana boats that went through—but no banana boats were going through. Fortunately, Annie and Fred deserted Louis and *Omoo*, at anchor in Balboa, and came to help us. We were able to borrow motor tyres as fenders from the yacht club, to be returned on the next yacht coming from Balboa.

Fred and Annie, experienced transitors, were full of cheery optimism, and when early the next morning our pilot and his wife arrived with lunch for us all, the passage began to appear to us more in the nature of a picnic than as one fraught with danger, damage and distress. The pilot seated himself and his wife in the cockpit and took charge of the ship, leaving us only the fenders and lines to look after, so we settled down to enjoy our freedom from responsibility. The water did boil up in the first two locks, but we were well secured, and in the last lock the current did try to drag us out before we cast off our lines, but all went smoothly, including a lovely sail of twenty-two miles across the Gatun Lake.

There is a great moment in every crossing of the isthmus, whichever way you are going, when suddenly you look down on a series of locks to another ocean, another half of the world. Whichever way we go we feel that it is our ocean, for both of us were born in England, lapped by the Atlantic, although we made our home on the Pacific coast of Canada. Perhaps not so eagle-eyed as Cortez, nevertheless we gazed on each other with a momentary surmise as we wondered—Fred and Annie too— what new adventures that pale ocean, fading into the sky, had in store for us.

Balboa was then, and probably still is, a good place to fit out for a long journey. There were several yachts being built or just completed by Americans working in the Canal Company; they showed a staggering efficiency and craftsmanship, which made me, unable to transfer a ship's lines to the floor, feel dreadfully incompetent. Here also were born great plans doomed to failure, whereas fortune rewarded us with success. Perhaps the fact that we were used to physical hardship, used to being out of touch with the so-called assets of civilisation, and by our—or, my—very incompetence, forced to rely on simple things like the wind and sails, had something to do with it.

Whatever they might have thought of our efficiency, these Americans were full of hospitality and kindness. By their clandestine aid we were able to provision the ship from the commissary, and if we needed any sort of ship's stores, there was a Norwegian double-ender, the property of a Mr. Harmon and his wife which was outfitted like a ship's chandlery and they never had to go further than their own fore peak to provide us with anything we might want, be it shackles or copper tacks or stainless-steel screws.

Such a wealth of stores made our mouths water and it was difficult not to take advantage of the Harmons' kindness. It was unlikely that we should be able to repay them; however, this sort of thing is normal in the cruising world. What is gained in one place is given to some other wayfarer somewhere else, perhaps even in a different ocean.

The Harmon's ship was in great condition, a strong Colin Archer type double-ender, she was just about to sail for Papeete with another couple and two elderly men, all of whom I believe were paying for their passage. We agreed to meet in the Galapagos. Meanwhile, *Omoo* had gone on her way to the Marquesas. The Ecuadorian Consul had refused to issue a passport visa to Louis, except in overtime hours. Louis was equally determined not to pay overtime, which was against all his principles, so they decided to miss the Galapagos Islands. Alas that they did so, for Annie could have written about the Galapagos Islands with all the gaiety and colour that filled the rest of her story of their cruise. For many years we saw no more of them, although like many cruising people who meet in different parts of the world, we kept in touch. Years later we found *Omoo*, in other hands, at anchor in Mombasa. She was still in good condition, but without Annie, Louis, Fred and the dog Tallow, she seemed forlorn. Years later still we were to stay with Louis and Annie in an old castle in Aquitaine, which they had made their home.

Our approach to get visas for a visit to the Galapagos Islands was different. "How ridiculous," said Beryl; "those two huge men going to the Ecuadorian Consul. I bet he's small and he's trying to show them how busy and important he is. Annie should have gone. She would have had no trouble at all."

"Well, you go and get ours," I suggested. "I won't come in."

Next day we drove to the consul's office in a borrowed car. Beryl went in and the door shut firmly behind her. It was a long half-hour before it opened again, and I could see a small, dark-haired man fervently kissing Beryl's hand. Rings and teeth were flashing as he waved good-bye to her. "Hasta la vista," I heard him call, "anything I can do, just let me know. Buen viaje."

"Of course there was no trouble at all," Beryl said, as she got into the car.

"Then what were you doing?" I asked.

"Having coffee. And very good, too."

I do not know whether we were unduly worried about toredo worms in those days or whether the paints were just so much worse, but we seemed to be continually in need of another coat of paint on *Tzu Hang*'s bottom. We had painted her in Barbados and now it was time to paint her again; there was a convenient hulk lying on the other side of the bay, against which it was customary for passing yachts to lean while their undersides were painted. We put *Tzu Hang* there and she took the ground on hard sand while we painted her between tides. The sunny side dried off well, but the side against the hulk remained a little damp for painting. In those days we tackled the job with enthusiasm, but in later years, as we stood beside her while the tide went out, or as she emerged on some reeking slipway, her flanks seemed to extend forever. There was always the same satisfaction, however, as with hair, hands, and face well smeared with paint, we walked round the clean smooth hull, once more ready to slip unimpeded through the water.

Early in January the trade wind reached across the isthmus to send us on our way down the long avenue of red and black buoys that led to seaward. The Islas Perlas showed hazily to port next morning, and soon after dark we were approaching Punta Mala. The lights of a big ship making up for Balboa showed ahead. I altered course to starboard. There was going to be plenty of room between us, and I sat in the cockpit happily awaiting the ship's passing, the rows of lights, and the thump of her screw. Suddenly she began to swing towards me until her mast lights were in line and both port and starboard light in view. I was horrified, not knowing what manœuvre she was carrying out, or whether she would correct her course again before running me down. Already her lights seemed to be towering over me, and I altered course to port. She rumbled past very close and then I saw that she was swinging back to her original course.

I felt outraged, as if she had deliberately tried to run me down, and my heart was still beating quickly when on a sudden impulse I looked astern. Far behind, another ship was approaching, and the one that had sent my heart into my mouth had only been making a definite alteration of course so that the other would know on which side she was passing. She had never seen *Tzu*

Hang's dim lights. It was a lesson I never forgot. Thereafter I never assumed that we had been seen by another ship unless she gave some indication of having done so, either by day or by night; when I saw a ship coming up ahead I always took a look astern to make sure that there was no other ship on the same course that might sandwich me in their manœuvres.

We had an uneventful passage to Chatham Island in the Galapagos, and as we approached Wreck Bay, the port of entry, we hoisted the Ecuadorian flag, which Beryl had made during the passage out of different pieces of coloured cloth. No sooner was our anchor down than we saw a small boat flying a large flag and realised that one of our colours, a blue instead of a black, was wrong. Thinking it was better to have no courtesy flag flying, rather than a wrong one, we hastily took it down. The Port Captain, the Medical Officer, and the Customs Officer came on board almost directly afterwards, but did not respond to our welcome and we trooped below in a harsh and pregnant silence.

Once we were all seated, the Port Captain cleared his throat and asked us to kindly explain why we hauled down the National flag, when we saw them approaching.

"Oh," said Beryl, "but I made one, and I found that I had used the wrong colour, so we took it down. We thought that you would be upset if it wasn't right. Here it is."

"But the colour is a bagatelle," said the Port Captain. "It is the gesture that counts."

"You don't mind if we fly this like it is?"

"But of course not. Let us go on deck again and hoist it."

We solemnly hoisted the flag to the cross-trees, and with good relations fully established, we went below to cement the structure with Barbados rum. It was a long time before we could get rid of them, and before they left they asked if we had seen Charlie Darwin. Such familiarity with the great scientist was so foreign to us, that we thought that they must be referring to some old whaling captain who had reti-ed there. They were so eager that we should come ashore to see him, to meet him, as we in our faulty Spanish understood the invitation, and the expedition was arranged for that evening.

After cleaning up, and dressed in our tropical best, the three of us rowed ashore at about the time of the "Paseo". We were met by the three officials at the end of the long and crooked wooden pier, which looked as if it were made of fence stakes but was in fact made from lignum vitae which is impervious to toredo worms. We walked a short way to the Botanical Gardens, where a few parched trees ringed with white stones cast thin shadows on the arid ground, and where at the end of a grassless pathway there stood a small bearded marble bust on a concrete pedestal.

It was not until we read the inscription that we realised this was the object of our visit, and had to adjust our faces rapidly to a look of gratification and awe, in spite of Clio's disappointed question of, "Is this all that we've come to see?"

We found the Harmons at anchor in Wreck Bay, complaining of a windless passage that thad forced them to motor the whole way. As they had only arrived the day before us, they must have had much the same weather as we had, but I suppose having started with the motor they never discovered that were was, in fact, a light following wind. They came on board to tell us that their voyage had not been a very happy one. "I have decided," Harmon said, "that I like fitting out but that I don't like cruising." With most of us it is the other way around, but then Harmon was an exceptional person. He told us that he had enjoyed his time in a Japanese prison camp. "Well, why not?" he asked us, indignant at our surprise. "I met my wife there. I had nothing to do except lie on a bed. I put on weight. I had no responsibility. I tell you," he said, "there were men who cursed me as they died, but I couldn't help it. I couldn't understand what they were so upset about."

Soon after they had left, their crew arrived in separate couples with tales of woe. We didn't think that they would get much further with their non-Pacific cruise, indeed we next saw the ship in a very run-down condition in Pango Pango, five years later, carrying copra with a native crew. A sad end to high hopes and a fine ship.

Ever since I had read William Albert Robinson's *Deep Water and Shoal*, I had remembered his description of the dark-haired Norwegian girl, Karen, with whom he had galloped over the hills around Progressor, and in my younger days I wondered why he had ever left her. Karen was married to an Ecuadorian long ago, and the mother of several children, but she still lived in Progresso. She was the doyen of single-handed sailor's girls, that they dream of finding, and loving, and leaving behind them.

As such, she had a mystique that dragged even portly yachtsmen up the long hot road, that danced and burned in the sun, to pay her court. We could not leave without doing so ourselves.

The road led upwards for about three miles, flanked by an uncompromising jungle or rocks, cactus and thorn. Along one side, all the way from Progresso to the end of the crooked pier, ran a fresh-water pipe which had been put in by the ubiquitous Americans during the war. Higher up we got into the country which is kept green by the mist and, judging by the state of the road, not infrequent rain. Here there was open savannah, with clumps of green trees and muddy ruts in the red roads. Progresso did not appear to have progressed very much since its inception. There were a few white-walled cottages with red roofs, which straggled higgledy-piggledy on each side of the rutted road, empty except for a variety of mongrel dogs, pigs and chickens.

The Señora whom we had come to visit, the slender Karen, was now a plumpish good-looking woman, with the blackest of black hair, a fair complexion that she had captured from the clear mountains of her birth, and a manorial air. She lived in the largest house of the village and welcomed us upstairs for coffee. One of her children, a fair-haired, sultry, langorous girl of about seventeen, played the guitar for us and sang a song of love. "It is very difficult here," said the Señora, with a glance towards her daughter that implied a house besieged by lovers of unacceptable qualifications. She told us of other yachts that had come to Chatham Island, of her husband who was away on the mainland much of his time, and of the difficulties of living in the islands. Like every European that we met in the islands, I felt somehow that she had lost her way. Her expression was generally serious, if not sad, but it lit up when she told us how a yachtswoman from the Pacific Coast had routed single handed a platoon of Ecuadorian infantry. She had motored up to Progressor in a jeep with her crew, who on arrival had not spared the bottle, first to refresh themselves after their rough ride and later to fortify themselves against the descent. On the way down they ran into the ditch and the skipper found herself stranded and badly in need of a cigarette. At this moment she saw a platoon of infantry marching up the hill and hurried down towards them in search of a nerve-steadying smoke. She was wearing a white dress and it was late in the evening. The leading soldiers came to a halt as they saw her, weaving uncertainly as a result of the accident and the rough road. There was a moment while those behind cried "Forward", and those ahead cried "Back", until a shout of "Phantasmagora, Phantasmagora", spread through the ranks, and the soldiers took to their heels, some of them not being recovered from the cactus until the following day.

From Chatham Island we sailed for Floreana, where Mr. and Mrs. Witmer with their two sons and a daughter had settled after the war in search of Eden. The yacht club at Balboa had provided stories about the settlement calculated to titillate the most unadventurous appetite, but the Witmers discovered that Eden had to be shared. A German dentist and his wife, having equipped themselves with stainless-steel teeth, had also set out for Floreana in search of a pastoral life amongst the thorns and cacti. The teeth chewed on something that they should not have done, for the dentist died of an internal poisoning and his distracted wife, found wandering on the beach, had been rescued by a fishing boat.

Unfortunately, their going did not leave the Witmers in happy and undisputed possession of the island, for they were next invaded by an Austrian Baroness and her lover. The Witmers had built a cottage "ariba" near a spring where they had started a farm, but the Baroness established herself and her lover in a cave close to this spring. She seems to have been a well-armed, dominant, and possibly insatiable woman, for she is said to have captured an Ecuadorian fisherman by shooting him in the thigh and holding him prisoner, while her former lover was relegated, or possibly promoted, to the duties of cook. In due course he escaped from the island with another man in a small boat; their bodies were found on the beach of another island with no water, and it was assumed that they had died of thirst. Shortly afterwards, the Baroness herself disappeared, and has never been heard of since.

The occasional reports brought in by fishermen or visiting yachts were the subject of endless discussion and speculation in the yacht club at Balboa, with fact and fancy deliciously entwined. The historian-in-chief and principle investigator was the senior canal pilot, a kindly yachtsman called Baverstock who made annual cruises to the Galapagos. Some years later when we met him on a passage through the canal, he told us that he had taken a couple of friends down to the islands, and while digging in a cave on the shore in search of some grisly evidence to show where the Baroness had gone, they discovered a pair of dentures. His friends, he told us, were furious when they got back to the yacht and found Mrs. Baverstock without any teeth, and Baverstock was forced to confess that he had stolen them while she slept, and dropped them on the floor of the cave to encourage the diggers and add zest to the search.

Floreana, in spite of its lovely name, had an unsavoury reputation as if it was bothered by some evil, perhaps from long ago. Disappearance, death and disaster haunted those who tried to make it their home, and soon after all these happenings, the Witmer's eldest boy was tragically drowned while fishing off Black Beach

It was with a feeling of some excitement that we anchored in Post Office Bay, where there is still a barrel used as a post office. As we came in to anchor everything was quiet and still, the waves just lapping the deserted beach but our chain running out made a prodigious clatter, and our voices sounded loudly. We did not go ashore that first evening. The sun was setting. A few birds made a sleepy twittering from the thick scrub near the beach and a fish rolled indolently on the surface near the boat. All was peace. Then suddenly from the hills above, there came a long gasping wail, a dreadful moaning that made our hair stand on end until it ended in a familiar, "Ee aw, ee aw, ee aw". "It's a donkey!" we all shouted in unison, laughing in surprise and some relief.

Next morning we went ashore and found the barrel, which was covered with names of ships and yachts that had made use of it as a post office. Held down to the top of the barrel with stones was a piece of paper on which there was some pencilled writing. I picked it up. "Help, help, help," was written across the top. "We have been marooned here. Please help us to get away." There followed the two names of the marooned sailors and the name of the yacht that had left them. It had a date of a few months past and I wondered whether they were still there.

"Well, if they've managed as long as this, they can go on managing. We can't take them on with us," said Beryl firmly, and I agreed. One doesn't maroon crewmen unless they are extremely bad ones, but I hoped that they had already found a passage to Panama or Equador. This, we discovered, had fortunately happened. Mr. Witmer told us later that they had had to look after them. One, whom he seemed to like, had been marooned because he happened to be ashore with the other, who was so awful that Mr. Witmer agreed marooning was the only thing possible. He thought, however, that he should have been marooned on some other island. We supposed, although he didn't say so, that he was thinking of a waterless one.

Next day, we sailed to Black Beach where there was an uneasy swell but a safe anchorage except in westerly winds. On the beach there was a small box-like cottage which the Witmers had built recently, where she and her remaining son lived, while Mr. Witmer lived with the daughter "ariba". There were several miles of stiff climbing between the two houses. Mr. Witmer cultivated the land and grew vegetables "ariba". Mrs. Witmer baked bread and cakes on the beach while her son did the fishing. The mountaineer and the seaman, the countryman and the coastal dweller, were all combined in one family.

We rowed ashore and paid Mrs. Witmer a visit. The little wooden shack was spotless and we were given tea and cakes. She was a middle-aged German Hausfrau, plucked from her natural element and transported to the wild, and so she had remained with extraordinary determination throughout all sorts of difficulties and vicissitudes. Even to have the material to make a cake seemed wonderful to us, but she was the sort of woman who would have sat primly erect on the threshold of hell. She was hospitable, but her conversation was stilted and reserved. There was no warmth in her. At least, not for us. If we wanted to go "ariba", she said, her husband would be down soon with water from the spring and he and their daughter would be spending the night. They would take us up in the morning.

Before tea was finished, we heard the jingle of harness and the shuffle of donkey's feet. Mr. Witmer and his daughter, with vegetables and water, had arrived. Mr. Witmer exuded vigour, but he also was reserved and gave the impression that, although he did not welcome visitors, he felt it his duty to offer such hospitality as he was able. He was dressed in a vaguely sporting way, as if he had just been up in the Bavarian mountains after chamois—perhaps rather as the head keeper than a great landlord, but he had something of the style of both.

We set off next morning along a winding mule track, hemmed in at first with thorn and cactus and later by dense guava bush. The Baron, as I had come to think of Mr. Witmer, set a smart pace, his muscular calves contracting and expanding relentlessly up the steep track. Behind him, his sturdy blue-jeaned daughter whacked and whistled at the mules. The Smeetons, soft from tropical sailing, were soon out of breath, although too proud to call for a halt. After an hour or two of vigorous exercise, we arrived at the farm. I had expected to see a vegetable garden, but here were acres of cultivation, as if Mr. Witmer expected an American fleet to anchor in Black Beach Bay. Sugar, thick-caned and green-leaved, stood ready for an army of cutters and a home-made press awaited the crushing. Whatever was crushed found its way to a home-made still—the secret economic foundation of Floreana, patronised by fishermen and the radio personnel. There were potatoes, over-grown cabbages, squash, peppers, carrots, peas and beans. This was no family vegetable garden, but a market garden—without a market. It takes men of vision to colonise a country, and we felt that Mr. Witmer's vision was years ahead of his time.

Besides the donkeys, Mr. Witmer kept pigs. They were the fattest and most indolent pigs that I have ever seen, and they lay, as if at a Roman banquet, under a huge avocado tree. From time to time a pear dropped off the tree and if it fell near enough to a pig it was eaten. Occasionally a pig would heave itself to its feet and roll off to the guava bushes for a change of diet. "The extraordinary thing about these pigs," said Mr. Witmer, "is that we don't get any fat When we render it down it all turns to oil."

When we set off for the beach, the donkeys were loaded with vegetables, limes, oranges and bananas. There was unlikely to be any scurvy on this voyage. At Frau Witmer's cottage we were given buns in pink paper bags to take on board. The bags had "Auf Bakerei Frau Witmer" printed on them. These were really people of vision.

That afternoon we sailed, unable to find out any more details of the Baroness' disappearance. I should have hesitated to ask Mr. Witmer, but Beryl plucked up sufficient courage to ask Mrs. Witmer. "I do not like to talk about it," she replied. "She gave us altogether too much trouble."

On our way from Floreana to Academy Bay, on Santa Cruz

Island, we called in at Barrington Island, which is, or was in those days, quite unoccupied. We had sailed late in the evening from Black Beach. A strange night, with dark tides and currents swirling around us; tide rips came chattering towards us, a hoard of little people whispering in the dark, busy on their own affairs, who were suddenly all about us and as suddenly left us again, rushing off into the night. *Tzu Hang* would dance and curtsey and swing her head this way and that as they passed. During my watch I saw a great splash like a shell landing in the sea and soon afterwards, while I was still wondering what had caused it, a monstrous ray flew out of the water not fifty yards from the ship and high enough so that I could see its black shape before it fell with a loud report back into the sea, sending out another huge splash.

Barrington has a narrow entrance on its eastern side, into a regular salt water lagoon. When the sun was well up so that we could see the reefs we went in and the entrance to the lagoon seemed to be alive with small rays moving out. They were not mantas, the one that I had seen jumping during the night, but looked more like sting rays, about two feet across. We could see seals lying on the beach at the far end of the lagoon and felt our way cautiously towards them, avoiding a half-submerged rock which was festooned with turtles. There appeared to be more rocks where we decided to anchor, and we chose some clear sand in which the anchor might lie, but as it descended through the clear water, the rocks took off and winnowed slowly away. The lagoon at Barrington was, and probably still is, one of the most unspoiled places in the world. It was alive with fish, turtles and rays. The beaches were loaded with sleek cow seals, so indolent that we could get within a foot of them before they would move. The bulls seemed to prefer the rocky shore to seaward, where they bellowed and snarled at us, disputing our right to use the goat track which followed the shore-line. A few pebbles would send them sliding indignantly into the sea, but it was advisable not to be on their direct route to the water. Behind the beach, if one sat for a moment amongst the thorns, the strong-billed finches of the Galapagos Islands would soon be fluttering round, and if we stayed still enough, would perch on hat or leg. On the rocks at the sea's edge, the primeval lizards sunned themselves and slowly clambered in and out of the sea.

In the days of the whalers, goats had been set free on Barrington, as on most of the islands, so that the whalers might find reserves of fresh meat. It was primarily to shoot a goat for ship's meat that we had put in, and as we lowered the anchor we saw a herd of brown and black goats with one or two lighter-coloured kids making off from just behind the beach. Next morning I set off on a goat hunt, armed with a 30-30 carbine.

The going was difficult, as it consisted largely of jumbled rocks without soil, for where there was soil, there was impenetrable thorn scrub. I suppose I was about two miles from the beach when I came upon the goats. All my old hunting instincts were unleashed. The wind was right, the sun was behind me, and the goats, as shy as any wild goats, were unaware of my presence. I settled myself comfortably on a flat rock, and waited for a suitable target to appear. The goats were moving slowly my way, the kids prancing and playing on the rocks, the females and one or two young males moving more sedately and browsing on the thorns.

I had forgotten all about meat. I ignored the tender young goats; I was waiting for bigger game. Presently it appeared. A fine old shaggy patriarch with a huge head of spiral horns. He stood on a rock, surveying his flock, and offering me a good shot, so that I dropped him dead. Never have I made a more stupid mistake. I found that by holding his forelegs over my shoulders, his head lolling to one side so that he threatened to overbalance me, his hind legs dragging, I could make slow and painful progress towards the boat. The sun was hot now, the goat smelled strongly, and I was continually stumbling, and all the time cursing my folly at having set out without a knife.

After an age of struggle, sweating, bloodstained, scratched and smelling, I saw Beryl and Clio making their way towards me. I let the hoary carcass slide to the ground and sat down to await their arrival. The euphoria of the chase had gone. I began to wonder whether my goat would be welcome. Beryl came agilely over the rocks and stepped up beside me. "What did you get?" she asked brightly. I pointed to where my goat was lying on its back, wedged in a crevice, every detail of its great age and sex displayed.

"Oh, dear," she said. "Oh, dear. It's an old Billy. Clio, come and see what Daddy's shot. I don't think we'll be able to cook it. It'll be as tough as anything."

"It had the best head," I said, crestfallen.

"I should have told you I wanted a young one. Anyway, I don't think he could have lived much longer, so perhaps it isn't so bad."

I felt that I had failed in man's most primitive duty—to provide suitable meat for his bride.

Next day we dropped anchor in Academy Bay, where across the bay the three Angermeers had made their homes along the sandy shore. They had left Germany before the war in a yacht of their own, bound for the Galapagos Islands, or round the world, or anywhere, for that matter, because they were light-hearted and young. They had only got as far as England, where they had enjoyed themselves so much that they had run out of money and had to sell their ship. I do not remember how they eventually came to the Galapagos Islands, although Carl must have told us. He was the eldest, bearded and with long hair, long before it became a fashion. He was the social one of the three, the poet and artist, well-mannered and at ease, a great raconteur and full of fun. They were all first-class seamen, the youngest being a fisherman and the middle one, Franz, the shipwright. The relationship between Carl and Franz was rather intricate, as Carl had married a European woman from Academy Bay, and Franz had married her daughter, so that Carl was the father-in-law of his younger brother.

Carl was soon on board to welcome us. He stayed for some time, a delightful visitor, and meanwhile *Tzu Hang* swung to the tide without pulling back on her chain. I had laid out a lot of chain and pulled astern on the engine to ensure getting the C.Q.R. well into the sand. I took Carl ashore in the dinghy and some distance astern of *Tzu Hang* saw a chain lying in the sand through about five fathoms of clear water. I called Carl's attention to it.

"Well, I'll be damned," he said. "I've often looked for that chain and never found it. It was left by a yacht that slipped her anchor in an onshore wind and never came back for it."

We had a good line and a grapnel as an anchor for the dinghy, so I suggested that we should try to grapple it. At the first pass, the grapnel hooked into the chain, and with a great deal of heaving and pulling, we managed to get a bight of the chain into the dinghy and fastened it to a thwart. We then started to heave in the chain, but after a few feet, it appeared to have stuck. By hauling the chain over the stern of the dinghy, until there was only an inch of freeboard aft, and then shifting our weight to the bow, we managed to break whatever was holding it free, and then, hand over hand, with a great deal of puffing, we brought the rest over in the stern, until the ring and stock of an anchor appeared, an anchor which looked familiar and soon turned out to be my own.

During our stay at Academy Bay, we took *Tzu Hang* into a shallow lagoon, just scraping over a sand bar as we went in, with Franz Angermeyer in charge. Here we propped her up on two poles, heaving down on them with a tackle attached to the shrouds and with boards fastened to the lower ends, so that they could not sink too far into the sand. We then laid out an anchor on each side and hoisted their hawsers to the mainmast truck. As the tide receded we felt at first as if a move to either side of the ship would topple her over, and when we clambered down into the water to start scrubbing, she looked most precariously balanced. The tide left all but a few inches of her keel, and as the deadwood here was copper-sheathed, it was of no consequence. The hull dried quickly so we covered it and ourselves in copper paint all one sunny afternoon, while we splashed about in the warm water and sand. On the way out, we touched the sand bar again, more authoritatively this time, and we were glad to be out, for there was only one more high tide on which we could get out that month.

One day, when rowing back from a visit on shore, we saw a pelican floundering in the water. We rowed up to it and pulled it on board. It had a double-barbed fish-hook caught in its beak and the top of its wing, so that its head was fastened back over its shoulder. Owing to the double hook we could not push it through the way of the barbs, so had to tear it out, breaking some skin in doing so. The pelican, looking very bedraggled, recovered quickly, and was soon on the wing again. Because of the slight scar on his cheek we could recognise him, and each time during the succeeding days when he flew close enough to *Tzu Hang* for us to be able to greet him, we felt that he was coming to thank us. At any rate, he wasn't scared.

There was a Norwegian family at Academy Bay who had a farm "ariba" and a daughter of Clio's age, so it was arranged that Beryl and Clio should go up to the farm and spend a night there. When they returned, Beryl told me that they had been awakened early by the crowing of innumerable cocks. When asked at breakfast by the family if she had spent a good night, she remarked on the number of cocks that had been crowing.

"Yes," said the solemn farmer. "Other people seem to raise hens, but we raise nothing but cocks."

Beryl pressed them to come and visit us before we sailed. The wife said that she would like to do so but that even the thought of getting on to a boat made her feel seasick. Beryl told her that we had some seasick pills and that if she took one as soon as she came on board, she would never feel the motion. The morning came on which we were due to leave and the Norwegian woman and her child arrived to say goodbye. I brought them out in the dinghy and Beryl gave the woman two pills to ensure that she should not feel sick. Soon she declared that she had never felt so well in her life and ate a hearty lunch. She was obviously enjoying herself so much that it began to look as if she would never go. Fortunately, the tide and a small wind came to our rescue so that we were able to say that we should be getting under way.

We met one other "character" in the Galapagos, and indeed anyone who went to the Galapagos with the idea of settling there had to be a "character". This was Sandy Sanders, who had once been Colonel Popski's driver, in Popski's Private Army. Driving with Popski had given Sandy such a taste for adventure that it is doubtful whether he will ever be able to settle for a humdrum life again. He was slight, fair-haired, grey-eyed, a typical New Zealander, hardy, independent and unflappable. The New Zealand Division in the Desert was full of men who looked and acted just like him. The only thing that was wrong for Sandy was that the war was over.

He had come to England as a seaman just before the war, and with the end of the war he turned to the sea again, in search of something that he had lost, so he set off with a Colonel and Mrs. Edwards for Cocos Island in search of treasure. One of the hazards of this much searched-for treasure is that rollers sometimes come into the anchorage; this is what happened to the Edwards' yacht, which was caught by them, washed up on the beach and broken. Cocos Island is only rarely visited by fishermen, so that the three of them had to settle down to a long stay. In such an emergency, at least, Sandy would never have been found lacking, and he must have tackled the Robinson Crusoe situation with enthusiasm. After a matter of months, a fisherman arrived who took the Edwards off, but by then the island had become too small for the three castaways and Sandy preferred to stay on by himself. Sometime later another fisherman arrived who took him to the Galapagos, where he decided he could find a degree of independence suitable to his temperament. What money he needed, he was able to make by fishing for the larger refrigerated boats which came through the Panama Canal from the United States to fish in these waters, using, however, the local fishermen in smaller boats to provide the catch.

Sandy had bought a cottage from an Icelander who had built it himself of stone right on the beach. It had the grace of a pill box in the "West Wall", and was rather a surprising choice of design for a beach cottage on the equator. Almost filling one of the small rooms was a paraffin deep-freeze which Sandy told us brought a constant stream of Ecuadorian women from Academy Bay to beg ice. Although the population of Academy Bay was small enough (there were only about three thousand in all the islands), the women, Sandy told us, were always pregnant, and had heard that iced drinks led to an easy delivery. He could not refuse them ice, he said, because of their condition and their belief in its efficacy, but he had begun to wish that he had never imported the vast white machine.

Sandy came on board to dinner, and dry understatements of adventure poured from him far into the night, so that in the end he slept on board. Part of my war had been in the desert, and at times I had seen jeeps, loaded with ammunition and machine-guns, water-tanks, and strangely-dressed soldiers, their faces as brown and crinkled as walnuts, setting off on, or returning from, some tryst with danger far behind the enemy's forward troops. I thought that I might even have seen Sandy. At least I knew those sunbaked shaking distances, the distant plumes of dust made by vehicles, the enemy aircraft quartering the dunes like a hawk in search of prey, the freshness of the morning air, the damaged and deserted vehicles left from some previous action which came to be milestones in the featureless wastes. Finding someone who knew these things, unleashed for Sandy, a long-restrained nostalgic waterfall.

Sandy had saved the deck watch from the wreck of the yacht on the Cocos Islands, and he insisted on giving it to us. We had been lent a deck watch by a friend in Canada and this was an exact duplicate, both Walthams. It was an extraordinarily generous gift, because routine necessities, or what civilisation had led us to consider as necessities, such as watches and clocks, could not be bought in the Galapagos, and there was no regular service between the islands and Panama, nor for that matter with Ecuador; nor perhaps was there in the islands any clock that kept time like this one. However, he insisted, and we were glad to have such an adventured clock on *Tzu Hang*. It is still *Tzu Hang*'s deck watch. Sandy was the sort of person who would always be ready to rid himself of possessions so that he might be free. Now he may have changed, as the latest news that we had of him was that he had a place "ariba."

From Academy Bay we sailed to Sullivan Bay on James Island where there was a strange rock pillar which had weathered into a network of holes so that it looked like an empty honeycomb. On the beach there was a very bad-tempered, solitary sea-lion who liked to dispute our right to walk on the sand. He had every reason to be bad-tempered because he had no women and half his tail had been bitten off, leaving a raw wound.

We could have spent months in the Galapagos, but I wanted to be off the Straits of Juan de Fuca, 4,800 miles away by the course we proposed to sail, before it was veiled by summer fogs. On this first long voyage we took care to select the most favourable time of the year for a trouble-free passage, not always with regard to the fastest sailing. I had decided April and May should be the best months for our passage north. Being unsure also to what extent we might expect to fill our tanks with rain water, I was reluctant to delay more than a day or so at anchor, having once left our brackish water supply at Academy Bay. We left a note behind in a glass bottle for Peter and Anne Pye in *Moonraker*, since they were coming to the Galapagos Islands in the following year, then set sail from Sullivan Bay on April 30. The note was picked up by another yacht and delivered to *Moonraker* when she arrived in Balboa.

Four thousand eight hundred miles stretched out ahead. What a long way it seemed! Twice the distance of our Atlantic passage; from south of the equator, across the doldrums, through the trades and into the westerlies. Perhaps it would not take so long if we made a good crossing of the doldrums.

CHAPTER NINE

The Long Road Home

If I were setting off again from the Galapagos Islands to sail to Vancouver, I would sail south-west as far as 3° S. and then west on that latitude as far as 118° W. From there I would sail north-west to 133° W. and then due north from there. If I had a good diesel motor and plenty of fuel, and was prepared to use it, then I should take a more direct route. The first route would follow the areas of least calms in April and it was the one that we intended to take; but I was eager to get north and in the end turned up too soon.

We sailed from Sullivan Bay on James Island on March 30, passing between Pinzon Island and Santa Cruz. There was a south-westerly current here and south of the passage we ran into heavy tide rips. The wind fell light during the night and throughout the next day we continued slowly on our way south. We were becalmed all that night in fog, with a very heavy dew, and next morning Clio, to her delight, brought me hurrying up on deck to see a ship—but it was April 1 and there was no ship in sight. The next night also we handed all sail and slept undisturbed until morning. This was not an auspicious start. In three days we had made about 160 miles and sixty of these were on the west-going current. However, by noon on this day, we had a fresh north-easterly wind in spite of a heavy swell from the south-east.

We made good progress all the next day with the same wind still blowing, and at 3° S. we turned on to a westerly course. There was a different atmosphere both within and without the ship. We were making about four knots with trade wind clouds above us, and the water cool, as if this was the Humboldt current that would carry us westwards, wind or no wind, until it was time to head north. The fourth day of April was a pleasant day, with the wind still light from the north-east and the current giving us about twelve miles a day. The sea was calm with an occasional swell rolling up from the south-east across the small swell set up by the wind. Clouds showed to the south-east, but above us the sky was blue, the sun hot and the water still cool. A lazy day with a murmur of voices coming up from below, as Clio struggled with her school correspondence course. We saw no fish and of birds, only small petrels that played around us, sometimes sitting in the water, and sometimes dabbing a foot in it as they flew as if to test the temperature.

For the next few days, we had light winds and variable weather. There were rain squalls hanging round that sometimes passed over us, giving us a good soaking, with all hands on deck busily soaping themselves in the free shower and catching water in buckets from the sails. To begin with, the water was too salty for drinking, but the sails soon washed clean and we were able to fill up our water tanks. We bathed over the side, floating with heads down over the sapphire depths which, as far as we could see, contained neither fish nor monster; but we floated for brief moments only, for even with no wind *Tzu Hang* seemed to roll herself along, as if the motion and the shape of her hull propelled her. Then we dried off on deck in the sun, with the salt pricking our skins. We could never get Clio to bathe off the ship when she was not at anchor, at least not in those days.

All the time, I was conscious of the doldrum belt above us and of the long passage to the north that lay ahead. To keep south and sail westwards with such exasperating slowness, as if we were already in the doldrums, seemed an unnecessary prolongation of the voyage. We decided that we would make 110° W. and then head up towards the equator. Because of the very light winds and the unusually confused swell coming to us from afar from both the trade winds, we found the rolling too trying on our sails to set a fore and aft rig, whereas the twin staysails, although far too small for these light airs, could be carried without risk of too much wear and tear. They were silent. The noise of the main and the genoa emptying and filling were an agony not to be borne. At least the current was giving us a hand.

We already had a lush growth of goose barnacles below the waterline and spent much of the day scrubbing them off, while hanging from a rope over the side. They collected on the log line, small pink mussel-like shells on a rubbery trunk. When our movement was so slow that the log line hung almost vertically below the stern, we hauled it in and coiled it on the deck.

At times I was bothered by the thought of never getting any wind again and of lying forever like some rotting hulk in the Sargasso Sea.

> "All in a hot and copper sky
> The bloody sun at noon
> Right up above the mast did stand
> No bigger than the moon."

Clio, however, enjoyed it. She found long, transparent snakes, built in segments and with faint dots of colour, and other slimy things which "with legs did crawl upon a slimy sea". She spent hours fishing for them with the bucket, but they were very fragile and soon dissolved away. The days dragged past, but were relieved by frequent bathes over the side. *Tzu Hang* was never too hot below, but the decks needed continual washing down. I can feel now, as I write of it and as I have felt so many times since then, the hot deck under bare feet, the splash of cool water as the bucket is emptied, and the cool wet teak.

On April 12, after twenty-four hours of very poor sailing, varied by short bursts of speed due to rain squalls, our total distance west was 1,020 miles, of which two hundred had been made on the current, in thirteen days. By noon we had another downpour, and after that a fresh breeze from the south-east. *Tzu Hang* turned her bow before it and started heading up towards the equator. To mark this slight change in direction and as if to show us that there were indeed monsters in the deep, a huge fish shot out of the water behind us and landed like a bomb with an explosive splash which still hung in the air although the fish had gone, by the time that we had turned to look. We were 108° W. and 3° 11′ S. and our course about 280°. The south-east wind continued all night.

The same wind held all next morning, but by the afternoon it had fallen light and was diverted by rain squalls; but next day the wind was so much in the east that we set the main and genoa and sailed due north. We were past the 110° meridian and when the sun set for the first time to port, we felt that we were at last on our way.

A faint hope—for the next week was spent largely in the same place—and, although we crept up to the equator and crossed it, whatever westing we made was counter-acted by an east-setting current running at about twenty miles a day. We first noticed this current on April 17 in Lat. 1° S., when we lost twenty miles, and my last plaintive remark in the log was made on April 20, when we were on the equator. During these four days we were carried eastward from fifteen to twenty miles a day, and the water was appreciably warmer. I next noticed a westerly set in Lat. 1° 25' N., so that this counter current probably extended for about sixty miles, running in a regular stream in opposition to and between the westerly drifts of the north-east and south-east trade winds.

After crossing the equator, out of an area of virtually no wind, we at last got into the true doldrum belt, which we had to traverse for about 600 miles before we got into the north-east trades. Other doldrum crossings that we have since made have been much more fortunate, for not only did this one extend much further than we had expected—including that part south of the equator for about 800 miles in all—with only a day or two of constant wind, but during all this time we had a confusion of swells so that *Tzu Hang* was frustrated by the movement and could never settle down to her sailing. It seemed that the north-east and the south-east trade winds were each stretching out a helping hand towards us, but always withdrawing it before we took hold.

The nearer that we got to the supposed southern limit of the north-east trades, the more infuriating became the delay and the awkward cross seas. Above us we could see the traces of the conflict between the winds. At least they were blowing up there. They sent their cohorts of clouds to join in battle. Sometimes there were skirmishers approaching from different directions, sometimes one army seemed to advance while the other fell back in retreat, sometimes there were clashes when they swirled and billowed together, and after brief combat fell apart and withdrew again. All this was far above *Tzu Hang*. Only occasionally did they come down to our level when, locked in dark struggle and striving separately about us, oblivious of where they trod, they seemed to hurl themselves upon us, so that we fled before them in pelting rain, blood from the wounds of war on the intertropical front.

Anyone who has made a crossing of the doldrums in a sailing vessel will know the feelings of hope and disappointment that attend the approach of the trade wind. It is like meeting at an airport someone whom you do not know, but who has been described to you. Person after person comes through the gate, and you think that this may be he, or that, until at last the one that you are waiting for walks through. Although he or she walks like all the others, is overloaded with baggage, and like all the others has an anxious, searching look, you are suddenly certain that this is the one that you have come to meet. So it is with the expected trade wind. Other winds have come and passed on, but suddenly this one reaches out to you and takes you by the hand and you know that you have got your wind at last.

So it was with us. The days had continued, some good, some bad, but usually only good in parts. I now had no fear of our running out of water, for our tanks were full, and we had even been able to wash our clothes in fresh water collected in the dinghy. Beryl, who had been bothered with boils ever since her carbuncle in Dominica, now had another on her knee, which worried me even if it did not worry her; but otherwise we were all in good shape. I was the most impatient to get on, but it was not until May 2 that I awoke about midnight to find that the rolling had ceased. I hurried aft and discovered a light wind from the north filling the sails. It had a different feel. There was a song to it. "I come from haunts of coot and hern," it sang. Well, not exactly. It had a lilting tune, a new consistency, a new temperature. It sang to me that it came from the Gulf of California, from the Islas Revilla Gigedo, and that for miles and miles now it would spread its magic carpet over the seas and carry us towards our home. It sang that it was the true wind, the faithful wind, the wind beloved by sailors, the wind of blue seas and the splash of spray on warm decks. We had taken the main down before turning in, leaving *Tzu Hang* to wallow in the confused swell under staysail and mizzen. Now we hoisted the main and jib so that *Tzu Hang* leaned and forged ahead with a new rhythm. "And suddenly everyone burst out singing," I thought. Next day *Tzu Hang* was still footing it sweetly to the north and within a few days Beryl's knee had healed.

Now the days were enlivened by good runs, by carrying the genoa as long as we dared, although sometimes we set a smaller sail at night. Now each day we tried to beat the run of the day before and guessed—to ourselves, because it would have been unlucky to mention it—how long it would take to get home. On May 5 we were in Lat. 13° N. and Long. 119° W. with many terns flying around us, while on May 13 we were north of the sun once more. There was a change in the climate. It was cool and fresh on deck and all night there was the sound of the bow splitting the wave tops, a steady crunching, and the merry trickle of water along the planking. We were averaging between five and six knots for every twenty-four hours of each passing day.

On May 13 in Lat. 24° N. we saw our first Black-Footed Albatross and from then on we had them with us all the time. It is a breathtaking thing to see for the first time the great wing-spread, and although they do not compare with the albatrosses of the southern seas, they are equally masters of the wind. To look across the rolling, and now rather greyer, seas, was to see somewhere the tilt of a slender wing showing above the top of a wave, or to see a big bird shoot suddenly high into the air, using the lift of the wind over a swell as a sail-plane uses a hill face. After gaining altitude like this, he would turn and swing along the line of waves, sometimes completely hidden in the valleys until far away he would shoot up once more, and then swiftly overtake us, turning his head as he passed as if to check that all was going well on *Tzu Hang*. All this without a flap of his wings.

They appeared to have large areas of responsibility, but only accompanied us so far. They stayed with us for a day or two, until we were able to recognise them and give them names, but sooner or later they came to the limits of their territory and handed over the duty of escorting *Tzu Hang* to more northerly and perhaps hardier colleagues. Every day was not a day of glorious trade wind sailing; we had one or two calms which did not last for long. On one of these we picked up two glass balls, lying within a few feet of each other. On these days the albatrosses always alighted near us, and if we were totally becalmed swam close under the rail of the ship, making occasional harsh squawks and snapping their bills, as if asking for food, but nothing that we offered them seemed to be to their liking.

At 30° N., right on the northern limit, the trade winds left us flat, but by May 20, fifty-one days out, they were back again.

On the following day I expected to pass close by the station of Weather Ship M, a station that has now been changed. I had promised Clio that if the weather were not too rough we would go alongside, and that we might persuade them to throw down some chocolate. Towards the end of the day, in spite of a fresh wind that had caused us to take in a reef, it was apparent that we would not make the station until well after dark. At about midnight I awoke from a sound sleep and saw a light flash along the beam above my bunk. I saw it flash again, the light coming through the skylight, just as if it were the revolving beam of a lighthouse! But we were supposed to be between five and six hundred miles off shore. Full of alarm, I scrambled aft and into the cockpit. A ship was overhauling us from behind and we were brilliantly illuminated by its searchlight. I knew that whatever was following us was almost bound to be the weather ship, but nevertheless I felt as if I had been caught out in a misdemeanour. I had been asleep and we were burning no navigation lights, although we had a stern light rigged on the mizzen boom gallows. I called to Beryl and soon her sleepy face, her eyes dazzled by the light, appeared at the hatch.

"There's a ship following us. Better get our lights up," I said.

"Whatever for?" she asked, not unnaturally. "It's got us in its light now, and anyway Eric Hiscock says that we are below the size for which lights are compulsory. I'll get the book."

"Damn Eric Hiscock!" I shouted.

"But anyway, it's too late now," she said.

In fact, it was too late to do anything without being observed, for we were shining in incandescent brilliance. I had not shaved for two or three days and felt every whisker glowing like a torch.

"I wish I'd shaved," I said to her, and as if to mock this ridiculous thought, the wind plucked the sarong that I was wearing from my waist, leaving me naked as a needle.

"For God's sake!" I cried to her now, feeling more naked than ever I had in my life. Beryl, partially incapacitated by laughter as well as the glare from the light, eventually passed up a duffle coat, and as soon as I was clad in this I felt better prepared to meet an angry challenge. Then she gave me the ensign, which I put in its socket at the stern.

The light was right above us now, shedding its brilliance in a tent around us so that we could see nothing beyond its walls.

Suddenly a great voice roared out through the loud hailer, shattering the night and making us both jump.

"Are you all right, are you all right?" it roared. "If you are all right, wave your hand, wave your hand."

We waved our hands with vigour and, as far as I was concerned, with relief.

"Do you need food or water?" the voice continued. "If you don't need food or water, wave your hand, wave your hand."

We waved again, and there was a pause as if the ship that was so close aboard us was considering what other kindness it could offer. Then once more the almighty voice was uplifted. "Well, good-bye. Good luck to our Canadian friends," it said. The light went out. We were in black darkness, but soon we could make out a tall bow swinging past and away from us, then the outline of a destroyer or frigate, an occasional light showing along the line of her hull, and could hear the rumble of her engines as she slid swiftly away.

"Well, wasn't that nice of them," said Beryl.

We both turned in, but we were so uplifted by this experience, by the feeling of kindness and consideration that the awesome voice had somehow inspired—almost the voice of Jehovah stooping in compassion over three small wandering mortals— that it was a long time before we could get to sleep.

The trade winds had come back, but not for long, as now we were in the Horse Latitudes, the area between the westerly winds and the trades. The trades had done more for us than we had expected, for they had held until May 23, when we were in 136° W. and 36° N. On May 27, in calm weather, we passed through hundreds of thousands of tiny jelly-fish, like small pale-blue biscuits, each with a triangular sail. I have often seen them since, one or two at a time on the back of a wave or half-submerged in our wake as we passed, but never a huge migration like this, all with their miniature sails set, stretching in all directions as far as the eye could see, and drifting together in packs. We wondered where they had come from, and whether they would reach the shore, and if that was Nature's intention.

Two days later we had a whale accompanying us. It was considerably bigger than *Tzu Hang* and when yards of whale had already appeared on the surface, its blow-hole came along, and where you would expect to see an end to this monster, a small dorsal fin appeared, so that there must have been yards more whale before its tail. This was submerged so that we never saw its whole length. It seemed to like our company, for it came with us first on one side and then on the other for about fifteen minutes. Now that we were getting into colder waters, there seemed to be more life about. One day I saw a Greater Black-Backed Gull, and as I associate this bird more with the proximity of land than with the open oceans of the albatrosses and the fulmars, it seemed to me to be the first herald of land, although we were still 650 miles away from Cape Flattery. It was May 29, we were sixty-one days out from Sullivan Bay, and our only contact with man had been the meeting with the weather ship. Not that we particularly missed our contact with man. Beryl never minds being alone for any length of time, provided that she has something to do. Clio had become accustomed to our way of life; she neither looked forward eagerly to arriving, nor regretted the lands that we had left. Nor did she ever seem to be bored, for she had already developed a great capacity for reading. I was probably the one who looked forward most to making our landfall, to meeting people again, and of course telling them all about our journey.

After light breezes, the wind came from the south-east and the glass began to drop. Soon we had it freshening to a gale from the south, while the seas mounted and chased us on our way to Cape Flattery. A seal joined us, sporting around us while we foamed along. He seemed to delight in diving from the top of a curling wave just about to break. The rough weather so confused my navigation that my noon fix put me somewhere ashore in Oregon; I hove to until I had worked out the error and checked the result by another sight. The seal put about with us and idled round the ship until we got going again, but by next morning, perhaps more assured of his navigation than I had been of mine, he was gone.

Now we had the wind in the north-west and a rising glass. All through the day, *Tzu Hang* raced towards Cape Flattery, while I was plunged in a flurry of navigation, luckily with clear skies, the moon and Venus to lend a hand. I figured that we would see Umatilla Light on the banks south of the Cape by 0200 hours next morning. I came on deck before two. Beryl was at the helm.

"No light?" I asked her.

"Not yet," she replied. "Sometimes I think I've seen one, but you can imagine anything. No. Not yet," she added more decisively.

I went forward and climbed the lee shrouds which were slack and wobbly. As I got a foot above the lightboard, I saw a light flash over my shoulder. I climbed down and went aft. "Well, it's there," I told her with enormous satisfaction. "We'll just check it." I stood on the mizzen pinrail and found I could see the light. "Flash and two and three and four," I counted, as homecoming sailors have so often counted the time between flashes of their welcoming lights. There was no doubt about it— Umatilla Light. I sat down beside her in the cockpit. It was a very special moment.

At first light, the wind had dropped, and as the day came we looked eagerly ahead, hoping to see Cape Flattery and the entrance to the Straits of Juan de Fuca. There was nothing to be seen—only the sea around us as there had been for so many days. Presently, the first rays of the sun caught a cloud above us and soon the eastern sky was red, and the haze that hid the land began to catch some of its colour. Slowly the red turned to gold, a glowing curtain, and through the curtain we could see the dark outline of the cape. It stayed just long enough for us to check our course and then it faded, leaving us once more surrounded by sea and haze and all the radiance gone.

We had our breakfast, and by the time this was over we were becalmed. The mouth of the Straits was still hidden, but soon the sun began to break up the haze into patches of fog. I could hear the sound of a ship's engines and presently a tug appeared with a long tow. Above us, hidden by the rising fog, an aircraft droned.

"Look at that tug with such a long tow. I wonder what it's doing out here," I said to Beryl.

She gave it a casual glance, and then took a protesting Clio down below for a last morning with the correspondence course. The sea was oily calm with a slow swell rolling in from the west. I stayed on deck, coaxing *Tzu Hang* along. All was quiet, the beginning of a summer day. The sun was just beginning to break through the haze, and in some places was already shining on the sea. Ahead, the engines of the tug hummed and there was still an aircraft somewhere above us. Suddenly *Tzu Hang* seemed to draw in her sides, and there was a loud twang, as if all her rivets had started. Two surprised faces appeared at the hatch. "What on earth are you going?" I was asked.

I had heard that noise before, but it was on a troopship when a destroyer was depth-charging close to us, after a submarine had attacked the convoy. "I'm not doing anything," I said, "but look at the chart. Does it say something about a bombing range?"

Beryl passed the chart up to me. We appeared to be in the middle of an area marked "Bombing Range". "That tug's towing a target and that was a bomb," I said.

"Oh, no," said Beryl. "Not now."

Perhaps post-war economy was working on our behalf, because there were no more bombs, and soon a wind came and hurried us round into the sheltered waters of the Straits. At one time the tide set us sharply in towards Tatoose Island and its outlying rock, so that we had to make a short tack to clear it. It was our first trip up the Straits, and as the following day was one of no wind, we had plenty of time to admire the scenery. Early next morning we were in sight of Race Rocks, with a tide carrying us down towards the mouth of the Straits. while just in shore a contrary current ran smartly towards them. With the help of the dinghy oars we managed to gain this current, but we need not have bothered, for a fresh wind sprang up and we tore round Race Rocks and, since we had no harbour chart of Victoria, sailed smartly in to anchor in Esquimalt.

We had not been there long before we were hailed from a small boat. It was Dick Goss, an old friend who had once sailed his own boat to the West Indies. It was Dick who had inspired us with the idea of bringing our own boat out to Canada, so that it was appropriate that he should meet us now.

"How on earth did you know we were in?" I asked.

"Well, you know the old saying," he replied; "a south-west wind with rain brings the ships home from Spain. That was what we had the other day, and I felt sure that it had brought you into the Straits; so today I rang up the lighthouse on Race Rocks and they told me that a yacht had just rounded the light, going like a scalded cat. I guessed it must be you."

CHAPTER TEN

Home From Spain

We were home from Spain, or nearly home; but before sailing the last forty miles we had to clear Customs. Our fate and our future were now in their hands. Since the day when we had first thought of the voyage, we had never asked whether duty had to be paid on a yacht sailed from England. If we had asked before setting off and been told that a third of the estimated value must be paid in duty, it is probable that the voyage would never have been made. It seemed best to meet these sort of problems as they cropped up and not to anticipate them. Like ostriches, we had hidden our heads in the sand, but now we had to raise them. I went ashore full of misgivings and telephoned the Customs Office.

The original object of bringing *Tzu Hang* out was to sell her in order to raise money to live on, but now, having with the help of the Bank of England discovered a way of transferring funds by way of the free market, whatever capital we had left, now much reduced was in Canada. During the voyage we had become more and more attached to *Tzu Hang*, and we had decided that we could not sell her, nor could we afford to pay a third of her value in duty. "Well," Beryl had said, "if they want us to pay duty we can go on to Australia or New Zealand, or whoever doesn't want duty. Round the world for that matter. At least we are free to do what we want now."

When two Customs Officers arrived they did not seem to be aware of their importance to us. They were smart, well-mannered, and enthusiastic. I rowed them back to *Tzu Hang* and down in the cabin brought out the ship's papers, certificate of purchase and our passports.

"Have you anything to declare?" one asked. "No tobacco, no

wines? Here," he said, "it's all on the paper. You had better look through it." There was no mention of yachts.

"We have some rum," I said, opening the locker door and showing him an opened demijohn of Jamaican rum.

Several hours later I took two merry customs officers back to their homes. We had been told to take down our Q flag and that nothing more was required of us. We were free to go. Next morning a mechanic put our engine right by pouring a little oil into the cylinder head and we were just thinking of getting up the anchor, when I got a message from the shore to say that I was wanted by the Head of Customs in his office.

"Now what?" I said to Beryl. "I suppose this is it, and they're going to make us pay."

"No," she said, "I'm sure it's all right. Probably something they forgot to ask."

"To ask for, you mean," I said.

On arrival at the Customs Office, I was sent up to an upstairs office. The Head of Customs in Victoria sat behind his desk with a dour look on his face. "Why didn't you report your arrival when you came in yesterday?" he asked.

"But I did," I said, much relieved. "We had two of your officers on board."

"That's strange," he said. "I heard nothing about it." He picked up the telephone. "Who were the two officers who boarded the yacht that came in yesterday?"

After a moment the telephone squawked back the information.

"Put one of them on the line," he said. A few sharp questions and answers followed. "It appears that they had some trouble with their car and didn't get back to the office in time to submit their reports," he said. "No, I don't want anything more. You are all through Customs. Sorry to have bothered you."

I left with a great feeling of well-being and hurried back to *Tzu Hang*.

"But is that all he said?" Beryl asked. "Didn't he ask about the trip or anything?"

"No. He just seemed to be rather angry and suspicious."

"I expect you were looking guilty," Beryl said.

"What for?" I asked.

"For seducing Customs Officers in the execution of their duty," she said.

From Victoria harbour, the distance by sea to our home on Saltspring Island was about 35 miles. In summer with light winds and narrow channels and strong tides we could get home easily enough in a day, but we had to show *Tzu Hang* to Fred Lewis on Coal Island.

Fred had been many things, from cattleman to sea captain, but the one thing he had never been was short of money. He was a perfectionist in all that he did, and if he had any religion it was an almost fanatical belief that man should be able to use his hands. Intellectuals were all right, but unless they could put in a fence post if required, or paint a boat, or use a hammer, he would think them only half a man. He approached everything from an essentially practical manner. Nothing was for looks alone. Everything about the place was functional and practical and of the best and most suitable material and construction, so that the island and everything on it had a beauty and a simplicity all its own. No one could possibly go to Coal Island without carrying away ideas for their own home.

Fred's great interest was the sea. He maintained a regular fleet of small ships for carrying to and from the island, for fishing and for marketing, and one larger ship round which everything revolved. When we first came to Canada he had a motor cruiser which, although beautifully kept up, had the practical lines of a small working tug, for which, no doubt, it could had been used if necessary. Most of the inside space was filled by the engine, which was polished and shining, and covered with dust covers when not in use. Very soon after our arrival he had bought a Fairmile, planked with mahogany, the hull still in splendid condition. He had replaced the engines with diesel engines and converted the ship to a yacht, but had removed all unnecessary deck hamper, so that she had beautiful long clean decks and, unlike so many converted Fairmiles, she had a look of simplicity and efficiency about her.

Fred was extremely intolerant of inefficiency or sloppy workmanship. To maintain the ships, to run the large workshop, to farm and keep the garden and the place in order, needed a large staff. Most of the men he employed stayed with him for years, and Coal Island always gave us the feel of a "happy ship". He was short with a mop of white hair and bushy black eye-brows.

We never knew his age, but during the time we knew him, he must have been under, and later over, seventy, always looking trim and in good condition. He was very fond of Beryl, who is intensely practical and always busy with her hands; he seemed to like me, although I am neither practical nor very efficient with my hands. Perhaps it was because of the way we had tackled our run-down farm, for he often came to see us and give us advice, and we, in the days of our 18-foot open boat and 3½ h.p. Briggs Stratton engine, often spent a night on Coal Island. He was a splendid host and, by all my standards, a great man; he was the only person that we had told of our intention to sail a yacht from England.

We came up under sail, loving the tree-covered islands and calm sea; then we started the engine for Iroquois Passage and took down the sails. Soon we saw with excitement the southern end of Saltspring Island, our home island, and then turned away from it to enter the harbour at Coal Island. Fred was soon on board and looking over everything. Beryl and I waited for his final opinion.

"Well," he said, "you've got yourselves a fine ship. She's really put together. You did well. Now you can come up to the house and all have a shower, before you eat." Each bedroom had a shower in the Coal Island houses. Fred would not allow a bath. "A dirty habit," he used to say. "Just sitting in your own dirty water and leaving those greasy lines."

Later, after a tremendous meal, Fred had good advice to offer. He had an idea of how well off, or not well off, we were. "Now," he said, "you've got to make up your minds. You have got to sell either the boat or the farm. It's no good trying to keep both. Either you spend money on the farm that you ought to spend on the boat or you spend money and time on the boat that you ought to be spending on the farm. A ship like yours," he said, "is going to cost you much more to keep up than you think. She'll want a good overhaul now, of course, and then, if you'll take my advice, Miles, you'll get rid of that junk-heap of an engine and get a new one."

Fred's advice was always good and we certainly didn't discard it straight away. We mulled over it before going to sleep. "I think we should ask Hugh Rodd about what sort of a price we might get for her, when we take her down for a haul-out," I said. Hugh Rodd was running the local shipyard, one of four brothers, all out from England, all extremely good with their hands, in spite of an English (Westminster) public school education.

After breakfast next morning, when we were getting ready to leave, I saw Fred talking urgently to Beryl, and heard Beryl saying, "Oh, no, Fred, you mustn't really. He wants to give us a new engine," she said, turning to me.

"I'm giving you a new engine," he said, but was unable to go on. There were tears in his eyes and the whole scene was charged with emotion. I realised that he was proud of his friends and that they had accomplished an undertaking that he also would have liked to have done. He was desperately anxious to show his appreciation and his happiness at our return. He was a great man; but he was also a humble and kindly man too.

We left, and in a couple of hours we had passed Musgrave's Island and were heading in for the Landing. We could see the truck on the wharf with Roy Smith, who had been looking after the place while we had been away, standing beside it. His healthy red face glowed like a beacon to guide us in.

Musgrave's Landing is a narrow pocket on the west side of Saltspring Island, sheltered from all winds except from the west; even from this direction there is only a mile of water across Sansum Narrows, and little wind, however hard it blew outside, ever found its way in. It extends for about 300 yards and is perhaps a hundred yards wide at the entrance; the fir trees go down to within ten feet of its rocky shores. A little-used Government wharf stood on its northern edge, and just beyond this there was a log shute, where the logging trucks sent their loads thundering into the water. They were kept there by a boom of single logs chained end-to-end, which stretched across to a dolphin, and then lay parallel to the shore towards the entrance. This boom enclosed a booming yard where the logs were made up into booms ready to be towed off by a tub to the mill. This yard narrowed the entrance to the harbour and increased the protection from any small swell that might find its way inside.

We tied up to the wharf in order to unload into the truck, but thereafter *Tzu Hang* always lay first to her anchor and later to a mooring, with a stern line to the dolphin. Here she was absolutely undisturbed, come wind come weather, and during the four years of her stay here came to no harm. Every morning, except during the week-end, the loggers arrived in a battered motor-boat, the rail and deck all scarred with boot spikes, and left again at six. Occasionally during the week-ends a motor cruiser tied up to the wharf and twice a week Roy Smith took his small motor-boat to fetch the mail. Otherwise, except on Sunday when he went fishing, it remained tied to a small float at the foot of the wharf. These and the squeak of brakes as the big logging trucks brought their loads to the chute, and loosed them with a prodigious splash and a far-carrying rumble, were the only activity that came to disturb *Tzu Hang* while she lay there. The loons and murrelet dived in the entrance and there was usually one of the loggers making up a boom in the yard, skipping light-limbed from log to log, pushing and coaxing until he had them in ordered rows, an almost silent ballet performed only for *Tzu Hang*'s benefit.

If we went there on a quiet evening, the landing was so still that it seemed as if all the trees were listening to the little talk of the bay. Sometimes we could hear it too—the patter of a mink amongst the rocks searching for shell-fish, a racoon washing some booty in the little trickle of water that ran down to the head of the bay, the rustle of droplets as a loon shook its head after a dive, or the soft plop of its diving. Sometimes, however, a startled heron would shatter the silence with its squawking, as it beat clumsily up from the edge of the water, its legs trailing like badly-stowed mooring lines.

"You've brought good weather," said Roy as we came alongside. "It's been kind of dull." The wharf was half a mile from the house, up a grassy lane which climbed parallel to the shore until we came to the gate about two hundred feet above the sea. We drove the truck slowly, noticing how the blackberries had spread or a rut had deepened. Roy's eyes, blue as the summer sky, were popping out of his red face in excitement. The jersey cow had had a calf, the bull was getting troublesome, some of the sheep had had twins, and so far he had caught no fish. The old blue house, which had never been locked, with its green roof, looked exactly as we had left it. Inside, Roy and his mother had cleaned everything and put flowers on the table for our return. How strange it seemed to us that we should have journeyed so

far, and experienced so much, and found no change at the end,
like a tale that is told.

And yet, there was one big change. Down at the landing lay
Tzu Hang, our new love. That night a furious thunderstorm
swept over us; the wind bent the trees and the rain rattled on
the windows. Beryl and I listened and thought of *Tzu Hang*
alone and untended.

"Do you think she's all right?"

"We ought to go and see her. Shall we take the truck?"

"No, let's walk and take a flashlight."

In a moment we had pulled on some clothes and sea boots
and were on our way. The rain was already over, but the wind
whistled around the house. The woods were black dark and the
path slippery, but no sooner were we into them than the wind
only stirred the branches far above us. Down at the landing only
tops of the trees were moving and *Tzu Hang* was not even restless
at her anchor chain. A whole winter and many storms had passed
before we could hear the wind blow and the rain on the roof
and not think about *Tzu Hang* lying in the little bay at her
mooring.

> *Uber allen Gipfeln*
> *Ist Ruh,*
> *In allen Wipfeln*
> *Spurest Du*
> *Kaum einen Hauch;*
> *Die Vogelein schweigen im Walde.*
> *Warte nur, balde*
> *Ruhest Du auch.*
>
> (Goethe, "Wanderer's Lullaby")

Tzu Hang's bottom was really dirty, her topsides were none
too clean, and it was high time that she was hauled out. We took
her down to Hugh Rodd's place to have her painted and the new
engine installed. Before doing this, however, we considered
whether it would really not be wiser to sell her after she had been
fixed up, and while her repute was still fresh from her voyage.
We asked Hugh Rodd for his opinion and suggested that if we
sold her we might, in a few years' time, buy another. Hugh had
already been right over her to see what required to be done.
Now he considered for a moment and then he gave his opinion.

"I think you'd be crazy," he said. "God led you to buy this ship, and he'd never do it a second time."

Neither of us has ever been particularly noted for wise decisions, but at least this was a happy one. It was no good keeping a yacht like *Tzu Hang* and not planning further cruises. "Australia in fifty-five," said Beryl—and this became our next target.

Tzu Hang rested in these once-idyllic surroundings, watching the numbers of motor-boats that passed the head of the anchorage or tied to the dock on week-ends, increase every year. Sometimes a cargo ship steamed down the Narrows on its way to Cowichan Bay to load lumber. By the time that she had rounded Separation Point, which lay between Sansom Narrows and Cowichan Bay, the remnants of her wash had found their way into the anchorage and made the ripples chatter on the rocks. They made *Tzu Hang* move restlessly at her mooring as if the sight of an ocean-going ship had set her thoughts wandering and made her dream of white horses and long swells.

One day, an extremely grubby little fishing boat came into the landing with a short mast on which a riding sail might be set. The galley chimney was smoking and smoke was also coming out of the hatch. The single-handed captain, looking as scruffy as his ship, sat at the helm while she chuffed past *Tzu Hang*, turned round and then lay off the wharf. I had just rowed back from doing something on *Tzu Hang* and stood on the wharf watching.

"Is that yacht for sale?" he asked in an educated English voice.

"No. I'm afraid she's not," I replied, not really expecting from the shape that he and his ship were in, that we had a prospective purchaser.

"I'd like to buy her," he shouted.

"I'm sorry."

"Well then, she can stay there and rot and be damned to you!" he cried, and forthwith chugged out of the anchorage again.

Later we were told that he was a survivor from the "Remittance Men". The Remittance Men always seemed to be looked down on by red-blooded Canadians, even those who are drawing unemployment pay, but I often think that they were largely responsible for making British Columbia. I also remember the war memorial in Duncan, with more than two hundred English names on it. I wonder what was wrong with them. Many of them must have been Remittance Men. Perhaps it was wrong that they should have had some money of their own, or wrong that besides working hard they had time to play, or that before going out to dinner they put on a dinner jacket, yet thought nothing of rowing three miles across the water in this unsuitable dress, in order to have dinner across the bay. They have become a fable of unwanted second sons, paid by their parents to stay out of England, a fable with little foundation in truth. If this were the last survivor of the Remittance Men, perhaps he had become solitary, missing his society, for he seemed to be a hermit living in a smoky ship rather than a smoky cave.

"If you look you'll see," someone told us, "that whenever he puts his head out of the hatch, he huffs to blow the soot off his eyebrows. But no one knows the channels and the anchorages up and down the coast like he does, or the weather, for that matter." At first I was rather shocked at the idea that he thought *Tzu Hang* was going to rot at her anchorage. Then I thought that he was only another odd-ball—they were all over British Columbia, including ourselves—and probably was quite able to buy *Tzu Hang* and our property three times over.

We had no intention of leaving *Tzu Hang* at her mooring. We were already planning our voyage to Australia. Meanwhile, she was out two or three times a week, over to Cowichan Bay or to Maple Bay for shopping or pleasure, sometimes to Coal Island, more rarely on an excursion to Victoria, and every summer we made a cruise of some sort. Our excuse for keeping her was to use her as a farm boat, but she had only one farming venture; this was to bring a large Suffolk ram from Maple Bay.

The farmer who sold him to us was a tall and enormously strong man with hands like a bulldozer blade. He swung the ram off the dock and lowered him by his forelegs on to the deck, which was some feet below the dock. Receiving him there was like trying to stop an "All Black" forward with his eyes on the touchline, but as soon as the ram sensed that he was surrounded by water he quietened down. Perhaps he was paralysed by fear. He took up his position in the middle of the deck just aft of the foremast.

The return passage was made without incident, except that our passenger was in a nervous state, and covered the deck in droppings. We anchored below the house and then hoisted him in slings on the dinghy boom and swung him outboard before lowering him into the dinghy. There he stood astride the centre-board, quite still, while we rowed him to the shore. Beryl sat on the stern thwart hanging on to the ram's quarters, while I squeezed as far as possible into the bow and rowed, meeting his black face every time I leant forward. It was fortunate that we still had the large teak dinghy that we had brought from England. The ram, for the only time during the rest of our stay on Saltspring Island, seemed to have a certain amount of sense, for he stood still until we grounded on the beach. By this time Beryl had decided that she had the wrong end, for he was still loaded, but I found it difficult to agree, having been overrun as he leaped for the shore.

Two of our friends who lived not far from Maple Bay, Raith and Vivie Sykes, often came over on the week-end to see us in a motor-boat that they had built themselves. They were at that time engaged in producing large numbers of broilers with great efficiency, and doing so well that soon there were numerous other farmers producing broilers and the market began to slip. Raith was already beginning to think that he would give the broiler business up and take a long holiday while he thought of something else. He had been a glider pilot at both the Normandy landings and at Arnhem, where he had been captured; partially owing to the treatment and hardships that he had undergone, he had developed arthritis which limited his activity. He was the sort of man whom one would always like to have with one in any adventure, a big man who found great joy in life, with a good sense of humour. Owing to the trouble with his feet, he shuffled about like a benevolent bear and, like a bear, I suspect that he would be quite frightening when angry. He was good with his hands, got through a great deal of work without talking about it, and certainly didn't take life too seriously. Whatever he did, like his car, an Allard, had style about it.

Vivie, or Vivien, as she was properly called, was a slim red-head of great vivacity and character. She was born in Canada but had managed to get back to England in the Red Cross before the end of the war. While working in a hospital she saw her tall airborne officer in his red beret and, having been warned that she should never allow herself to be alone with him for a moment, particularly in the linen cupboard, immediately fell in love. We

THE SEA WAS OUR VILLAGE

had already suggested that when we left for Australia they should come with us as far as Hawaii. They jumped at the idea. The same day they came down to Maple Bay and, as we left under the engine, Vivie saw the engine exhaust water gushing out of the exhaust. She really didn't know very much about boats then, but something was obviously wrong. She cupped her hands and shouted after us, to Raith's shame and disgust.

"You're leaking, you're leaking!"

Raith's voice came clearly across the water, "Vivien, really! it's going out, not coming in."

In order to see whether they would like to come with us on a longer cruise, the year before we set off for Australia we made a short cruise up the west coast of Vancouver Island as far as Port Alberni. There was a bad weather report, but we set off anyway, thinking that we'd make Victoria harbour before the weather really deteriorated. It was a mistake and we missed our tide round Trial Island. Then, with a steadily rising head-wind and a contrary tide, we were soon overtaken by darkness. No matter how many times we tacked across the Straits we always seemed to be back in the same place. It was a filthy night.

To begin with, there was some excitement in trying to make up against the tide and wind, and finally we got up to Port Angeles and went about for Victoria. By this time we had all lost our tomato soup suppers. To be wet and miserable and seasick was nothing new to Beryl and I, for we thought that it was a necessary evil that we soon got over; but it was a hard initiation for Raith and Vivie.

As we approached Victoria harbour, I got Vivie to read the lights from the light book. Something was wrong. Either she had the wrong place or I had, so that in the end I decided to put to sea again. We put Vivie and Raith to bed on the main cabin floor, thinking they'd find less motion there, and the dog took up his position between them—the same Poopa that we had brought from Madeira. He also was seasick. From time to time Beryl shone her flashlight on them from the cockpit; we could see two miserable figures lying there, white faced, with the dog sitting hopelessly on his haunches between them, swaying to the roll of the ship.

"They'll never go on with it," Beryl said.

During the night the wind switched to the north-west, and as the light began to come we made in again for the harbour entrance. Beryl and I had quite recovered already and, after a really nasty, rough night, felt happy and exhilarated as we came into the harbour. We tied up to the wharf opposite the hotel. Vivie and Raith were sound asleep, although still rather white faced. Beryl and I stepped over them to the fore cabin, wondering whether they'd wake us up before they left.

They did wake us up, and we found that breakfast was cooking and everything had been cleaned up. Raith even brought me a cup of tea in my bunk.

"What a hell of a night," I said.

"Wasn't it!" Raith said. "I'm afraid we were not much help, but we'll do better next time. When are we leaving?"

We left with the tide, a few miles only to Sooke; it was a gentle sail in perfect weather—the other side of the medal.

That cruise, like the others we made, round Vancouver Island and up and down more sheltered channels, gave us a variety of experience, rough weather, fog, lazy sun-baked windless days, and a few days of sunny sailing. Most of all, it gave us experience of fog. We groped our way out of the Straits of Juan de Fuca; we found the Swiftsure Lightvessel rolling, and fortunately bellowing, in dense fog and on a grey sea that mingled with the fog, so that for a moment she seemed to be suspended in the air; we rounded Cape Beale without seeing it and found our way up Trevor Channel, seeing only rocks and waves breaking like little black shoes and a petticoat hem beneath a grey crinoline. It was these days that gave me a confidence in fog navigation, perhaps an over-confidence, but it never brought us into trouble. No one, however, can have confidence in fog when on a shipping route. That is something always to be avoided.

The British Columbia coast, however, is not an ideal cruising ground, except for motor-boats and motor cruisers. There is too little variety in the anchorages; too many tall dark trees that hem them in; too little wind in summer, or too much in the wrong direction, blowing up a sound when you want to come down it and down it when you want to go up. We enjoyed our cruises, but they only served to whet our appetite for going further afield. Vivie and Raith were also affected. They decided that they would sail with us to Hawaii when we left for Australia in the following year.

CHAPTER ELEVEN

To San Francisco

We set sail for San Francisco and Hawaii on September 4, 1955, intending to make a two-year cruise in the Pacific. We had sold the farm and were footloose. The world was open. Our intention was to return to B.C. at the end of the cruise and to get land again with an anchorage for *Tzu Hang*.

Land is a hard mistress and sets its shackles on you. The more you have put into it, the harder it is to break away. Beryl and Clio had loved their life on Saltspring Island; for them leaving was particularly hard, especially for Beryl, who had given so much of her imagination and energy into making the place. Once we had sailed from Musgrave's Landing she closed her mind to what was past and done with, then looked to the uncertain future with all the enthusiasm and excitement that is part of her character.

Clio was fourteen, tall for her age, with long legs, widely-spaced grey eyes and well-shaped but usually grubby hands. She was condemned to struggle with another school correspondence course. She was entirely happy at leaving school and starting off on another journey; she shared her bunk with the dog Poopa and the Siamese cat Pwe. As we sailed from Musgrave's Landing, she was preoccupied about a mouse that she had smuggled on board, and how to keep the knowledge from the cat, the dog and myself. Fortunately, Beryl persuaded her to put it ashore at Coal Island, where we called on our way down, without the rest of us learning her secret. She was still a great reader and we were well-provisioned with books. She was also a useful hand at sea, although preferring drama rather than routine chores.

Pwe, the Siamese cat, we had bought as a kitten a year before, so that it might be prepared for a seafaring life. The lady from whom we bought it let us have it at a reduced price, because, she said, "It's going to have such an interesting life." Little did she know. Before the cat retired from the sea she had had adventures in ports all over the world, had been overboard on several occasions and had even had a shocking experience in a Paris sewer. No long-cruising yacht should be without a cat. They are soon quite at home, always charming companions, and provided that there is room for plenty of sawdust so that their litter box can be replenished daily, they are not offensive in any way. We became quite choosy about the cat's litter and after round the world experience found Mediterranean pine to be the best.

Vivie and Raith joined us in Victoria, but when we wanted to leave next morning, the dog was missing. Love, during the four years that we had lived on Saltspring Island, had passed him by. There had been no bitches on our side of the island; nor on our brief trips to the mainland had he ever lost his heart until now. We hunted for him all over the place and eventually found him with a troop of nondescript dogs, battle-scarred, dirty and exceedingly pleased with himself. He was most reluctant to leave and put to sea.

We made only a short sail to Sooke, a secret little village, tucked away behind a curving channel and a sandbank, so that it might have been a hundred miles from Victoria, which we had left only a few hours ago. The great thing about beginning a voyage is to start on the right day and preferably at the right hour; it is best if one has only to go a few miles before anchoring, in calm water, to settle down in peace, and to have a good night before putting finally to sea.

Next morning we left with the tide. A sunny September day with a feeling of Fall already in the cool air, as good as wine for a stirrup cup as we started on our adventure. As *Tzu Hang* sailed down the lovely sound, we recognised landmarks that we had come to know during our various passages through the Straits. The maples and dogwoods were already on the turn along the water's edge, illuminating the greens of the forest above them. Soon the southern shore was lost in mist and in the afternoon Callam Point appeared—a grey hump crowned with firs on the edge of the fog. The light wind dropped altogether, and I decided to push on out of the Straits with the motor. Fond hope. The battery was quite unable to turn the engine; after a time Raith and I discovered that the engine was full of water and the gasket was broken.

There was no wind. On these occasions it is best to count blessings; fortunately, we were well off the shipping route. We drifted slowly out towards Tatoosh Island with the tide and presently came slowly back again. So we spent the night, drifting here and there, but able to check our position from the fog horns that boomed and barked dismally all night. During our time in British Columbia, we had become accustomed to fog and, though no sailor enjoys fog, we were not ever anxious.

Neah Bay, on the south side of the Strait, was the nearest port where we could get a new gasket. Early in the morning a light breeze got up so we were able to sail back towards Waadah Island, which is near the bay's entrance, guided first by the sound of the fog horn and then by the sound of early fishing boats putting to sea. Over the sound of motors, outboard, inboard, heavy-duty and marine, which filled the fog on all sides, we heard the noise of a bell buoy. We brought its sound on to the right bearing, then turned and headed for the harbour entrance, allowing for the tide, which was running against us, and continually checking the bearing of the bell. Presently a light flashed dimly through the fog; we checked the flashes and found that it was the harbour entrance buoy. The wind dropped, but *Tzu Hang* continued to ghost in with the sails and everything on deck damp and dripping. Inside the harbour the fog began to thin and the wharf lights appeared, paling now with the coming of daylight. It was 5 a.m. when we anchored and went below for a huge breakfast. It was our first port and as usual things had not gone as expected; but we had brought *Tzu Hang* in under sail on a failing breeze in fog and against the tide; that was enough achievement for the first day.

Neah Bay was a most unattractive place. I do not expect it is much changed now. Some commercial fishing boats operated from the bay, but most of the life of the little town seemed to depend on those who came to fish for sport. I cannot feel great enthusiasm for trolling with a plug bait when it is a matter of luck whether a fish takes your plug and no great skill is needed to bring it to the boat. I met one fisherman who had a bare-breasted mermaid with a gold tail, a small plastic mermaid, which he said was an excellent lure. I saw one old man back from fishing who looked tired, cold and ill; unwisely I asked him if he had had any luck and he replied angrily with a short "No." No wonder he felt angry, for he had been out in an open boat since before daylight in fog and a roughish sea and was returning to little comfort; for, apart from a few sleazy lodgings, a shabby pool-room and an even shabbier cinema, there seemed nothing for visitors other than the fishing.

The day after our arrival in Neah Bay, a cold wind came rushing suddenly off the hills while we were at breakfast. Clio looked out from the hatch and remarked casually that we were a long way from the shore. So we were, and dragging our anchor rapidly across the bay. It took yards of chain before we brought up again, and a long row back for the mechanic who was fixing the engine. During our short stay at Neah Bay, Poopa behaved abominably whenever he was taken ashore; to get him ashore we had to climb a vertical steel ladder up the side of the wharf, and during the ascents and descents, no matter what difficulty was encountered he remained relaxed and confident in our arms. As soon as we forgot about him for a moment ashore, he was off in search of new adventures. The cat preferred to remain on board, but she caused us great anxiety by walking out to the end of the bowsprit whenever we rowed away from the ship.

On September 8, we were all ready to go. The local weather prophet had told us to expect the first south-east gale. "They mostly come on September 12," he said. We filled up with water at the wharf and, since there was no wind, motored out until we were well past Tatoosh Island, passing it for the fifth time but seeing it only for a second, so often does the fog hang about the entrance to the Straits in summer. In the afternoon, *Tzu Hang* picked up a light breeze from the south-west, and headed south close-hauled on the starboard tack. The mountains of Vancouver Island soon dropped out of sight in the haze.

The passage to San Francisco was not uneventful and, reading the log after so many years of sailing, I am astonished at how many things went wrong, and also how cautious we were. The fact was that although we had sailed *Tzu Hang* out from England and had had her by then for nearly five years, we were still rather inexperienced yachtsmen.

By the time that Vancouver Island had disappeared we were

becalmed, about forty-miles off-shore, with poor visibility and fog in-shore. We put up a riding light and turned in. Morning came without sunrise; only the darkness turning slowly to grey, and the grey slowly lightening to show a listless moving sea, which merged imperceptibly into a dull and stationary sky. All through the night there had been a strange little chattering noise about us, and now we saw numbers of small green birds, like flycatchers, although I did not identify them at the time, circling the ship and landing exhausted wherever they could find a foothold.

Pwe turned into an evil demon, and stalked them wherever they settled. We put her below but she popped out again whenever a hatch or skylight was opened. We tried to scare the little birds away but they were too tired to face the grey emptiness about them, and soon fell victim to the cat's quick crouching rush. Some we put below in a place where she could not get at them, but they died in an hour or two from exhaustion. There had been no wind to blow them off their migration route, so it must have been the fog that confused them.

We were about the same distance offshore when night fell. As we were still near the entrance to the Straits we kept a watch. The sails were down and a riding light burning. At about midnight, while Raith was sitting in the galley reading, Pwe jumped down from the deck on to the chart table and from there on to the cabin floor. She was carrying something in her mouth which was fluttering and chattering angrily; as she got to the saloon it escaped from her.

Pwe began to growl, and whatever she had been carrying in her mouth scolded back from under the cabin table. Between these two and Raith, who felt himself in need of reinforcements, we were all soon awake. Raith shone his flashlight and discovered a large bat under the table. It had big ears, a doggy face, and an alarming array of white teeth. With its back to the wall, or in this case the starboard seat, it was putting up a ferocious show of resistance, while Pwe crouched in front of it, growling angrily but reluctant to come to closer quarters. Raith, since it was his watch, was told to remove it. He caught it in a towel, but on his way aft to the hatch if fluttered and Raith, with what can best be described as a girlish cry, let it go again.

We all turned out, except Poopa, who continued to hog it

in Clio's bunk. While Raith searched in the after part of the ship with his flashlight, the rest of us hunted in the main cabin and the galley by the aid of the ship's lighting, which was never very bright. As Raith bent down to look under the bridge deck, the lower half of his body filling the small door that leads aft, I saw something hanging on the seat of the baggy old trousers that he was wearing.

"Raith," I called to him, laughing, "it's hanging on to your backside."

He backed out and stood up under the doghouse roof, turning towards me, his big friendly face beaming, but I could see a hint of suspicion in his eyes. "Don't be so silly," he said, and turned back to his task.

I looked again more closely. The large bat was indeed hanging upside down attached to the seat of his trousers, a veritable vampire of a bat. I got hold of Beryl. "Look," I said, pointing at Raith's backside, which again filled the doorway. He heard our laughter and turned round again, like a horse backing out of its stall into the stable alley.

"It really is there," I said.

"Nonsense," he replied, but this time the doubt in his eyes was more evident. He felt gingerly behind him and the result was surprising. "Oh," he shouted and jumped round to present his backside again. "Take it off, take it off!" His behaviour was not quite what one would have expected from an ex-Airborne Division officer, who had put his glider down on the Normandy beaches and at Arnhem. We caught the bat, still firmly attached, in a towel and released it into the night. It was the sort of bat that would make nothing of forty miles if it flew in the right direction.

We had a flukey wind at times during the following day, and a rough sea sent to us by some more distant disturbance. By midnight we were only eighty miles on our way. The night was dark and cloudy with occasional rain, no moon and only occasionally a dim star showing. At about one in the morning we were hit by a strong squall from the south-west; it came without warning, hissing out of the dark night, and almost at once we were spinning along with our rail in the water and carrying too much sail for the wind, with everything except the lee shrouds humming tight. Beryl and I clawed down the mizzen and stifled its frenzy, then brought the jib in, fighting the wind for every foot of it with the spray slapping over the bow; this left *Tzu Hang* under main and staysail. Raith, hearing our struggle, came up into the dark careering night; as yet he had not been in a hard blow, nor was he very familiar with the ship, so that the best that he could do was to take the helm, which he always did very efficiently. He could feel the tension in our movement and in our voices until we had the sail stowed; as we had a cup of cocoa in the cockpit afterwards, he told us that the noise of the wind and the excitement had made his heart beat quickly. Beryl and I felt very salty. Later in my watch there was a heavy thump at the bow, and then another on the keel amidships which lifted the ship in the water. We slid off and I looked aft to see the dark shape of wreckage falling astern. It looked like a wooden quay and some of its piling, and this time it was my heart that was beating quickly as it disappeared.

It was by then the twelfth of September, and if the weather prophet of Neah Bay was right, we might expect our gale. We had been out for three days and had only made 120 miles, having had, except for the one night, calms and light head winds; so we hoped for a change. The glass was dropping as the wind began to strengthen from the south-east and by ten in the morning we had a head wind blowing up to gale force. We hove-to under the mizzen with the staysail aback. The mizzen was too strong for the staysail so that *Tzu Hang* kept fore-reaching and taking some hard thumps from the sea; this was the first time that we had ever hove-to for any time and were not sure of the correct combination in this sort of wind. It was an uncomfortable night. As *Tzu Hang* came up to the wind the mizzen fluttered violently until the mast shook and she fell away again. On the following morning the glass shot up and the wind went to the west, so we set off again. As we did so, the starboard hatch-cover that had been taken off and not yet stowed, disappeared downwind and into the sea. With a big sea still running and half a gale blowing we did not try to pick it up again. Poor Beryl; it was a new one that she had just finished making.

After blowing freshly for most of a bright sunny day, the wind became light and patchy. There was a lumpy sea running and the boom began to bang about so that we brought down the main and tied it loosely on the boom. During the first night watch

I thought that we were running into a belt of fog. The sky was very dark, but I could see a lighter band lying right across the sea beneath it. It turned out to be the lighter sky under a dark line squall that was approaching; suddenly it rushed upon us, heeling us right over. There was a sharp jar from the mizzen mast and the mainsail tore itself from its loose tyers and started to flap violently, the heavy reef cringles flogging the deck and making a hideous noise below. As I tried to get the sail under control I felt as if I had to turn away to breathe, and the wind blew my mouth into a strange shape and took my words away as I tried to shout to Beryl. It was over in a moment; we then noticed that the weather mizzen shrouds were slack, and found that the pin of the big shackle that fastened the after mizzen shrouds to the chain plate had sheared. It must have been a very strong wind, but even if I had recognised it as a line squall I should have done nothing about it as we already had the main down. Good seamanship is a mixture of common sense and experience. We had never been caught by a line squall with the sail badly furled before; I do not remember whether it ever happened to us again, but it certainly would have done if it had not been for this experience.

Our troubles were not yet over, although we were half-way to San Francisco; in spite of the slow start we still hoped to make the whole passage in a week to ten days. The glass was falling again and the wind backing as we pitched into a nasty southerly swell. *Tzu Hang* was sailing herself close-hauled on the starboard tack with one reef in the main. We were all at breakfast when a big jolt shook the ship as if we had run into a log, and at the same time something crashed on to the deck. As we tumbled out of the hatch I saw something fall from the lower starboard cross-trees, and almost at the same time discovered that we had no backstay. We hurriedly set up the port backstay which had been slackened off and fastened to the shrouds; at the same time put *Tzu Hang* on the port tack. Then we brought down the main and hove her to.

All *Tzu Hang*'s rigging was new stainless steel which had been spliced up for us in a shipyard in Seattle. One of the backstay splices had pulled, and the resultant strain on the after main shroud had caused another shackle pin to shear. When *Tzu Hang* was re-rigged two years later we did away with all shackles in her standing rigging. We were lucky not to lose the mast, but hove-to on the other tack, she was safe enough. First we slackened off the rigging screw which held the after main shroud, then filed out the hole in the lug on the mast fitting and put in a stronger shackle. Meanwhile the wind had strengthened to gale force again and we could not, or perhaps did not want to, fit a new backstay until we had a better opportunity.

Next day the sea was down enough for me to go aloft. When Beryl and I are alone and someone is required to go aloft, she prefers to go rather than to hoist me in the bos'n's chair; with a man and wife crew this is perhaps the best arrangement if the woman does not mind working aloft. In a rough sea a life-line should be passed around the mast and fastened to the chair, being released and refastened at the cross-trees and other fittings which may interfere with its upward progress. Even with this life-line it is still necessary to hang on with arms and legs, and while working to hang on for dear life with the legs. The higher you get, the more violently does the ship try to swing you off and, in spite of good thick trousers, bruises and nips on the inside of the thighs are the order of the day. On this day I had no excuse to stay on deck, with four people to hoist at the main halyard. We had a spare jib forestay which I took up and fastened to the backstay shackle. At that height there was still a lot of motion, and as far as I could see in all directions nothing but heaving grey sea. I was glad enough to get down without dropping a spanner. We set up the new backstay with a handy billy, as it was too long to attach to the lower part and the Highfield lever.

The passage was obviously going to take longer than we had expected, so Beryl and I began to wonder whether, in suggesting that Vivie and Raith should come with us, we had made too little of the frustrations, discomfort and futile movement of the bad periods. They seemed to be standing it well, not liking it more nor less than we were. Vivie, who was supposed to be teaching Clio, felt a little seasick most of the time, but apart from an occasional exasperated "Clio, you clot!", there was little sign of tension below, and none on deck. They were good companions.

At this time of the year one can have summer or winter weather on this coast. *The Pilot* describes the weather that we had had so far in these words: "These gales, with the heavy south-westerly swell prevailing in winter, cause a heavy confused sea which taxes the weatherly qualities of a vessel to the utmost. They spring up gradually from the southward and increase in strength, with a rapidly falling barometer. When the barometer becomes stationary, the wind shifts to the south-west and blows heavily with clearing weather and frequent rain squalls. The barometer rises when the wind hauls to the south-westward, from which point it generally blows from ten to twenty hours." This describes the weather that we had had nicely, although ours were only the first gales of winter and not as bad as those that would come later. Now we were to experience a norther.

The Pilot says: "Strong north-westerly winds prevail along the entire coast (in August) . . . the north-westerly winds frequently reach a velocity of seventy miles an hour. . . . The severe north-westerly gales generally last for two or three days and continue through the night with little or no diminution."

The norther arrived on the eighteenth. We hove-to for the night under reefed mizzen and staysail, and this time there was no shaking and she remained well-balanced. In the morning a tanker spotted us and stopped while *Tzu Hang* drifted down towards her. Beryl and I sat in the cockpit drinking huge cups of tea out of empty mugs, hoping to dispel any doubt in the captain's mind that we might be in need of assistance. He was watching us through glasses from the wing of the bridge. Eventually we had to start the staysail sheet and sail away, and the boat moved so easily that we wondered why we had stopped.

The tanker was running light with her screw half out of the water. It gave a few slow flicks; then she gathered way and moved off on her course, the thump of her screw coming clearly through the water against our hull.

Looking back on that norther after many years of sailing, I think that I was far too cautious, for we ran with very little sail or no sail at all, when I might have made up for the delays already encountered. On the other hand we had a pretty strong wind, and having lost one backstay I was frightened that I might lose the other, so was content to sail slowly southwards. On the fourth day the wind had eased considerably and we were able to lay a course for Punta Reyes. Morning came and no Punta Reyes, visibility being poor. Fortunately, the sun appeared and we were able to get a fix and found that we were a little further out than we had thought and just south of the Farallones. We laid a course for the Golden Gates and picked up Montara light soon after dark. Since I didn't want to enter in the dark, we hove-to for the night.

Morning found us deep in fog. We went towards the lighthouse until the swells began to hump in shallow water, then laid a course for the bridge. The fog soon cleared and we motored under the bridge and down to St. Francis Yacht Club. There were all kinds of people on the breakwater to shout "Mind the shoal!"; but it was clearly visible, and once it was avoided we were directed to the visitors' float. There was someone to take our lines, to tell us to make use of the club, and to offer us that breathtaking hospitality which makes one feel at home almost before one has arrived.

Vivie and Raith took rooms ashore and we felt almost sorry that they would not be mixed up in the higgledy-piggledy jumble on the yacht for the next few days. If they wanted to get rid of us they were out of luck, as we made great use of their flat.

CHAPTER TWELVE

San Francisco to Hawaii

St. Francis Yacht Club was quiet and sheltered; the only traffic on the road between the yacht basin and the club consisted of the cars of members or sightseers, who drove slowly down the road, watching the yachts sailing in the harbour or looking at those moored in the basin. There was no danger for dogs or cats, and both Poopa and Pwe found sufficient scope in this quiet area to satisfy their desire for exploration.

When we went to the town we left them both on board and they both invariably sat in the bow to watch us go. Poopa assumed a ridiculous look of disappointment and obedience, while Pwe, who had no hypocrisy in her make-up, watched us go with ears pricked and solemn blue eyes, betraying no emotion. We knew perfectly well that the moment we were out of sight Poopa would jump on to the float and go exploring round the club-house, while Pwe would stretch and go below to await our return. Pwe's time for exploration was at night and she always seemed to be particularly interested in other people's yachts. If caught out by daylight and the movement of people, she had an alarming habit of not returning until night, and as she had probably stowed away for the day on another ship, we were always worried that they might sail away with her. This danger was not so great in yacht harbours, but in commercial harbours she could not resist a fishing boat and it was a wonder that we never lost her.

Poopa was usually irresistible to anyone who met him on his promenades. Cooks fed him, children gave him sweets, and old ladies found it quite impossible to pass him by. Although a small dog, he had an alert and masculine air, and was always very busy on his own affairs. One day Beryl and I were talking to a well-dressed elderly man who had a poodle on a leash; he asked us whether we came from the Canadian yacht and while we were talking Poopa arrived and sniffed at the poodle. The elderly man aimed a vicious kick at Poopa, which he avoided with ease as if admiration was not all that he encountered during his explorations.

"Go on," I said. "You can kick him if you wish. He is our dog."

"I'm so sorry," said the man. "I just don't know what he's done to Cholmondeley. He's disrupted Cholmondeley's whole day."

Cholmondeley did look upset and he also looked as if he needed a little disruption.

While we were in St. Francis Yacht Club, John Guzzwell arrived in *Trekka* at the beginning of his circumnavigation of the world. He told us that just before we left, he had been in McQuade's, the chandlers in Victoria when we were getting some ship's gear and, although we were both sailing to San Francisco, he had been reluctant to introduce himself. He was young, athletic, powerful, and very reserved. He gave us an impression of great reliability; all the strength of his character seemed to flow through his hands which were so skilled and sure in carpentry.

Trekka was lying only a short way from where we were moored. A little jewel, beautifully built and tended, looking frail in comparison to *Tzu Hang*, but feeling remarkably robust when one stepped on board. She was painted blue and carvel built, her planking glued edge-to-edge and so wonderfully finished that John was often asked what she was made of. *Trekka* was eventually sold, made another circumnavigation, and is probably still going strong. We have lost touch with her, but fortunately not with John, who is still sailing and building yachts.

A week before we were ready to go, John set off for Hawaii from Sausalito, to which we had both moved. Sausalito always seems to be in the sun when St. Francis is in the shade, although they are only separated by little more than the width of the Golden Gate Bridge. There was just the suggestion of a breeze, but it was sufficient for *Trekka* to sail. One or two reporters were down to see him off, one of them a woman; as *Trekka* disappeared round the end of the floats, she turned to me and said, pointing to a square houseboat decorated with window boxes and geraniums, "There is another adventurer."

"What does he do?" I asked.

"He's living there, trying to find himself," she replied.

Our biggest adventure in Sausalito was Captain Wagner. He hit us like a cyclone. We were coming back one day, our arms full of parcels, when we were stopped by a dumpy, close-cropped man who was tying up a nice-looking yacht at the float.

"Are you the folks from the Canadian yacht?" he asked. "I've been meaning to make your acquaintance."

"That's right," we replied, while he beamed at us, short-sighted and friendly. He looked at our parcels.

"You haven't been to those ships chandlers?" he asked. "They're ruin, you know. How much did you pay for that rope?"

We told him.

"I knew it! I knew it!" he cried. "They have no principles. Now, if I'd known it, I could have got it for you twenty cents a pound cheaper. I was a captain in the Navy, you know. Yes, sir. I was a captain, and I've got all kinds of influence. Everyone knows me round here, Captain Wagner is the name. Now, as soon as I'm fixed up here, I'm coming right over to you and we are going to make a list of the stores that you want. I'll get them for you and I'll bring them here in my car."

In a short time he was sitting below with Beryl, his agile mind darting from one item to another, suggesting things that we had forgotten and improving on the suggestions that we made. Beryl is always entranced with a bargain and Captain Wagner was a catalogue of bargains. Thereafter, he appeared every evening, and every evening, in addition to a car-load of stores, he brought a bag of doughnuts for Clio. It seemed that one of Captain Wagner's numerous interests had to do with doughnuts, and that doughnuts do not keep. Every evening he collected the surplus doughnuts from a bakery and distributed them to the Sea Scouts, the Younger Daughters of the Revolution, or some such hungry organisation, among which he now included *Tzu Hang* and her crew.

Two days before we left for Hawaii, we saw a familiar beamy yacht anchored off the yacht harbour. It was Tony and Bridget Reeves in their *White Hart*. They were both English and had been fishing for several years on the British Columbian coast, and had done very well at it; now they were off to cruise the Pacific islands for a year. They had often put in to see us while we were

149

at Musgrave's Landing, the two yachts lying at anchor together below the house; they had some of our bottled fruit on board and we had some of their canned fish. Tony had been one of the last fighter pilots flying in Malta during the bad days before relief came and had later flown Typhoons in Normandy. He was a sturdy and extremely self-reliant character, and would never come and have a bath at the house because he felt it a betrayal of boat and bucket with the life that he had chosen.

Bridget, his artistic and courageous wife, had no such misgivings. She and her small son loved to wallow in hot water on the rare occasions during the fishing season that they came ashore. They had built their ship in the Cayman Island with all kinds of adventures, and sailed it up to Vancouver at about the same time that we had sailed from the Galapagos Islands. Having a powerful motor and a large reserve of fuel, they had kept closer inshore.

"Come and tie up to us," Tony said, "and we will give you dinner before you leave." We agreed to move out the following morning and tie to them. It would be that break from the shore without actually starting off, that Beryl and I think so valuable.

That evening, Captain Wagner arrived with a final instalment of stores. Beryl had been looking for a stop-watch to time the development of her Polaroid camera films, the process being not so sophisticated as it is now. She had not been able to find anything cheaper than five dollars, so she had handed over the task of finding a cheap one to Captain Wagner. He, being unable to resist a bargain, had bought her a twenty-five dollar watch for fifteen dollars. Beryl, when she heard the price, gave an involuntary gasp, which was all the reward that Captain Wagner required. Clio and I knew that it was a gasp of dismay.

There were no doughnuts. I do not think that any children were shy with Captain Wagner—certainly not Clio. "Captain Wagner," she said, "you've forgotten the doughnuts."

"Sure, I've forgotten them," he replied, "but don't you think that you might take a look in the car? There just might be a bag there."

He followed her up and presently we heard them giggling on the deck. There were five large boxes of doughnuts, five hundred doughnuts in all.

Next morning, we tied up to the *White Hart* and divided the doughnuts. We were rolling in a slight swell and kept snubbing at our lines until one broke. One of the characteristics of the British Columbia coast is a pair of fishing boats tied together, one at anchor, to which the other is made fast. To prevent their boats snubbing, they make fast each to a motor tyre between them which acts as an efficient shock absorber, while a motor tyre may also be fixed to a bight in an anchor chain for the same purpose. Now Tony introduced us to this practice and we lay quite comfortably beside him.

Vivie and Raith came on board again. We finished our stowing and spent our time on one boat or the other, the gentle movement preparing Vivie again for the sea. Next morning, October 15, the Reeves and ourselves set off in different directions. We expected to be returning from Australia and New Zealand in the following year and Tony told us that he also would be returning and might be in Fiji. "See you in Fiji," we called as the boats drifted apart, although I did not think that any of us expected to meet before we got back to Canada. Then Tony and Bridget, the professionals, efficient and salty, with *White Hart* so powerful and beamy, moved off up harbour; *Tzu Hang*, looking quite slender and yachty in comparison, carried her crew of amateurs towards the Golden Gate Bridge and the open sea.

There was a light breeze blowing from dead ahead as we motored under the bridge. We kept under power until we were clear of the channel, passing six destroyers in line ahead on their way in. We dipped our ensign to each in turn and two of them replied. Once clear of the channel we set all sail and *Tzu Hang* sailed herself quietly to the south-west. It was another grey day, grey sea and grey sky; in a very short time we were out of sight of land, and might have been hundreds of miles from anywhere, except that a small grey land bird came fluttering in hopelessly inefficient flight over the sea. It perched on the log line and spun round and round until we brought it in and loosened its feet from the line. After a rest it set off again, but fell three times into the sea. Each time it got up again, and the last time it struggled once more after *Tzu Hang* but could not catch us. We hove-to and it settled on the deck, sheltered behind the rail. It was exhausted and during the night it died.

Half-way between San Francisco and Hawaii there is a high pressure area, which moves higher up in summer and lower down in winter. The winds revolve round it in a clockwise direction and, if no other weather system is jostling it, a northerly wind should take a sailing ship from south San Francisco, until she finds the north-east trade winds to carry her across to Hawaii.

In winter when the high pressure system is further south a succession of lows moving across the north Pacific, and the winds in San Francisco may hold more in the south; but it was October so we hoped to find a north wind to take us down. If we headed straight for Hawaii, our course would take us through the centre of the high pressure area and we would expect calms. The best rule for a passage to Hawaii is to get into the trade winds as quickly as possible; the question for which every navigator, either on his way to or from Hawaii, needs the answer, is the position of the centre of the "Pacific High".

On our journey down to San Francisco, we had all that we wanted of strong winds and rough weather. Now we were going to have too much calm weather with baffling light airs from the south. For eleven days we fuddled slowly to the south, with never a fresh or favourable wind and only one sunny day. On that day, we saw two Tropic Birds sitting in the water. These birds, also known as the Bosun Bird and Crater Bird, have long red or white central tail feathers, which they keep cocked up when on the water. They can be met with anywhere at sea in the tropics, and call you up on deck with a high-pitched, tern-like cry; you will see them, brilliant in their white plumage, delicate as a Japanese drawing against the sky, close above the mast-head and demanding attention.

On the same day we heard two fishermen miles away off the California coast talking on their radios. The radio hams are the worst wafflers on the air, but fishermen, and more so their wives, run them a close second. "Ain't having no luck today," said one. "Der's no fish around. Ain't seen one de whole day. Tink I go home now, George, monkey around wid de garage and play wid de baby."

On November 26 we found the trades. In the morning we were wandering slowly to the south, with a light and variable head-wind and, as usual, a grey and overcast sky. We were becalmed at mid-day and took down all sail; we might have bathed, but the see looked dull and unattractive under the grey sky. In the afternoon, the sky began to break up into low cumulus and the sun to shine patchily, but at sea level everything was still, breathless and waiting. For us, ignorant people of the land, it was just another dull day, but the things of the sea knew that a change was here. First there came a whisper, a breath, a feeling of expectancy; then a distant murmur, gradually taken up and growing in the sea and sky around us. Softly at first, but steadily growing, came the wind from the north-east, and all the surface of the water around us took form and purpose, while the little waves chattered merrily as they ran past.

Whenever the trade wind comes, it seems to make a studied and dramatic entrance. It comes like a jolly aunt to lost and hungry children, with rustling skirts and good humour, to take them home to tea. It always brings joy and relief with a promise of sunshine and good passages. In *Tzu Hang* all spirits rose immediately and we were soon bowling along under the twins, with the sheets led to the tiller so that she sailed herself, as she had done across the Atlantic a few years before. That night, during my watch, *Tzu Hang* rolled along with her characteristic trade wind motion, her lights shining green and red on the two headsails and on the mizzen boom gallows the stern light—an ordinary hurricane lamp—lighting the cockpit. On each side the wavetops glowed with green phosphorescence and the wake glowed for a long way behind. The mast wove its long slow pattern across the stars, and a shadow arrived with a soft plump on the bridge deck. It was Pwe on her routine patrol. She disappeared towards the bow, reappeared on the other side, said a few words to me and then disappeared below.

Next day, the trade wind was still blowing. Fair and fresh it came, rolling the little broken cumulus clouds across the sky, here and there tossing up a white flash of spray on top of the regular lines of the sea. On deck, Beryl was rubbing tallow on the staysail sheets where they passed through the blocks on the ship's quarter. They were subjected to continuous work here over a short length, and the tallow on the hemp sheets prevented wear; later we used it with the same result on terylene sheets.

Raith, sitting in the cockpit wearing a blue checked shirt and a red handkerchief round his neck, lit two cigarettes and handed one down to Vivie below. They were getting short of cigarettes and now if one smoked, the other had to smoke too. I was trying to persuade Raith to tell me about putting a glider down at Arnhem.

"Do you make a figure of eight and come in slowly?"

"Good Heavens, no! You come down as hard and as fast as you possibly can to get out of the Ack Ack."

I looked at him, smiling, bronzed and relaxed, then tried to picture him, his face lit by flares and flashes, straining to select a landing in the murk below, diving steeply with no engine to pull him out of trouble, and so many lives in his hands. The peak moment in a lifetime, perhaps never to be equalled again.

Below, on one side of the cabin table, Vivie was sitting reading, her red hair in careless curls about her head, waiting to hear Clio's lesson; on the other seat was Clio, in shirt and shorts, lying on her back fondling Poopa with her bare toes.

"Vivie," she said, "Poopa is going grey."

"Clio, for God's sake. Get on with it."

Beryl went below and started to gather some things together for lunch on deck. Orange juice, bread and cheese, olives, salami, chocolate biscuits and, of course, doughnuts. They had kept for two weeks and we still found them good.

"Lunch is ready," Beryl called, so Vivie, Clio and Poopa hurried up on deck. Young faces, sunshine and bright sea.

In the evening we played some games in the cabin while *Tzu Hang* sailed along by herself. One of the most popular was called Clue, a murder game played on a board. We also played a game in the form of a story, each player writing a paragraph and then folding the paper so that only the last word showed, then passing it on. The tone of this game usually became low. Best of all, we enjoyed a form of Dumbcrambo, when one player would act to his side, without speaking, the name of a book, or a play, or a proverb given to him by the other side, with a time limit in which his own side might guess what he was portraying. In the cramped and heaving little cabin so far out in the Pacific, we had a great deal of laughter and more fun than ever I had in troopship, tramp or liner.

Our biggest problem when planning this trip had been the question of Clio's education. During our first voyage from England to Canada she had been away from school for a year. On the ship, in fair weather and foul, she had sat with her nose pressed to the Canadian school correspondence course. Her mind wandered as freely as any child's mind can wander from the task in hand, but for five or six hours a day, every day at sea, it was intermittently and irresolutely applied to her lessons. At the end of the passage we decided that we could not again expose her to correspondence courses supervised by her parents. It was bad for parent–child relationship. At the end of Clio's first term after our arrival in Canada, she was higher in her class than she had ever been before. It looked as if the interlude had done no harm, so we began to plan another trip with, hopefully, someone else to supervise. This is what Vivie was doing now.

The correspondence course is for children way out in the sticks who, because of lack of companionship, establish a companionship with their teacher by correspondence; they look eagerly for the return of their corrected papers, become enthusiastic and try to do well. Yet the last thing that Clio wanted to do was to establish a companionship with the teacher who corrected her papers in Canada, and by the time that they returned she had quite grown out of them. The papers have to cater for a variety of children of different races and origins, and some of the subjects, to a much-travelled and widely-read girl of fourteen, seemed elementary and repetitive. I suppose the real difficulty was that we were too far away. She seemed to be learning as much as she learnt at school and we hoped that in other ways she would be learning far more. The Vivie era was good; but alas, all too soon it came to an end.

One day we were rolling along on our way. The trades, never very boisterous on this passage, were blowing force 3 to 4, with a regular swell. We were all on deck. Suddenly Vivie, who had been watching Pwe stepping along the rail outside the shrouds, gasped, "My God, the cat's gone!"

We looked, appalled, and saw for a moment her dark little head, as she swam in our wake, until it disappeared behind a following swell. Before it reappeared I heard Beryl say in a matter-of-fact way, "I had better go, too," and she immediately dived over the side.

Man overboard in calm weather, or trade wind weather, is not so very far removed from man overboard in a rough sea. Even in trade wind weather during the Trans-Pacific race to Honolulu, a man had recently been lost overboard and had been twenty-four hours in the sea until he had been picked up by his own boat just as the search had been called off. Every helmsman must always know what action he will take if a man goes overboard, and the possibility should always be somewhere in the skipper's mind. No doubt it had been in mine—a subconscious fear—and I reacted quickly, unnecessarily alarmed, for Beryl was a good swimmer. We were unlikely to lose sight of them, but the distance widened surprisingly quickly between them and the stern of the ship.

I shouted to Vivie and Clio to let the headsails down, chucked a life-belt over, remembering not to hit Beryl on the head with it, but finding her already too far away to get near. At the same time I put the helm hard up and called to Raith to start the motor. *Tzu Hang* swung ponderously into the wind. Beryl had got the cat quickly and was now trying to collect the life-buoy, not because she was in need of it, but because she didn't want to lose it. She put the cat on the life-belt, but Pwe, seeing *Tzu Hang* swinging away, jumped off and swam like an otter after her.

There was a roar from the engine which then died and stopped. "Turn on the bloody gas, for Christ's sake!" I shouted. But actually the fault was mine, as I had throttled down too soon and too much. Meanwhile Beryl, deserting the life-belt, had caught Pwe and was half-pushing her, half-carrying her towards the boat. The engine had started again and we were under control, except that Vivie was fumbling with the ladder as she tried to hook it over the rail.

"Can't you bloody well fix that ladder?" I called to her.

Vivie gave me a sultry look.

With everyone on board again, I felt angry and ashamed at my own alarm. Yes, "man overboard" when a ship is under way is almost always an emergency of sorts; to realise the full horror one should read the account of a man lost overboard at night, the desperate search and the failing cries, so dramatically told by Peter Hayward in his *All Season's Yachtsman*. The most important thing to do, at almost any risk to the gear, is to stop the ship, then to keep her stopped until the lost shipmate is spotted or heard, and can be kept in sight and hearing while the ship is manœuvred. To search without knowing his exact position is often to draw away from a swimmer quite capable of reaching the ship without help. At night to search rather than stay stopped can be the best way to ensure his end; yet to lie stopped, drifting away, waiting for a shout, may be deserting him. A skipper must stop and listen until convinced that there is no one near, and only as a last resort retrace the ship's course as slowly and silently as possible.

There are ways of ensuring that crewmen do not go overboard, such as using safety lines; there are aids to their discovery— lights and whistles in their lifejackets—if they do. But who wants to use safety lines and wear lifejackets on a starlit tropic night? In times of danger one is prepared for danger, but it is in times of relaxation and peace that danger so often strikes.

When becalmed, as happened frequently, then we went over the side for a bathe. Swimming with goggles, one could see to a tremendous depth, could almost feel giddy with the height. Sometimes a little shoal of fish lurked suspended in space twenty fathoms below the ship, but usually there was nothing to be seen except one or two small striped pilot fish that stayed close to our stern. One day, a great number of bottle-nosed porpoises came to visit us, sending Poopa into paroxysms of excitement and frightening Pwe, who for the first time realised that there were monsters in the sea. She would not go beyond the cockpit coaming and sat as thin as a fence stake, craning over its edge with her ears flattened nervously. They made a much bigger impression than her ducking had done, and from then on she treated the sea with greater respect.

Poopa was always delighted if porpoises came to play. He stood in the very bows of the ship, barking excitedly, and the moment that they left the bow, rushed from one side of the deck to the other, wherever they appeared. Most of all, he appreciated a visit from a whale and when down below he could hear them from some distance. Then he would jump off the bunk, his feet skidding on the deck, and rush to the ladder barking and whining until someone put him up, as he was unable to negotiate it without assistance. Even in his worst paroxysms of excitement, he took very good care not to go overboard.

On the twenty-fourth day from San Francisco, after a slow but very pleasant voyage, we hoped that we might see Mauna Loa outlined against the setting sun. The sun set as a red ball almost down to the sea, but there was no sign of land. Perhaps it had set in the saddle between Mauna Loa and Mauna Kea.

"Will you wake me? Please wake me long before daylight,"

said Clio as she turned in. I woke her just before five. She came sleepily on deck and sat with me in the cockpit in her duffle coat.

"I don't see anything. It's just the same as any time. Isn't Poopa lazy?" said Clio.

"Get him up then."

"No. Poor Poopa."

Pwe arrived on deck and disappeared forward. When she returned to the cockpit, Clio took her inside her duffle coat. The sails began to show, the sky behind us to lighten and the stars to fade. A faint finger of light moved across the sky.

"A flash! A flash! I saw a flash! There, over there!" cried Clio, pointing towards the port bow.

It came again, a pencil of light passing briefly, elusively across the sky. We counted the seconds before it flashed again and found it was Cape Kumukahi light. The darkness faded and slowly the daylight came. The flashing light for a few moments showed its source, then paled and disappeared before we could see the land on which it stood. Then, high in front of us, the outline of a mountain began to appear, much higher and fainter than we had expected. Gradually the outline grew firmer and took on colour, a warm rose from the unseen sun, until there shone before us the Twin peaks of Owhyhee, as Captain Cook called them. Not covered in snow, as they were when he arrived on his last voyage, like us coming down from Canada; but still it was one of the most beautiful landfalls of the world.

CHAPTER THIRTEEN

Hawaii

We kept well to windward of our harbour until we could recognise the low promontory east of Hilo Bay; then we turned and with a fresh wind on the beam came spinning down for Leleiwi Point. No sailing is as good as sailing with land in view after a long passage. *Tzu Hang* seemed to feel the same excitement as her crew and raced gladly along while we sat on deck trying to pick out the various landmarks. Below the brown slopes of Mauna Loa, now disappearing into cloud, was a forest area falling steeply to low slopes of sugar cane close to the sea. It was scarred in places by black and grey lava spills. The cane fields below shone green in the sunlight; the land under cultivation and ready for planting was a warm fertile red; here and there were sugar factories marked by their tall chimneys; the blue of the sea turned to the palest green by the shore.

There was time to have lunch on deck as we approached the breakwater, which was about one and a half miles long, and every hundred yards or so was marked by a fisherman with his pole; we found out later that they were almost invariably either Chinese or Japanese. Poopa sat in the bow wrinkling his nose to the land smells and, knowing nothing about quarantine regulations, was obviously anticipating a run ashore. The cat was uninterested and lay in the sun. We passed the head of the breakwater and started to beat up towards the small harbour at the head of the bay. The wind proved too strong for the old cotton main, which split from luff to leach into a flapping fury. Having hastily stowed this sail while continuing to tack under mizzen and headsails, we tried the engine and found that it was overheating. It seemed that we were being subjected to "the slings and arrows of outrageous fortune" or, in other words, were at panic stations; so we

159

selected an anchorage in the lee of Coconut Island, left the channel and anchored there. Later, several people told us how beautiful the ship had looked coming in under sail; "Serene" was the word one of them used. They should have been on board.

No sooner were we unhappily anchored, overlooked by the hotel on Coconut Island, than we saw *Trekka* coming out of the small inner harbour. It was to be the first of many meetings in different harbours and anchorages. John looked brown and fit with *Trekka* as smart as when she had sailed from San Francisco. He had had a better start than we, but otherwise his weather had been much the same as ours and he had taken only four days longer although half our size. He had a friend with him, the purser of the *Hawaiian Pilot*. *Trekka* sailed up to us, and they let her ride behind like a dinghy, while they came on board. Vivie and Raith had divided their last cigarette a few days before; now they anxiously watched the purser take a packet out of his pocket, light a cigarette and return the packet to his pocket again. "Please," said Vivie, in a little wheedling voice that Clio had certainly never heard before. "Could you please spare us a cigarette? Half a cigarette would do."

I went into the harbour on *Trekka* to clear customs and quarantine and to sign a guarantee that the animals would not be allowed ashore under a $200 bond. From then on, we were dogged by the secret service of the quarantine authorities who were apt to turn up at any moment to find out whether the animals were still on board. We went back, intending to tow *Tzu Hang* into the inner harbour, as soon as the breeze was down, but found Raith smiling and the engine running; he was even better pleased when he found that the purser had fallen for Vivie and sent her a present of a carton of cigarettes.

We tied up in the small inner harbour with stern anchor and two bow lines to the quay. By pulling on one of the bow lines we could step off the bowsprit to the quay, but this was beyond the capacity of the cat and dog so they remained disgruntled but safe on board. We were alongside the Coastguard vessel, whose crew had a small canteen with changing rooms and showers ashore; they hospitably gave us the use of the showers and a washing-machine during our stay. A quarter of a mile from the yacht there was a small store at a cross-roads where we bought milk, eggs, fruit and bread. If we had to do more serious shopping we went to town, crossing a creek where all kinds of gaily-painted fishing sampans were moored. This was quite a journey, but it was almost impossible, even without an overt signal, to go far without being given a lift.

John had been offered a lift by a Hawaiian who had read about him and where he had come from in the paper. "So your father was English and your mother is South African," he asked. After a silence and one or two sideways glances at his big, fair-haired companion, he continued, "Well, you've certainly taken after your father then."

The Hawaiian Islands consist of eight large islands and numerous small ones running from south-east to north-west over a distance of about 350 miles. They lie roughly in this order: Hawaii, Maui, then, south of Maui, Kahoolawe and Lanai; then Molokai, Oahu, Kawaii and Niihau. Kahoolawe is a military and naval preserve, while Niihau is private property. The north-eastern sides of the islands are apt to be windy with frequent rain squalls, particularly in the afternoon, but the south-western sides are sunny and dry. Owing to the north-east trades, the best way to cruise the islands is to start with Hawaii and end with Kawaii so that the winds may be more favourable. The channels between the islands are usually blustery but seldom dangerous. The only threat to the southern sides is caused by the Kona wind in winter, it is a south wind which can blow strongly. The only harbours on the southern side that give protection to these gales are Lahaina, Honolulu, Pearl Harbor and Nawiliwili. There is usually plenty of warning and time to get round to the sheltered side if a southerly gale is developing, but often these depressions bring only light wind, overcast and rain. Apart from these rare winter storms the southern coasts offer splendid cruising in sunshine and sheltered waters, with occasional fast and wet dashes across the channels; there are many attractive and often unfrequented anchorages.

We did not plan to stay long in Hilo, but a strong Kona wind blew for two or three days after we had arrived. We were glad to be safe and sound in the harbour; the wind howled over our heads, while twigs and leaves blew off the eucalyptus trees which grew behind the Coastguard's quarters. Not a swell stirred in the little harbour and behind the quay we hardly felt the wind; but if we had arrived a day or two later we would have been hove-to outside. The Kona blew itself out and we were told not to worry about another gale for a month or so. Directly the "weather man" told of a return to trade wind conditions, we began to think of leaving.

Before we left, Beryl was determined to walk to the end of the breakwater; it consists of enormous boulders piled one on top of the other. Every step was a sizeable jump so a walk in no way describes the feat of physical endurance required to reach the end. Beryl did not yet know John well enough to cast her toils about him and force him to accompany us on these expeditions, but although Vivie and Raith started she was unable to overcome their combined resistance after the first hundred yards. They sat on a stone in the sun to watch a fisherman. By half-way Clio had become interested in photography and in the crabs that came up through the crevices of the reef on which the breakwater was built; but once Beryl has embarked on any such project, it has to be pursued to the end, so that we finally arrived at the last stone and the ultimate fisherman, an emaciated Chinese.

We left Hilo in the afternoon, having arranged with John to sail south about round Hawaii and to meet in Kealekekua Bay, where H.M.S. *Resolution* and *Discovery* were anchored when Captain Cook was killed. When we got outside, there was a very light wind with a swell that emptied and filled *Tzu Hang*'s heavy sails; John quickly overtook us and then, to our chagrin, pointed higher and left us behind. We held on to the north on the starboard tack until we could clear Leleiwili point and then went on the port tack; at first it looked as if we would never be able to clear Cape Kumukahi, the most easterly point of Hawaii, but the wind was freshening steadily and *Tzu Hang* started to point higher and to sail better. When night came, the light was dead ahead and by this time we began to think that we must have passed John. A dark night it was, too, with just the steady flash, flash, flash of the lighthouse to relieve it. It was Raith's watch, but I stayed with him in the cockpit and later he with me, while we tried to steal a little more to windward round the Cape. *Tzu Hang* had her rail down and her lee deck awash, but for a long time the light stayed right on the bow.

One hundred and seventy-eight years before, and at about the same time of year, *Resolution* and *Discovery*, on their way back

from trying to discover the north-west passage, were also trying
to round Cape Kumukahi. At four in the afternoon, as we had
done, they had "made sail and stretched to the north". At midnight *Resolution* tacked, but *Discovery* did not see this and continued to the north. At six in the evening of the next day, Captain
Cook wrote in his journal, "the southermost extreme of the Island
bore south-west, the nearest shore seven or eight miles distant,
so that we had now succeeded in getting to windward of the
Island, which we had aimed at with so much perseverance".

We were doing better, but there was not going to be much to
spare in rounding the point. The flashing light came closer and
began to climb higher, until it started to draw round towards
our beam. It was difficult to tell just how far off we were. A large
fishing boat rounded the point in the opposite direction, but giving
it more room than we were doing. We strained our eyes in the
darkness, trying to recognise some form of rock or cliff below
the light or to get a sight of breakers; we were unwilling to tack
yet feared to hold on. There was a rumble and spatter close to
starboard so that for a moment we held our breaths. It was nothing.
Only a wave breaking, still in deep water. The sea was dark and
silent again except for the rush and flurry of *Tzu Hang*'s movement. The light drew abeam, hanging over us, and then drew
on to our quarter. Now we could ease the sheets and run south
with the wind on the port quarter. Raith turned in and Beryl
came up for her watch. I sat with her for a time while the light
dropped away astern and we opened up the distance between
Tzu Hang and the coast.

Early next morning we gybed and headed for the southernmost
point of the island, Cape KaLae, the fabled point of departure
of the Hawaiians on their journeys to the south. We had breakfast
on the way; nothing is as good as Beryl's porridge at sea, cooked
in milk and swimming in condensed milk and brown sugar,
doubly good after a night of watch-keeping, and trebly good
when you realise that you have not felt in the least seasick on a
first night at sea. It was followed as always with fried eggs,
toast and home-made marmalade. On top of all this we were
running with a splendid fair wind down a new and beautiful
coast with every prospect of being in an anchorage that night.
This is the way to be completely happy. There was no sign of
Trekka and in fact I knew that she could not possibly have kept

up with us during the night. There were no lessons for Clio today. We sat on deck watching the land to starboard.

From Mauna Loa and from the Kilauea crater south of it, the black streaks of the lava flows scarred the green hillsides. In places the lava flow had poured over the cliffs and into the sea. One explosion had split a whole hill-side. Red cones, black cones and grey cones were scattered about the southern slope of the island. A great pot had been simmering there under the thin skin of the green earth, which had suddenly boiled over and burst apart, shouldering the green into valleys and islands between rivers of lava and deserts of ash. It was still simmering, and from time to time overflowed again.

The land was largely uninhabited. Here and there we could see a few cottages and a white church showing the course of a road, here and there a fishing village on the shore marked by coco-nut trees and small grass huts; since the whole southern side of the island sloped down towards us we got a good idea of what was there. There was far less than when British sailors first found their way along the coast; Captain Cook wrote of this southern point of the island which *Tzu Hang* was now approaching, "On this there stands a pretty large village, the inhabitants of which thronged off to the ship with hogs and women." Only the lighthouse and it's buildings are there now.

Tzu Hang was flying as the wind freshened towards mid-day. Many hours in his glider behind a towing aircraft had helped to make Raith a good helmsman, but now he had his hands full as the boom was as wide as it would go, lifting against the preventer guy as *Tzu Hang* rolled violently in the steep following sea. We were cutting KaLae too fine, so took the main down and ran on under the mizzen with the staysail boomed out to starboard; this enabled us to give the point a little more room, while the coast slid past like the landscape in a train window.

Once round the cape we were out of the full blast of the trade wind and the water was as calm as a lake. There was still enough wind squeezing round the corner to send us along at a good pace to the next point, twelve miles away; but there the wind dropped dead. In the calm water we saw three triangular fins cruising together and for the time being dropped the idea of the bathe that we were contemplating. Ahead of us there were two brightly painted outrigger canoes. I started the motor and we went up to them; they were Hawaiian fishermen, friendly and smiling, with their canoes full of fish.

I asked them about the anchorage at Milolii, and was told that it was a good anchorage and that I would be able to see where to drop the anchor in sand.

"What about the bathing?"

"Good bathing, good bathing."

"What about the sharks?" I asked. "We have just seen three."

They all burst out laughing. "Very friendly sharks," explained one of them. "Much trouble for fishing and taking fish and breaking nets, but not dangerous." He was a tall, well-made man, his skin shining in the sun, a rag knotted round his head and a coloured cloth round his loins; his broad feet amongst the fish in the bottom of the canoe, he was standing as if unaware of any movement. He told us the names of the sharks, and that they lived in three different bays but that they met every day at ten o'clock and went for a stroll together until four. "They'd never hurt anyone," he said, and they all went off into peals of laughter again at the idea.

It made me think of the life insurance man that we had met in Hawaii who told us that he had nearly had a nervous breakdown trying to sell life insurance to the Hawaiians. "All they do is laugh," he said, "and what the hell they've got to laugh at I don't know."

Milolii was a narrow little habour backed on all sides by coral reef. There was a small wharf and some buoys to which one or two boats were moored close to the reef. The few houses of the village were hidden by ironwood trees and a grove of coco-nuts. Behind the village and on each side of it the lava flows had seared the land, leaving only a blackened stony waste with cactus and scrubby thorns where lizards and a few goats could find a living. I could see the coral clearly as we crept in and chose a small patch of sand in which to drop our anchor; it was plainly visible, with every link of chain leading down to it, and the little multi-coloured fish moving like hover flies about it.

We went over the side into the water in goggles and fins, paddling about and watching the busy life of the reef, exploring caverns and coral heads; we were quite enchanted with this new world, for this was the first time that we had seen it. It was quite an ordinary reef as reefs go, but all so new and wonderful. Presently the fishermen returned to their village in their outriggers, with small outboard engines sending them hissing through the water. One man sat at the engine and one stood in the bow with his arms folded, looking like the painted Hawaiian chief on the road signs. We bought some of their fish, which we had for dinner. They tasted like mackerel.

Next morning, still with no sign of John and *Trekka*, we hauled up the anchor and set off in a flat calm under the engine for Kealekekua Bay. Captain Cook in his journal wrote, "At daybreak on 16th, seeing the appearance of a bay, I sent Mr. Bligh" (later Captain Bligh of the *Bounty*), "with a boat from each ship to examine it . . . at eleven in the forenoon we anchored in the bay, which is called by the natives Karakakooa. The ships continued to be much crowded with natives, and were surrounded by a multitiude of canoes. I had nowhere in the course of my voyages seen such a multitude of people assembled in one place. For, besides those in canoes, all the shore was covered with spectators, and many hundreds were swimming round the ship like shoals of fish."

There was no wind and we continued under power right into the bay. On the starboard hand as we entered there was a long, low, scrub-covered point; the back of the bay was faced by steep cliffs from four to six hundred feet high; on the port hand as we entered was another long, low point with a white lighthouse built on a mass of black lava at the end. In the north corner of the bay a steep footpath winds down from the cliffs to scrubby thorn trees which border the sea, and which border the bronze plaque in shallow water where Captain Cook was killed.

In Captain Cook's time, below the cliffs in the northern angle of the bay, there was a large village, and near the Morai in the southern corner there was another large village, separated from the former by the sweep of the bay. Both these villages have gone, and when we were last there, there were only a few modern Hawaiian cottages hidden in the trees in the southern angle of the bay, at the village of Napoopoo.

To come in from the sea and to anchor as *Resolution* had anchored and almost in the same place gave us the most extraordinary feeling of living in history. The huts and the thronging, laughing Hawaiians have gone, but little else has changed. In front of us was the beach and the piece of ground near the Morai where the sail-makers were repairing sails and the carpenters the mast when the first shots rang out and the hubbub and confusion arose at the northern end of the bay. We could imagine the excited figures running along the top of the cliff to give the news of Captain Cook's death to the priests at the Morai and to the inhabitants of the village at the southern end of the bay. In front of us was the Morai itself where Mr. Bligh and the marines had defended themselves; perhaps that was the cave in the cliff where one of the Hawaiians had put up such a stout resistance when the marines and sailors drove off the men who, after Captain Cook's death, were harassing them at the water point. The water, too, is there, although it now runs through a pipe, and near the Morai there is an old monkey pod tree that must surely have witnessed these events.

Close to the Morai there is a memorial to William Watman, a seaman of the gunners' crew on *Resolution* who was buried in the Morai before the tragedy destroyed good relations. The Morai itself is an acre of black lava rock piled in two platforms and on it there was a paw paw tree from which we got fresh fruit every day of our stay.

In the northern corner of the bay there stands a white stone memorial to Captain Cook; on a small piece of land leased in perpetuity to England, it is surrounded by posts and chains like a pump on the village green. It is a desperately unimaginative memorial which, perhaps, one day may be changed; surely more appropriate would be a model of *Resolution*'s questing bow and bowsprit, pointing the way through so many uncharted seas; I am sure that Captain Cook, wherever his roving spirit may be, would like it better.

John appeared the day after we arrived and anchored beside us. On each halcyon day that we spent there, Raith rowed Vivie and Clio in to the beach where they did lessons at a table under a thatched roof which had been provided either for picnickers or for the sale of baubles when tourist boats came in. Later, not being an over-enthusiastic swimmer, Raith rowed in with the lunch, while Beryl led John and I to the beach with her tireless easy stroke which always leaves me puffing far behind.

John was an impetuous rower and once when borrowing our dinghy broke an oar where it had become worn by the oarlock;

from then on we had to paddle. One day we set off together to see Captain Cook's memorial and on the way back were passed by *Captain Cook*, the glass-bottomed tourist boat from Kailua. We were both well-tanned, wearing swimming trunks, and paddling our uncoloured fibreglass dinghy. As *Captain Cook* passed us, a stout tourist wearing horn-rimmed glasses, a brilliant Hawaiian shirt, and smoking a cigar leant over the rail and shouted aggressively down to us, "Hey, you there! What's that canoe made of?" The two natives—John and I—were dumb and sullen at being thus addressed by the dominant race.

While in Kealekekua Bay John explained how he baked cakes in the pressure cooker. Beryl immediately set about baking one herself, and in due course it was turned out for tea. We all were loud in our praise, except John, who was silent.

"What do you think of it, John?" Beryl asked, eager for admiration.

"Well, it's all right," said John, "but you can make them light and fluffy too."

From Kealekekua, John went on to Keauhou, a little port that was too cramped for us, while we went south a few miles to Honauhau, the City of Refuge, where in the old days anyone fleeing from justice or the anger of the king could find sanctuary. Its walls, made of lava blocks and boulders, and in most places fallen down, enclosed a large area of short grass and palm trees where goats and cattle were grazing. There was an old Morai there but the place had nothing like the historical atmosphere of Kealekekua Bay. The lack of it was compensated by a splendid reef, full of towers and caves, and a big overhanging cliff of coral which we did not like to swim beneath. There were innumerable brightly-coloured fish and the most attractive was a little solitary charmer of the most brilliant blue; but we saw nothing that looked edible, unless it was for Pwe.

Ashore in search of eggs we found an old lady living in a small house overlooking the harbour. She was the district nurse, and talked of her hens as if she was running a home for old people. They were not all that old, as we got some eggs. She also had a young bitch that had just come into season; she could not tolerate the idea of a union with one of the village dogs, but had noticed Poopa on board. "He's such a bright, well-bred looking little dog," she said. "Couldn't he be allowed ashore just this once?"

Clio was delighted at this praise and her heart bled for the little dog who had now been cooped up for six weeks on the yacht.

"Oh, Daddy, couldn't he?" she asked. "I'm sure that it would be so good for him."

"No, certainly not," I replied. "It might cost me two hundred dollars, if not a jail sentence, and anyway I've signed a bond to say that I will not let him ashore."

"But you didn't say that you would not allow a dog on board," said Beryl, who always has a solution, although it may not be within the letter of the law. "Why not bring her out to the boat? After dark, of course," she added.

That night, the shore party set off. Raith and I waited on deck with Poopa. After a time we could make them out on their way back to the yacht. There was a furtive air about the loaded dinghy; the oars were being dipped with extravagant care and the sound of whispering came across the bar. Poopa was the first to see the bitch in the boat and the stillness of the night was shattered by a volley of barks and growls which was answered by a shrill and hysterical yapping. We were "blown", or would have been, had there been anyone to see.

The furious cat was locked in the "head" and to Poopa's astounded delight the bitch was left on deck while we all hurried below. Later, when we took her ashore, Poopa did not even bother to look after her; thereafter he was more relaxed and happy on board, thinking, perhaps, that all things come to him who waits. Many years later Beryl and I were again in Honauhau. There were definitely signs of a Poopa strain in many of the village dogs.

From the City of Refuge we went on to Kailua, where we got some rudimentary spear guns. From then on it was almost impossible to get John and Clio out of the water once they had set off on a fishing expedition.

Kailua was not our sort of place, as there were several hotels and shops there that catered to tourists. We wanted less accessible harbours and the more deserted they were, the better we liked them; the beauty of travelling in your own boat is that you can find them.

We stayed in Kailua a few days and one afternoon were taken to see the petroglyphs. We did not understand what we were in for and, as the invitation included lunch, we were far too well-dressed for the long underground exploration that the search for petroglyphs involved. People who come from yachts have usually all kinds of clothes suitable for underground exploration and very few suitable for lunch; so it was most distressing to find ourselves crawling underground in a lava tube, dressed in our best lunching out clothes. A lava tube is a cave in petrified lava, made by a bubble of gas either escaping or being imprisoned in the lava. In this case, the tube was several hundred feet long, very hot and not high enough to permit walking or low enough to enforce crawling when best clothes were at stake. We did a Cossack shuffle in which Clio, being the youngest and most supple, suffered least.

The petroglyphs are rock-writings found in some places in Hawaii; nothing is known of this script except that it was written by a people who lived in Hawaii before the Polynesians came. In the writing, male and female figures are recognisable in various forms of juxtaposition, drawn as a child might draw, with rectangles, lines and circles for bodies, arms and legs. For the rest, it seemed to be mostly lines and angles. We took some photos using the flash on someone else's camera, which meant that our cameras were not always pointing in the right direction when the flash went off; I got a picture of a cigarette pack, of Raith's leg, and another of Beryl looking very disgruntled in her best shirt, with some blood on her forehead where she had struck the roof in one of her Cossack hops.

We decided that we should give a drink party on board before leaving Kailua, to which both invited and uninvited guests appeared. It was disastrous. The swell made several of them seasick and I had to take one white-faced lady and her husband home aboard the dinghy in a hurry. On account of the broken oar I had to kneel in the bow and paddle Indian fashion, while she sat on the centre thwart facing forward, supported by her husband in the stern. I heard him say to her, "Be sick in the boat, not overboard. You'll have us all over." The upturned bare soles of my feet were right in the line of fire. I managed to get my insteps on to the gunwale and in this intolerable position, which no Indian could have supported, I paddled furiously for the shore.

We were grateful to Kailua for one particular reason. I found there a carving in wood of a woman's face; it was a beautiful

Hawaiian face, sad but tranquil, one hand resting on her cheek and the other hand holding the wrist. The driftwood from which it is carved is not a Hawaiian wood and it branches above her face, giving the impression of a medieval hat. The top had had a small iron wedge driven in as if to split it, but the wedge is still there and all round it has been drilled by toredo worms during its voyage in the sea. I gave it to Beryl and we mounted it on our cabin bulkhead. It was carved by a Polish Hawaiian. Later, when we discovered that *Tzu Hang*'s name meant "the wooden ship under the special protection of Kwan Yin", Goddess of Mercy and Protector of Sailors, we felt that the face, full of compassion, was that of Kwan Yin. She was with us in all our subsequent adventures in *Tzu Hang* and is now fastened to a wooden post supporting a beam in the living-room of our home, close to two pictures of *Tzu Hang*, one under jury rig in the Southern Ocean, and one rounding Cape Horn. In both of these affairs she, in her tranquil way, took part.

CHAPTER FOURTEEN

Maui

John left Kailua the day before we did, missing both the cocktail party and the petroglyphs, neither of which he would have enjoyed. He did not enjoy small talk with people whom he did not know and with whom he had no particular common interest, then he would have seen no point in an uncomfortable underground journey to see the unintelligible writing of an unknown people. *Tzu Hang* left in the following afternoon with a light off-shore breeze that did not take us very far. We changed to the engine and continued until dark, watching the coastline slip quietly past with its alternating patches of lava, trees and sandy beaches. At nightfall we stopped and, as were all clear of danger, put up a riding light and turned in. The current which runs through the Aleinuihaha Channel met the current running up the coast, and there were some tide rips about us, whispering and chattering in their own peculiar language of the sea. The wind soon arrived, finding its way down the skylights and hatches, blowing on our faces and awaking us to reluctant action.

The Aleinuihaha Channel has a bad reputation, as the trade winds funnel between the high mountains on Maui and Hawaii to blow strongly. The wind was back and ready to let everyone know about its return. Beryl and I reefed the main, set the storm jib and took down the mizzen while Raith took the helm. *Tzu Hang* sailed easily and swiftly across the channel, the loom of the lights showing on the other side. She passed the island of Molokinni at daybreak and we made our way towards the small port of Maalea.

Maui consists of two mountain masses separated by a narrow flat neck about six miles across and four miles wide. The western end of the island, which is supposed to represent the head of the old Polynesian god, is topped by Mount Puukukui, just short of six thousand feet. In the centre of the eastern half, which represents the shoulders and upper half of Maui's body, is the crater of Haleakala, with the highest point on its rim over ten thousand feet. Maalea is on the southern side of the neck, and as *Tzu Hang* sailed up to it we could look across on the port hand to a wild jumble of broken green-clad peaks, the West Maui Mountains; on the starboard hand the great slopes of Haleakala rose up through scrub, ranch land, and eucalyptus plantations to the crater's rim. As *Tzu Hang* approached Maalea she passed a canoe-load of stout Hawaiians going out to fish on the reef; they overflowed its sides and the little craft, half-submerged by their weight, had all it could do to keep the important parts of its outboard motor out of the water. As they passed, they shouted with deep musical voices, "Aloha! Aloha!" with the accent on the last syllable, making the word sound like a war cry. Inside the harbour we moored with two bow ropes to a quay and a stern anchor out; thus the cat and dog were secure again, which was just as well, for the sleuths of the Quarantine Service came burning up the road in a jeep in the hopes of collecting two hundred dollars if they had found one ashore.

At Maalea we met Stew and Darrel Milligan; it was a lucky meeting, for they did all kinds of things for us while we were in Maui. They drove up to the quay and then walked over and asked if they could do anything to help. We pulled *Tzu Hang* in until Darrel could step on to the bowsprit. Women do not often succeed in boarding a ship over the bowsprit and still looking their best, but this one contrived it with an easy grace. She was followed by her husband who made a dive for the dinghy. "Fibreglass," he said. "Wonderful stuff. I have just put some on the boat I built. She's over there." We had already noticed the boat, which was marked not only by an undistinguished appearance, but also by various signs of amateur craftsmanship.

"You ought to meet John Guzzwell," I told him. "He is on his way to Lahaina." We had in fact just seen him heading that way beyond the harbour entrance. Stew was eager to meet another small boat builder; he was tremendously proud of his boat and we wondered rather anxiously whether John, who was straightforward to the point of bluntness and had no subterfuge, would be able to admire it. Stew was in charge of labour relations with the Puunene

Sugar Company, a born arranger, who tackled everything with a boyish enthusiasm. He said he'd arrange for us to make a trip up to the Haleakala crater the following week and would drive us up from Lahaina, where we were due to meet John.

Next morning we pulled *Tzu Hang* back on her stern anchor, hauled it on board, and sounded carefully out, although the darker blue of the dredged channel showed clearly. An old fisherman, hunched on a stone at the end of the mole, his hands listless on his rod, watched us go with disinterested eyes. Once past the outer buoy we made sail. The breeze came lightly from the sea and *Tzu Hang* slid steadily along a few cables off-shore. The deep water and the reef's edge were clearly defined. We could see the traffic on the road, the sugar cane behind, the red, rich, ploughed land running up to the West Maui mountains, which thrust their bush-covered edges into the sky in places so steep that it seemed impossible that any vegetation could cling to the cliff face.

I saw Vivie sitting on the doghouse slowly shaking her red head with a puzzled look in her eyes.

"What on earth are you thinking about?" I asked her.

"I was thinking about me in a yacht off Maui," she replied.

As we approached Hekili Point, where an old sugar mill hides its ruins in a dark mass of mango and banyan trees, and a rickety pier thrusts out into the sea, we could see what appeared to be a pass leading through the mountains. "Look at that," I heard Beryl say. "That would be fun."

I knew at once that she was contemplating an expedition through the mountains. During much of my life with Beryl, her ideas of fun have from time to time resolved themselves into what seemed to be a struggle with exhaustion, starvation and thirst, and then realisation that the fun was to be found in the mere matter of survival. It certainly adds spice to adventure. We both loved freedom of movement and hated to limit it by carrying large packs of provisions, tents and bedding; both of us preferred to walk forty miles with a ten-pound pack rather than ten miles with a forty-pound pack, but a ten-pound pack sometimes found us rather short of equipment if the expedition was prolonged or bad weather intervened. This predilection for fast movement and light loads has led to one or two uncomfortable nights, but if benighted on a mountain, we have had enough clothing and food to see us through the night. That is the main thing. The pleasure of unburdened climbing compensates for the minor discomforts of a little hunger or cold. It is a question of outlook. Some people take pleasure in the enormous loads that they carry and the efficiency of their bivouacs; others in the distance that they can travel and the speed that they can go. As I listened to the enthusiasm in Beryl's voice and looked at the jagged green peaks, like the quarters of a half-opened lime, I knew that sooner or later we were in for a rough passage.

At Lahaina, a crowded little port which is reached by passing down a buoyed channel, with breakers foaming on the reef on each side; then doing a right-angle turn through the side of the breakwater, we dropped our anchor across the channel by the breakwater wall and pulled back with our stern to the quay. Behind us was a huge banyan tree spreading its shade so widely that its branches were supported by posts; the similarly spreading and almost as ancient hotel that must have known high times when the whalers anchored off Lahaina in Kahoolawe Roads.

Stew Milligan arrived to say that he had arranged for a couple of pack horses to take our food and bedding down to the rest-house in the crater, and that he would drive us up to the lodge where we could pick up the horses next morning. John, in a kindly and unnecessary return for the meals that he had with us while we were together, said that he would scrape down *Tzu Hang*'s mast for us while we were away.

We picked up our horses next morning and set off up to the rim of the crater and then down a zigzag path to the crater floor where it crossed a many-coloured moonscape for several miles. The path wound through black dunes of ash and across cliffs of red shale until it came out on the other lip of the crater, then slanted down through scrub and grass to the rest-house where we spent the night. We were above the clouds or in them, so the slope disappeared into mist. It was cool and fresh after the heat below, and I felt as I had so often felt in India on reaching the hills after the heat of the plains, it was a feeling of energy, almost of weightlessness, as if one could float away.

We were back next day and found John with a long face. "Your mast has about had it," he told us. "There is a big patch of rot and the glue has gone at a scarfe. You might be able to patch it, but it looks to me as if you need a new mast."

175

Beryl and I were appalled, but Stew, who now had seen *Trekka* and realised John's superb skill as a carpenter, was unperturbed.

"What's the worry?" he asked. "If you want a new mast you've got the right man here to build one for you. Haven't they, John?" With his easy, out-going manner, as he put his arm round John's shoulders, I realised how he came to be a labour relations officer. John looked surprised. "What? Here in Maui?" he exclaimed.

"Sure. Why not? You could do it, couldn't you?"

"Well, there's nothing to building a hollow mast," said John, "but I've no tools, no glue, no clamps, no wood and no place to build."

To Stew this presented no difficulties. "I'll take you over to Puuene tomorrow," he said. "We've got everything that you need there in a big modern planer mill, wood and everything. We'll fix it all up."

John was silent, but I could see that at least we were half-way to getting a new mast.

Next day we all drove over to Puuene. Stew showed us round the mill, planers planed, saws whirred, routers routed; to Beryl and me it seemed a very modern and highly mechanised mill. John observed everything but said nothing; he was like a general on his annual inspection who leaves everyone on tenterhooks as to whether his report is going to be good or bad. Stew became more and more enthusiastic and persuasive, and we became more and more doubtful whether the mill had met with John's approval. His face brightened a little in the wood shed and at the end of a long and non-committal tour, John said that the mill would do and that he would make the mast for us. Stew had been so enthusiastic about his mill that I thought he might be upset at John's lack of it; but he recognised John's acceptance as high praise from a perfectionist, and winked at me. John has written about building the mast in his fascinating story, Trekka *Round the World*; we lost it later in the Southern Ocean, but that was in no way due to his workmanship which was, and always is, superb.

A few days later we sailed round to Kahului and anchored together a short way off the beach for the commencement of operation "New Mast". We had not been there long before a big man and two boys swam out and climbed on board; he was a doctor, Guy Haywood, right on the beach was his house, which he and his wife, Anita, made available to us for whatever we wanted; into it they took Raith and Vivie, during the rest of our stay.

From where we were anchored in the harbour we could see the narrow cleft of the Iao Valley, leading into the West Maui Mountains; our thoughts began to turn to week-ends and to the pass that we had seen from the other side. It was said that there was an old Hawaiian path, but that no one had attempted it for twenty years.

On the first week-end, Guy Haywood drove us all up the Iao Valley and we started off to reconnoitre a way through. The scrub on this side was dense and progress very slow. Like a file of pilgrims on some holy path, we repeatedly measured our length on the ground as our feet went through into pitfalls concealed by the dense vegetation. Eventually, much to Beryl's disgust, I decided on a withdrawal, determined that we should at least equip ourselves with cane knives before starting off again.

The valley itself looked as if it might once have been the crater of a volcano. It was enclosed by a ring of mountain peaks, which were connected by precipitous, water-grooved, knife-edged ridges. The whole ring of mountains shed their waters into the valley by numerous streams, which cut their way across its floor to join the main Iao stream under the southern wall. This stream then burst out of the gap through which we had entered.

Straight across from where we were and about four miles away, the lowest part of the valley wall could be seen; it was about four thousand feet high and deeply grooved by water. The narrow ridges between the grooves looked as if they would give access to the wall, which appeared to be the watershed between the north and south mountains, and was probably the same ridge that Beryl had seen through the pass from the other side. Even on the steepest faces there seemed to be some vegetation clinging, but there could be very little soil, and it looked as if we would need a rope.

With a reluctant and still protesting Beryl, we headed down one of the side streams until we could hear the roar of the Iao River below; then we slipped and scrambled diagonally down the slope. It was a wide, fast stream, full of rocks and boulders, with deep pools and runs. By skirting, wading, crossing and recrossing, but mostly by jumping from boulder to boulder, we were able to make much better progress than we had made on the plateau above. John and Clio were soon way ahead of Beryl and I, leaping lightly from rock to rock their shouts and laughter occasionally sounded above the noise of the stream.

We decided to try again, but from the other side, where there should be less vegetation; there we might use the stream bed to get out once we had crossed the divide. Meanwhile, Christmas and a Kona storm intervened.

The Kona storm blew for three days, while the wind whistled over the narrow neck of land between the mountains, and reached seventy miles an hour on the airport. The rain poured in torrents, flooding the gay little market square and filling the dinghies. *Tzu Hang* rode to two anchors, with over thirty fathoms of chain out in a depth of three fathoms.

On the first night of the gale, John had dinner with us as usual. The wind changed to the south in the afternoon, and had piped up all evening until it was blowing strongly. We played games after dinner, and later he left in our dinghy to return to *Trekka.*

"John's a cool customer," I said to Beryl. "If it had been me, I would have been up and down all evening, making sure that my boat was all right."

"When you were his age, you didn't worry either," she said.

I was still wondering just what she meant by this remark, when there was a mournful hail from outside: "*Tzu Hang,* ahoy!"

We hurried on deck; John had just tied the dinghy to a cleat and come on board.

"*Trekka*'s gone," he said. "Can you come with me, Miles?"

"Good Heavens, where? Yes."

"I think I caught sight of her near the breakwater."

It was as black as pitch, with stinging rain, and even here in the lee of the shore there were little white tops everywhere. He shone his flashlight again and away over by the breakwater there seemed to be just a flicker of a reflection which might come off her polished hull. We jumped in and I rowed as hard as I could, while he directed. The dinghy, helped by the wind and the sea, flew through the water. We had almost a mile to go, but soon he said, "That's her. I think she's still all right."

The waves began to build up as we got further out and the dinghy to surge and lift on their points. *Trekka* was fifty yards from the breakwater, and drifting on to it when we caught her. John jumped on board and gave me a line. I tried to keep her away by rowing, while he pulled up his anchor chain. After a few fathoms the anchor came up with the chain wrapped round the fluke. He cleared it and dropped it again, and then went below for the Seagull outboard engine. He pulled it out from where it had been stowed on its side, and clamped it on the stern. It started first pull, and was soon plugging away through the dark, towing me in the dinghy back to *Tzu Hang*. It had been a near thing for *Trekka*, as she would not have lasted long if she had got on to the breakwater wall. She had fouled her anchor when the wind changed.

The Kona wind was barely over when we had another near disaster. Again we had been playing games after dinner, with John on board. There was an awkward swell running in the bay. *Tzu Hang* was rolling at her anchors, and it was a dark and wet night. I had gone on deck to check that all was well, and as I walked forward I heard a faint and desperate squall from Pwe, in the water somewhere near the bow. She had fallen in and was now trying to scrabble up the smooth side. The piteous cry ended in an ominous bubble. I did not know how long she had been in but it sounded as if she was very near the end now. I dropped over the side and could just make her out against the side of the ship. When I grabbed her she was limp and very far gone.

I trod water, holding her up with one hand. I hate using the word, "help". Instead I shouted, "Hi, there!", but it sounded rather ineffectual. There was nothing to hold on to except the bobstay, so I swam amidships, still holding Pwe up in one hand, to the porthole of the head, into which I could hook my fingers. I shouted again, "Ahoy, there!", and could still hear laughter and talk from the saloon. There was no avoiding it; I bellowed for help. Again the laughter came faintly from the saloon. I gave one more shout, feeling that all Kahului must hear: "He-elp!", I bawled. This time there was a satisfactory silence, and then a clatter from the hatch. I shouted to Clio to get the steps down, and heard her calling delightedly, "Daddy's in! Daddy's in!"

She put the steps down and Beryl arrived to take Pwe.

We decided to make the next attempt at going through the

West Maui Mountains on the New Year holiday when the mill was closed and no work could be done on the mast. Stew had heard about the old Hawaiian trail and thought it started in the Olowalu Valley, the valley that we had seen on our way to Lahaina. He suggested that we should see the Head of the Water Conservation Board who kept a check of the rainfall and would know of any paths; however, he was not at all helpful, and said that it was quite impossible to get through. He told us that there was a path leading to a rain gauge while beyond that there was nothing but bush and mountain so that even the water board men would never think of attempting to go further. He suggested that we should go up Mount Puukukui and that we could get half-way up by car and spend the night in a Government rest-house. He did not actually say that we would get him into trouble if we tried to go through the mountains, but I suspect that he feared it. Stew saw at once that we were on the wrong trail.

"We'll have to give it a miss," he said, and the moment we were out of earshot, "All right now, when can I drive you over for the start?"

He dropped us on the evening before New Year's Eve at the end of the Olowalu Valley, and we hurried up one of the overflow beds of the stream and through a thicket of Kiave trees. The stars were already beginning to show when we stopped; Beryl spread out the food while the rest of us collected wood for a fire. The food consisted of a dozen eggs, a slab of chocolate, eight oranges, a loaf of bread, a small pot of peanut butter, some raisins, tea, sugar and milk. John, Clio and I looked at each other with anxiety.

"But you can't want more," said Beryl, "we are sure to be in tomorrow night," and later, when someone upset the billycan of eggs which were being scrambled, "Well, that simplifies breakfast."

The stars began to cloud over, the mosquitoes hummed savagely and the bushy mattress that we had cut resolved itself into a heap of leafless faggots. Presently a light rain began to fall. We all huddled together under the one blanket that we had brought and composed ourselves for the night. An uncomfortable bed has one great advantage—it is easily left. Before the hill-tops showed against the sky we were up and coaxing the fire to heat the billy.

The first few miles were along the stream bed, with here and there the signs of a path. Presently we came to the rain gauge built up above flood level; the debris of past floods in this narrow valley with its steep catchment area showed that we might have to take to the hills in a hurry if the Kona storm, which was supposed to pass west of Maui, hit this area. Beyond the rain gauge there was no sign of a path. We followed the stream while we could, but at times the depth of the water forced us out on to the steep, jungle-clad banks where the going was slow and difficult. We followed one tributary, a dark green tunnel which trended to the east and eventually showed us hills that we could not recognise; but they were not the watershed that we were in search of. We retraced our steps and tried another tributary, which led us first one way and then the other but finally settled on a northerly course. As long as we could keep climbing and heading north we knew that we must eventually reach the watershed.

This stream soon began to narrow and led us to a succession of waterfalls up which we climbed, making use of the 100-foot nylon cord. The waterfalls became steeper and narrower until finally an overhang forced a traverse along the side of the rocks that contained it. There were some palpitating moments until we were all assembled by a gnarled old tree which clung with roots like crippled fingers locked into cracks and crevices in the rock. The difficulty about these slopes was that shale and scree lay at a steeper-than-natural angle, held by the flimsy vegetation which only found life on its rocky bed because of the moist climate. An unwary step was liable to break up the whole fabric and send it sliding. Once out on to the ridge at the side of the waterfall, the slope became easier but the bush thicker, so that we had to chop and cut the whole way.

The spur petered out and we angled diagonally up the sides of the hill, across spurs and gullies, until we came out on to something bolder and more definite than any ridge that we had been on so far; the sun, now sinking fast, told us that we were heading in the right direction. Up we went until it looked as if the ridge that we were on had only five hundred yards to go before it joined the main ridge of the watershed. We had left the trees far behind and now had only dense, short scrub to compete with; it sometimes locked across the rocky knife-edge on which we were climbing, so that we had to force our way through a kind of rabbit tunnel to keep contact with the rock. I couldn't see the difficulties ahead but it did not look as if we could make the watershed that night. I looked down to Clio and asked, "How is it going, Popsy?" She turned away and bit her lip, and Beryl and I realised that our fourteen-year-old had had enough for one day. We had been going for fourteen hours, an hour for each year.

Beryl swept her up in a whirl of enthusiasm to find a camp-site on this impossible ridge. Great clouds were piling up from the south and I dreaded the arrival of a Kona in such an exposed situation; but Beryl and the others refused to consider any retrograde movement in search of better shelter. We managed to clear a small platform on the ridge. John and I were on opposite outsides and were roped together so that we could not fall off on either side. Clio was next to me and Beryl next to John. John and I struggled all night for our outer edges of the blanket. We had been in water or under waterfalls for most of the day and now a numbing cold crept up from our wet feet. For greater warmth and security, John put his arm round Beryl and said to her, "Beryl, you know, if I were ten years older and you were ten years younger, I don't think Miles would like this."

Suddenly, from far down the coast behind us, came a faint popping and banging of fireworks. Lahaina was celebrating the arrival of the New Year. We all turned on our backs, linked arms and sang "Auld Lang Syne" to the huge amphitheatre of the hills. The dark vault of the sky took the words from our lips and scattered them in tiny noises. I think it was one of the nicest New Year nights that we have ever spent, but someone said to me later when I told him about it, "I wonder if you really are as certifiable as you sound?"

We were up next morning before the stars had paled. There was no fire to be made as we carried no water. We divided the last two bars of chocolate and set off while the coast below us was still wrapped in the night. Soon we were out of the scrub and on to the real ridge of rock, sparse earth and heathery shrubs. The climbing seemed much more exposed, although it looked as if the ridge "would go". At the very end there had been a slip on the face of the ridge exposing the rock face and leaving a crumbling overhang. I was in front grumbling and complaining, convinced that I should never find a way up, while Beryl from below kept telling me that it looked all right. Eventually I managed it, but only to find the few feet that remained even more precarious. Beryl came up to join me and we decided that John could lead on a traverse below us, reversing the order of climbing. I looked down to explain the new procedure to Clio and John, whose eager young faces peered up at me over a bush like hawks in their eyrie.

John led off while we secured him and Clio from above. He made the slope of the main ridge and then climbed up to its edge with that easy balance that we had noticed so often on *Trekka*. When he got there he called to us that he could see the Iao Valley below. From then on it was just a matter of getting down. All day we slid, traversed and scrambled, using water courses until they dropped off into waterfalls, then traversing out to the spur that enclosed them and down the spur till we could make use of the water course again. Presently the valley levelled off, the stream began to widen out, and the going to become easier.

When darkness fell we had reached a deserted clearing on the bank of the stream. John tried for an hour to get a fire going from damp wood, but to no avail. We ended by mixing milk powder and peanut butter with water from the stream. It had the consistency of cement and tasted much the same. We slept until the moon was up and then continued down the stream. We were each armed with a long stick to probe the waters and support our jumps from boulder to boulder. The trees and bushes that interlaced over our heads, the dark secrecy of the banks, the moonlight on the rushing waters and wet boulders, the leaping figures, all would have made a strange and eerie picture if there had been anyone there to see. But presently the shadows began to assume their natural colours and an ebullience of spirits to show in the younger members of the party. They were soon leaping far ahead and showing no signs of fatigue. In two more hours we were on the bridge where the road to Kahului crosses the stream; out of a wild, exciting and almost unvisited country and into civilisation again.

Almost immediately, a car skidded to a halt beside us. "Are you the hikers?" a girl asked excitedly.

"What hikers?" I said suspiciously.

"I guess you are," she said. "Jump in. My house is just round the bend." She laughed as if at her own thought that the description might suit us too.

"Could we use your telephone?" I asked. "Of course," she said. "The Press wanted me to ring them, too, in case you came out."

When we got to the house she gave us coffee and biscuits and went to the telephone. When she got back she looked surprised. The cups were empty and the biscuits had gone. I telephoned Darrell and found that Stew was off in an aircraft to see if he could spot us. No sooner had I rung off than I heard the putter of a small aircraft on its way up the valley. I looked out and saw him climbing slowly and struggling with air currents and down drafts in the narrow hills. "Why the hell does he want to look for us?" I asked anxiously. "I wish we could let him know we are out." Someone suggested a mirror and the girl said that she had one on her dressing table. It was one of those old-fashioned round mirrors. We dismantled it and took it outside, then flashed it on a near hill for direction and up at the aircraft. Almost at once it turned and came down the valley, waggled its wings over our heads and made off back to the airport.

Presently Stew arrived in his car. "What were you doing?" I asked. "You weren't really getting anxious about us, were you?"

"No, sir," he said. "But I knew about that mass of food that you were carrying, and I wanted to lay on lunch for the right time. Into the car, now, and mind the steaks."

We had to submit to an interview with the Press.

"Are you professional hikers?" they asked.

"What are professional hikers? We walked through for fun."

"For fun," they said. "That beats everything." The pencils scribbled busily. Next morning it was in the papers. "The walk was done with khaki and denim trousers," it read, and, "the horizontal slopes were negotiated with the help of a rope."

While we were away Vivie and Raith had looked after Poopa, Pwe and *Tzu Hang*. Their being with us had given us a freedom that we would not normally have had, for we could leave *Tzu Hang* without worrying. By the time that we had arrived in Honolulu it was time for them to go back to Canada. As the aircraft carrying them home climbed into the night sky, I am sure that they looked down, trying to spot *Tzu Hang* and to say goodbye to her. But they were not saying goodbye to the sea. The seed had been sown. A few years later they had a ship of their own, and by the time that we arrived back in Canada they were almost ready to leave on a voyage to New Zealand, which they completed successfully. For the time being we were going to miss them, the easy companionship and the laughter and the silly games that we played in the restless cabin.

Tzu Hang spent the rest of the winter in Honolulu with one brief visit to Kauai when we left *Tzu Hang* at Nawiliwili and did a hike along the worth-west cliffs to a valley below the Kilohana Lookout. It was a good walk with, at times, the path clinging to vertical cliffs and great drops to the breakers thundering in on the beaches below. It was done in our usual campaigning style and we had a couple of wet nights out. The beauty of the Hawaiian Islands is that there is no threat from the weather, there are no snakes, no scorpions, no leeches, no ants that we have met with, and consequently, as many recent visitors have discovered, no great hardship in a bivouac on the beach.

Honolulu was a great event in Clio's life. A circus was coming to Honolulu, organised by a Masonic sect known as the Shriners; Clio was taken on as an assistant, with the job of looking after the animals in a mixed animal act. During all the time that the circus was there she was as busy as a girl could be, working for a Mr. Kristensen, a Dane with a Palomino horse on which he gave a demonstration of haute école, and which she groomed and polished all day. She also looked after a dog, a goat, and a sheep, and two guanocos which all took part in the not-so-haute-école part of Mr. Kristensen's act; they performed free in the sawdust ring and sometimes, if things went badly, out of it, in which case it was Clio's job to recapture them.

One night Beryl and I were out to dinner and we did not get back until well after the time that the circus was due to end. Through pouring rain I drove to the circus ground to collect her, not a little worried that I had left her so late at night with what I imagined were rough and tough circus hands. I found my way to the entrance of the big top which was still glowing with light although there was now no one about outside. In the centre of the ring some bales of hay had been pulled together in a circle and several hands were sitting there listening to a story by the lion tamer, while the rain thundered down outside. Clio was sitting amongst them, her elbows on her knees, her chin in her hands. The story had just ended and I called to her to come home.

"Oh, Daddy," she protested. "Couldn't I wait a little longer?"

"Good God, child," I said, "it's after twelve. No. Come on. I've got the car outside."

She got up and walked across the sawdust to me then we turned and made for the exit. I was aware of a disapproving silence behind me and presently the lion tamer shouted after me, "Why didn't you bring her a coat?"

Clio made several appearances on television with various animals and when her birthday arrived the day before we sailed, Mr. Kristensen, looking very dashing in a broad-rimmed western hat, the lion tamer, the bear man, and several other of the hands came to tea on board. Her cake was covered with circus animals and clowns. Beryl and I could not understand the Bronx accent of the bear man, but Clio interpreted and the party went with a swing. Clio was desolate at leaving next day, but no more than Mr. Kristensen who, when he said good-bye next morning, could not prevent the tears from rolling down his cheeks. Some months afterwards, when we were in Australia, Clio had a letter from him. He was giving up the show business, he said, and wanted to give Clio his beautifully-trained Palomino. Unfortunately he was then in California and Clio was about to go to school in England.

CHAPTER FIFTEEN

South to Fanning

It must have been on the day we sailed that I saw John step on to *Trekka* watched by a small crowd, although there was usually a small crowd looking at *Trekka*, attracted by her small size and her neatness. As he slid through the hatch and disappeared below, a Hawaiian girl called out excitedly, "You see? He fits!" It was March 4 when we both sailed for Fanning Island, just over a thousand miles south of Honolulu, en route for Samoa, Tonga and New Zealand, confident now that we would not meet any hurricanes in the Samoan area.

As we got away from the shelter of Diamond Head, the sails of the yachts outside the harbour began to lose themselves against the narrowing band of houses and hotels, until only one small sail remained. *Trekka* was hard on our heels. Presently the houses began to fade and disappear over the horizon until only the blue and still unspoiled hills remained. By the time the lights began to flash it was time for them also to disappear, and by midnight all that we could see of Honolulu was the loom of the light on Diamond Head and the constant stream of landing lights, suddenly illuminating, as the aircraft from so far away began their approach to the airfield.

We made good progress that night with the wind south of east, so that *Tzu Hang* was close-hauled in order to get to weather of her landfall and well up-current with the westerly drift. It was a rough night and Clio looked pale; she was heartbroken at leaving behind the lions, the Palomino, the guanacos and the goat, not to mention her circus friends. Beryl and I did not feel too good ourselves, but the motion eased after the old jib split from luff to leach so we had to set the storm jib instead. Before breakfast we were in trouble again when the headboard of the old mainsail split off, giving Beryl a prodigious amount of stitching in the morning, although fortunately the wind was down so that we did not feel we were losing too much time. *Trekka* saw us that evening but soon the wind was up again and we had left her behind. Both our animals had lost their sea legs; Poopa had to be escorted to the mast like an old man being helped to the "lou" in a hospital, while during the night Pwe gave us a terrible fright by squalling and bellowing as if someone had her by the tail. Beryl was trying to calm her and Clio to calm Poopa but none of us could think what was the matter until I saw that she was staring at the deckhead. I went on deck and found a large flying fish in the scuppers. It was some days before she was confident enough to go out once more on her flying fish patrols.

The next day was one of the nicest that I have ever had at sea. We were making good progress in the right direction and rapidly approaching the Inter-Tropical Front. It was good to be off again on our travels; in a few days we were going to see our first coral island and we had all got over our squeamishness. That evening the sky was covered with a giant canopy of lacy clouds pulled down at the four corners as if pegged to the horizon, and showing clear areas below the arch of its sides. Above us, the cloudy veil was so thin that the blue of the sky could be seen through its mesh. We seemed to have a powder blue and silver laced cloth from Damascus spread over our heads.

Our fifth day out, with 500 miles on the log, was a grey, depressing day. We could not hold our course, but as we were well east of the Fanning Island meridian this did not worry us. By noon *Tzu Hang* had made 120 miles in the last twenty-four hours and soon after that the wind dropped. It was a pause only, for it came back from the west, catching us aback; by the time that we had this sorted out, the rain was falling in torrents. *Tzu Hang* was into the Inter-Tropical Front with a vengeance. The sea was quickly flattened by the downpour as the rain streaked across its surface, each drop sending up a little spout of water which left a floating bubble, like a silver spangle, floating for a few moments until the water that formed it disappeared in the source of its origin. Each drop an allegory, to be born again somewhere in vapour, to travel and finally to rejoin the sea.

For the rest of the afternoon we sailed through tons and tons of falling water, and it was only in the evening that the wind settled in the east and the rain steadied to something less than a downpour. By two-thirty in the morning we had the main reefed, the mizzen and staysail down; but still *Tzu Hang* had all the sail she needed. By noon we had 150 miles on the log, which was skipping along the tops of the waves. I set a course for a point thirty miles east of Fanning Island and calculated that we had 320 miles to go. The *Pacific Pilot* warns that the island should not be approached unless a ship is sure of its position, on account of the treacherous currents, so we hoped to get out of this streaming world before we got much closer to it.

During the last two days of the voyage we experienced a thirty-mile set to the north on each day. John in *Trekka* a day or two later had the same set. Not only was *Tzu Hang* a long way short of her log, but when I tested the engine I found that the water pump was not working and that I was unable to mend it. The engine was dismantled and I was thoroughly disgruntled. Beryl, as usual, bore my impatience with stoic calm, and Clio, happy that the engine had somehow prevented further study with the correspondence course, was in the fore cabin, busy with her art, which now had a Dame Laura Knight flavour of clowns and circuses. "I haven't absolutely decided," she told us, "whether I shall go into the circus business or not."

On the tenth day the bad weather was behind us and we had glorious sailing with a fresh wind. We began to experience the excitement of an approaching landfall. Terns and boobies were round the ship.

"At four o'clock," I announced, "we'll see Fanning."

At four o'clock we all climbed the rigging but could see nothing except the blue of the sea around us, stretching forever and away. Beryl and Clio went below for tea but I refused to leave the cockpit, yet determined not to look towards the horizon for another hour. In the end I looked after half that time and was rewarded by the sight of a thin double line as if a soft pencil had been drawn along the canvas of the sky where it joined the sea. On the next wave I saw it again, and almost as I looked it turned into the tops of palm trees just showing above the line of the sea. How low it was and how wide it was! How surprisingly wide, when half an hour before we had seen nothing from the cross-trees.

"Land Ho!" I shouted, and there was a momentary silence

instead of chatter below. Then a rush on deck, a barking dog handed up first, Clio crying, "Where, where?", a wife saying "Nonsense," and lastly and most sedately, a cat.

We altered course slightly to clear the western end, and presently hove-to for the night with the island in sight to starboard, checking our drift by the angle of the log line. A lovely, peaceful night. No rushing through the darkness, no pounding waves, no water sluicing down the deck. The hatches were open and it was cool below. From time to time one of us put a head out to listen for breakers, but no tumbling rumble made our hearts beat faster. At first light I went up with my sextant to get a sight of Jupiter but there was no need. To my surprise the island was there, a little closer than when we had last seen it before darkness fell. Now it was clearly defined, a break in the reef, palm trees, a point.

Beryl was up and laying down the law. "First we'll have breakfast and tidy up," she said. "There's no point rushing in at this hour."

By the time we were ready it was just eight o'clock. We hauled up the mizzen and staysail and loitered in to Whaler Anchorage off the cable station. There were no signs of life. We could see the cable terminals, a few rusty barrels, a dilapidated wharf and red corrugated iron roofs showing between green bushes and over white sand. There was a sandy bottom at five fathoms, but it would be a restless place to stop. We decided to go on along the southern shore to English Harbour and the entrance to the lagoon. *Tzu Hang* slid along in calm water. The entrance to the lagoon was easily distinguished by a high flagpole on Weston Point and by the stream of light blue water ebbing from the lagoon—light blue because of the coral sand that it carried with it and dropped in its path. We could see the stream boiling and writhing with the tide, running between dark-blue banks of ocean water for a mile off shore. Inside, a small boat was towing a lighter, and presently a launch appeared and came out to us. Bill Frew, an Australian working for the copra company, came on board. He was as brown as a teak log and wearing a strange straw hat pulled down fore and aft like a cocked hat.

"No engine?" he asked. "Well, we will give you a tow. I'd better go back in and arrange it with Phil Palmer—he's the manager of the copra company. Tide changes at two so I'll be right back out."

At two they were back, this time with Phil Palmer in command, a vigorous figure with a voice like a waterfall, loud and unceasing. He soon had us in tow, explaining that he was not an Australian, although he talked like one, but a "Pommy". "Been with the company twenty years," he said, "except for the war. They told me to go and dig for gold," he said, "and I certainly found it for them," with a wave towards the copra sheds and the trees. He turned out to be well-read, a skilled ham radio operator, a natural seaman, and a rare enthusiast. As we arrived in the anchorage, his two teen-age daughters waved from the shore.

Beryl and I were to visit other reef-bound coral islands in the years to come but this, our first, was also the best—a classical coral island. The many-coloured lagoon was so wide that only the trees showed on the far edge. The rim was so narrow and low and the island so isolated that it felt as if it were more sea than land. The island seemed to have more of everything than the others. More burning sun and blistering coral sand, more sea birds crying, more squalls sweeping darkly across the lagoon and temporarily obliterating its peacock brilliance, more crabs, more coco-nut trees peering anxiously into the afternoon wind.

"It's not a good anchorage," said Phil Palmer, "but if you drop your hook in line with those two beacons you should be all right. Where is the I.T.F.? We've been expecting it any day." After a moment's consideration I realised what he meant and was able to tell him that we had come through the Inter-Tropical Front and left it behind only yesterday.

Fanning Island was first discovered by Captain Fanning of the trading ship *Betsy* of Boston with a cargo of fur from Masa Fuero, bound for Canton. The island was later settled by Captain English from Manihike and operated as a copra estate. In 1857, William Greig, after hunting for gold in California and Australia, heard that a bookkeeper was needed on Fanning Island and got himself a job there. Captain English seems to have been in some sort of financial trouble and Greig was able to get the island in payment or part-payment of his debts, but Captain English gave his name to the harbour. Greig was joined by an American, George Bicknell, and both of them married Gilbert Islanders. The Island went through various ups and downs, and when we were there was owned by Fanning Island Plantations Ltd., under the able management of Phil Palmer, who also operated the copra on Washington Island. Hughie Greig, the grandson of William, lived on the island in Greig's house, and ran the labour which was recruited from the Gilbert Islands.

When we met Hughie Greig, who was over eighty but still very hearty, he told us of the German raid on the island in 1914. He had been out shooting and camped for the night; then next morning he smelled coal smoke and heard two explosions. He was then employed by the cable and wireless company and they had been warned that they might be raided. He was a member of the island defence force, but they only had a few rifles.

He hurried back to the station and found it completely deserted and the clacking of the relay machines ominously silenced. He regained his room, exchanged his shot-gun for his rifle and, with a quickly beating heart, poked a hole with his bayonet through the blind on a window that looked out to sea. There was the long grey shape of the *Nurnberg*, so soon to do such damage at the battle of Coronel and soon thereafter to be sunk at the battle of the Falkland Islands. She was lying close in-shore, but on the beach there were one or two boats from the warship with officers and men ashore; to his surprise the whole of the cable station personnel with their wives and children were there watching the cutting of the trans-Pacific cable. The affair had the atmosphere of a picnic and everyone was taking photos. Hughie felt rather stupid peering through the hole in his blind with his rifle in his hand. After the Germans had gone, Hughie, who was a good diver, was able to recover the ends of the cables and they were soon spliced up and in business again.

Three days after our arrival we saw *Trekka* in the channel. John had experienced a rugged trip, as *Trekka* had not been able to sail with her twins so John had been forced into a lot of steering. If left to herself she had headed up rather closer to the wind than John wanted to go, so he had made do with about three hours' sleep in twenty-four. He had also met with some heavier weather than we had and at one time had been hove-to. In fact, the Inter-Tropical Front had arrived at Fanning Island, and for those three days we had wet squally weather. Phil Palmer had been surprised at the way our anchor had held but we found later that the chain was wrapped round two coral heads.

Soon after John arrived we moved over to an anchorage behind Cartwright Point on the other side of the channel. This was a much more secure place where we could safely leave the boats during the hike round the island that we were contemplating. Ashore there was an old copra shed where we mended sails and had lunch every day, calling it The Grange. We had hung the mainsail up in the rafters and the cat was resting in its folds when some Gilbert Islanders came to talk to us. One of the girls happened to look up at the sail and saw the cat's blue eyes and whiskered face looking down at her. She let out a scream and took to her heels, running like an antelope. None of us knew what was the matter, until one of the men who had pursued and caught her, dragged her back.

"She has seen a demon in the rafters," he explained.

The lagoon was about twelve miles across and thirty-three miles round, the greatest width of the rim being only half-a-mile. We had to time our walk so that we might cross at low water the two boat passages in the reef, Shark Passage and North Passage. John and Beryl were determined to live only on coco-nuts during the walk, but Clio and I carried fruit juice, prunes, biscuits and some "pinias" made from sugar dates and nuts, food for Indian pilgrims, that we had eaten in the Himalayas. I carried the food and Clio helped me eat it.

We crossed the entrance to the lagoon in the dinghy, leaving the cat on *Tzu Hang*. As far as Shark Passage our path lay through coco-nut palms and across occasional salt-water channels. The going was good and the sky cloudy with a cool trade wind. For most of the way we were accompanied by fairy terns, little white birds with large black eyes and black bills. They were particularly interested in Poopa and hovered a few feet above his head. These terns lay one egg in a slight hollow on the branch of a tree, but make no nest. Both the male and female sit on it in turn. Hughie Greig told us that he had often watched them changing over and had never seen an egg knocked to the ground.

For several miles the path led through coco-nut palms, first on one side and then on the other of the narrow strip of land between lagoon and sea. It passed a deserted labour camp with a lonely frigate bird tethered to a post which hissed at us. The islanders capture frigate birds and then tame them. Once they are tame they attach coloured streamers to their wings and let them go. Then when they hold up small fish which have been caught in a net for bait, the birds come dropping out of the sky with their small coloured cotton streamers, each to his own mistress, for it seemed to be usually the girls that had them as pets.

A little further on we came to another channel which led from the big lagoon to a small lagoon within the island rim. We waded through at its narrowest point and picked up the trail again as it meandered through the trees. As we began to turn the corner of the island and approach the trade wind side, the path petered out and the going in the shade of the trees became littered with branches and old husks. We took to the mud flats on the edge of the lagoon and soon the coco-nut palms on the right gave place to hardier tangles of scrub and small trees, an impenetrable growth, leaning away from the wind. Beyond them we could hear the booming of the waves on the reef.

Along these salty flats were all kinds of shore birds, many of them migrants from the far north. The finest of these was the curlew, a russet-rumped fellow down from Alaska, but his anaemic whistle could not compare with the wild haunting and cascading cry of the ones that I was familiar with in England. He called "curlew", all right, but the last note fell as if he was wearied by the heat and there was no attempt at the final repetitive whistle.

We now began to feel the heat ourselves, and the glare from the white salty flats was as bad as that from a snow field. The white coral grit began to get into shoes or sandals and rub the skin off heels and toes; there was no antidote to this as our feet were not hard enough to go all day barefoot. Beryl was the most remarkable figure; she wore a large planter's straw hat, dark glasses, and a handkerchief tied over her nose. The whole was topped by a sunshade that she had bought from some Chinaman in Honolulu; it was encircled by a slogan, "God protects the righteous", and "step by step one goes a long way".

For the time being, the wild scenery and the bird life made us forget the hot sun and our sore feet. We found frigate birds sitting on low bushes like old discarded clothes on a hedge. Clio was convinced that she could catch one, but her stalking was always spoiled by Poopa who arrived importantly on the scene and sent them flapping awkwardly off their perches until, windborne, they turned into a thing of grace. In the tangled mass of trees and scrub which now covered the strip of land between the lagoon and the reef there were hundreds of boobies—blue-faced, red-footed and brown. They were living side by side with frigate birds, who catch them on their way home from fishing and force them to disgorge. This piracy at sea seems to have no effect on their relations at home where they shared the same bushes in amity.

We decided to cross the strip of bush and to walk on the seaward side of the island rim. On the outside of the strip of sand and scrub, between it and the reef, was a narrow, shallow lagoon; outside this is a regular wall of flat coral slabs, so regular that it appeared to have been artificially laid. Outside this again we could see the dark hurrying tops of the waves before they broke on the reef; the up-flung spray of their breaking being in general hidden from us by the reef wall.

We splashed in the water along the edge of this shallow lagoon, frightening numerous little puffer fish into blowing themselves up so that they floated helplessly belly up and we were able to catch them in our hands, where after a short time they deflated and slipped away through our fingers.

When we arrived at Shark Passage it was at low water and not more than a couple of feet deep and five hundred yards wide. It narrowed towards the reef and in the boat passage there we could see the ocean waves jostling together and then turning into lazy ripples as they reached the lagoon.

As we waded across we saw one or two small sand sharks which scurried away from us and provided no justification for carrying Poopa, who waded, swam and splashed across with us, always with his curly tail wagging above the water. The sand was covered with prickly sea urchins which only Poopa seemed unable to see. He trod squarely on one, yet seemed to have received no damage.

Once across the other side we tried splitting some fallen coconuts, but the labour seemed barely worth the trickle of juice that came out at the end. The sun was now fierce and we began to walk with dull determination, each following his or her own bent and no one talking. North Passage seemed a desperately long way ahead; the undergrowth was too thick to permit walking in the shade, so we were forced out on to the burning, shimmering salt flats, which often turned into clinging mud. After a time we could make out the Gilbert islanders' camp at Tara Fefe, which lay opposite *Tzu Hang* across the lagoon and was therefore the half-way mark.

When we arrived at the camp, the islanders gave us fresh

coco-nuts to drink, each with a bit of husk attached to the shell to make a handle. Never was a drink so good. We drank in front of a semi-circle of laughing, white-toothed men and women, while naked children swarmed round us like flies, which were also prevalent. They seemed to live in conditions of appalling squalor in their camps, with no attempt at any cleanliness. Most of the money that they earned was spent in the company's store, but the clothes, canned goods and other stores that they were able to buy were locked away against their return to their homes. Single men had a return trip every eighteen months, married families every two years. For the time being, all that they seemed to need was a corrugated iron roof, a grass mat, some coco-nuts and fish from the lagoon.

About a mile beyond the village I found that I had left my camera behind on a tree where I had rested before reaching the village. I turned back while the others waited. This was the low point of our journey and it was made worse for me by finding my eyes affected by the glare, like snow blindness, so that I had difficulty in seeing. I was so pleased at finding my camera where I thought I had left it, that I began to feel better immediately, and when I got back the others were well rested and eager to go on. We continued for another six miles, sometimes in jungle, some-times on salt flats, sometimes losing shoes in the mud and always in trouble with coral grit; the sun was getting lower and its heat was spent. Darkness was falling as we reached the passage and a point on the chart called Pono Tai, where the crossing is a mile wide. It was time to halt and wait for the moon and for low tide. We lay down in a grove of coco-nuts and from time to time a nut fell to the ground somewhere near us. Clio, Beryl and I huddled together for warmth as the night had turned cool and sometimes a rain squall swept over us. Poopa was in great demand as a hot water bottle while John, grumbling that he had not come all this way to be hit by a coco-nut, kept changing his position to one of imagined greater security, only to change again as he heard another nut fall.

After a few hours of restless turning, the moon was high enough and the tide low enough for us to start our long wade. I led, carrying Poopa in order to avoid an affair with a shark. The moon was bright enough for us to see deep water and to keep to the shallows, but it was a long wade and Poopa grew to the size of a Great Dane and was passed from hand to hand as each of us in turn wearied. No strange monsters bothered us and after a time we arrived at a sandy island. Here we rested and opened a tin of fruit juice; even Beryl and John had a taste. Some more wading and we were across. We struck out through planted coconut trees which grew on cleared land, knowing that now we had only six miles to go to the Cable Station, where we planned to hold up the duty operator for a cup of tea.

The whole way was contested by land crabs which scurried across our path. For all their desire to avoid trouble it was sometimes impossible to avoid treading on them, and joining them full-length in the grass.

We were in fine form now and arrived at Napari by 2 a.m. to find the duty operator fast asleep under a mosquito net. He got us tea and biscuits as we had hoped, because fortunately he was the mess secretary and had access to the mess.

We were soon under way again. Only another six miles. The moon began to sink, the land crabs scurried, and our feet felt suddenly very sore. Bend after bend in the road failed to reveal the white shape of *Tzu Hang* in the bay. Only thirty-three miles behind us, but we felt as if we had walked fifty. And then suddenly we were home. Pwe let us know in a very loud voice exactly what she felt about the desertion.

The hero of the expedition was Poopa. He had not walked half a mile for five months and here he was as busy and enthusiastic as the moment when he started out, having had to do with at least a hundred land crabs, let alone all the interests which suddenly beset a sea-going dog when first he gets ashore.

Before leaving Fanning Island, Beryl insisted on swimming across the entrance to the lagoon to recover the dinghy. We had another dinghy which Clio sensibly rowed across, as I could not help thinking of the large barracuda head that was mounted in Phil Palmer's study; however, we dutifully swam across and thereby completed the circuit of the island under our own steam.

We left as a dark squall obliterated the island behind us and stole our wind, so while *Tzu Hang* rolled and flapped, *Trekka* slipped away ahead. Sometime after supper I could see her small light in front. Beryl had made some cocoa and I went below to drink it with *Tzu Hang* sailing along nicely by herself. Before I had finished my cocoa I looked out and there was *Trekka* beside us. I could have pitched my cup on to her deck. Her stern and running lights were burning but there was no one on deck.

"John!" I called. "*Trekka* ahoy!" But there was no answer.

"I expect that he is cooking his dinner and couldn't hear over the primus," said Beryl. Whatever he was doing, it was a narrow escape for *Trekka*, and I could not sleep for the rest of the night for thinking of it.

The morning came, a dull grey morning with squalls all round. Fanning Island was long out of sight, but all kinds of boobies and the fairy terns came to see us. "Only a few miles over the horizon," they seemed to say, but it was unlikely that we should see their bright lagoon, the grey reef and the coco-nuts forever peering into the wind again.

CHAPTER SIXTEEN

To Samoa

On this passage, owing to the presence of the Inter-Tropical Front which piled huge thunder clouds one on top of the other and sent black squalls chasing each other across the sea, we were treated to the most wonderful sunsets and cloud effects.

The sun disappeared behind the horizon in a stupendous burst of colour. Sometimes in a blazing golden flash as if from a huge explosion, while opposite, the sky was all roseate and grey like pigeon's breast; sometimes it set like a red hot iron from the forge, darkening in patches; sometimes it caught the summits of cloud mountains to the east in a golden light, while far below, the sea was already dark. Each night Jupiter chased Venus across the sky—she lit her lamp over the glowing traces of the vanished sun. And with all this beauty, so little sound—only the hush of the wave at the forefoot, the creak of a block like some small sea bird and, with the lightening wind, the tug of the boom against the sheet. It felt very good to be alive.

On Friday the 13th Poopa ate the fudge that Beryl had made, but we made a run of 170 miles, and on the next day of 130 and on the next of 145. With the wind just abaft the beam, a hot sun and dry decks, this was the fastest and most comfortable sailing we had done. *Tzu Hang* sailed herself and scattered the flying fish ahead of her like spray.

During our stay in Fanning, Clio had brought a small lizard with a stumpy tail on board, which we christened Mr. Greig. He now made an appearance, looking rather fatter than before. She had also brought some lizard's eggs on board in a ball of grass in a coco-nut shell. These hatched out and from time to time emaciated little lizards appeared about the boat. Mr. Greig stayed with us as far as Tonga but then withdrew into some secret place and was not seen again.

We had intended to pass west of the Danger Islands. On the fifteenth, when I hoped to be well west of them, my sight put me to the east and I had to assume that I was in an east-going current. I did not want to pass them by night on the east side for fear that we should run out of the east-going current and into a west-setting one which might put me on to them. We therefore held on to the west until I was assured that we were out of the easterly set and well to the west of the islands. It wasted a day but was a reasonable precaution, as the current normally runs strongly to the west and they are better passed on the west side.

A day or two later we expected to make Tutuila by noon. I was sitting in the cockpit at breakfast and looked casually to port. There I saw the islands of Ofu, Olosega, and Tau, so beautifully named and so unexpected, as I had been thinking only of our landfall on Tutuila. For a moment I felt as the early discoverers must have felt, and have since come to think that there is nothing so nice as an unexpected landfall.

Soon afterwards, the first pinnacle of Tutuila appeared, and then more blue peaks and points as the land grew wider across our bows. Presently we could see the passage between Tutuila and the small island of Auunu while the land began to take on new shapes and colours. The north coast was wild and rugged with great fingers of scrub-covered rocks pushing up out of the surf. As *Tzu Hang* closed the passage we could see houses on each side, some of American timber construction and some Samoan with palm thatched roofs supported by posts and open-sided. A bus was running along the road by the beach and be-cause we had not seen one for some weeks Clio called, "Look, look! A bus!" Poopa started barking as if he'd seen a whale.

With a following sea and wind, *Tzu Hang* ran quickly through the passage but, as it was already beginning to get dark and we had no chart of Pago Pago harbour, we hove-to for the night, five miles south of the harbour entrance light. Next morning I made a chart from the pilot book and went in under sail since the water pump was still out of order. We had some difficulty in recognising the entrance to the inner harbour until it opened out behind Goat Island. We gybed *Tzu Hang* and went in under a single headsail, and as *Tzu Hang* came abreast of the old Navy wharf I saw a familiar broad-beamed Norwegian double-ender, lying at anchor in sad disarray.

"Isn't that Harmon's boat?" I said to Beryl, thinking of the smart yacht that had sailed with us from Panama a few years before. It turned out to be the same ship, but she had changed hands and was now working as a copra ship between the islands. Her hull was a dirty grey, her spars black and her decks all stained with copra; but at any rate she represented an anchorage. We made towards her but before we reached her a voice hailed us from a converted minesweeper at the wharf, the *Manua Tele*.

There was just time to turn up into the wind and to tie alongside with, it must be admitted, a moment's aid from the waterless engine.

The *Manua Tele* had been bought by the people of the islands that we had seen on our port hand coming in, but for the time being had been taken over by the Government. Both the captain, Bob Page, and the engineer, Jim Sword, were American and both married to Samoan girls. Jim was the son of a Scot who had settled in Fiji and his grandfather on his mother's side was also a Scot who had been in sail. While we were in Pago Pago, Jim Sword made for *Tzu Hang*'s engine a new pump which was better than the original, and we made great use of the *Manua Tele* and particularly of her shower. As soon as we were secured, Bob Page called down to us that he would get the doctor, and would have some coffee ready when we were cleared.

The doctor came on board. He had a small military moustache and was dapper in white shirt and shorts with little white socks. He gave us the most penetrating look, as if to search out not only weaknesses of the body but weaknesses of the mind, but after a few questions pronounced us fit to go ashore. Dr. Edgar Martin was born in Austria but is now a Canadian, and he and his gentle wife, Marie, took us under their wing during our stay. Edgar always spoke in careful, well-considered phrases, and whatever he said was always worth listening to; so much so that we were often caught out by his humour and found ourselves listening seriously to something that was betrayed as nonsense only by the twinkle in his eye.

Two Government officials came down to the wharf, perhaps to assess our social status, and I was asked if I'd like to meet the Governor that afternoon. I was taken to unobtrusive Government offices which looked as if they might have been converted from an old store and presently shown into an inner sanctum, where a small, white-clad, narrow-faced Governor was sitting behind a long mahogany table in front of large crossed flags. It was all strangely different from what would have happened in a British Colony in the Colonial era. First of all, I do not think that I would have been asked to meet the Governor, and if I had, our meeting would have been much more informal. He might even have been a yachtsman and come down to the boat. On this occasion, after one or two formal pleasantries, the Governor cleared his throat, and, with a "that reminds me" of a professional raconteur, told me a story. I felt like an audience at a public dinner, and took the end of the story as a sign for my departure, which indeed it was. As I said good-bye, the Governor asked if we would care to come to a reception for General Dolittle who was going through on his way to Australia to celebrate the anniversary of the battle of the Coral Sea.

We arrived at Government House next afternoon and found that cars were depositing their occupants at the foot of the hill from which a single police car was doing a ferry service to the top. A Samoan Chief and his wife will fill any car, so there was a considerable back-log waiting at the bottom. At the top of the hill there was a large concourse of Chiefs and wives, with Government officials of the American administration and their wives. Everyone who was anyone in Samoa was there, some having spent all day travelling. The chiefs wore coat, shirt and tie, and below this the lava-lava held up by a low-slung, broad belt. Below this again, bare legs and feet that could have supported mountains.

They were all obviously enjoying themselves, happy to be at the party, and looking forward, as Beryl and I were, to drinks and cocktail snacks. Beryl had refused to give us tea on this account.

Presently the Governor and his wife with General Dolittle and his wife appeared in the hall and the long line of visitors began to file past. General Dolittle wore his renown with complete unconsciousness; he was, in my brief impression, small, unassuming and friendly. Yet he had an air of greatness; an aura caused by the admiration and respect of all those round him. We walked on down a hall and out on to a lawn where we stood about awkwardly, not knowing anyone. In fact, most people seemed to be in this situation and there was no one to act as host and put them at their ease. We waited perhaps for an hour until the last visitors came down the hall and out on to the lawn. Then the First Secretary appeared. We all perked up, thinking that we now would be told where the drinks were. It had been a long hot afternoon.

"Now that you've all seen General Dolittle," said the First Secretary, "you may go. Please use the gate at the bottom of the garden."

We left, but in doing so caught a glimpse of the receiving line, waiting, not now for guests to come, but for guests to go. The Samoans, their appetites unappeased, had a dazed look as they went down the hill. With their strict rules of etiquette and hospitality they needed time to adjust themselves. Not so the Americans. "What on earth did you think of it?" they asked. "Never has such a thing happened in Samoa before." A New Zealander who had come from Fiji and had a job with the Administration was so upset that he became sick and went to bed. A few days later we met him looking better. "I feel O.K. now," he said. "I hear they gave the General a real bonzer party in Fiji,"

We had dinner with the Martins. Edgar told us about his time in the Belgian Congo working both as a doctor and a biochemist, and of the rivalry between the Missions that employed him, where the dying could be turned away unless they were converts to the sect from which they sought succour. He also told us of how he had practised Yoga under an African teacher and only gave it up when he found it was leading him to strange esoteric experiences which were better avoided. One of the results, he told us, was to relieve him of all sense of physical desire.

"Was that why you gave it up?" asked Beryl.

"Well, partly," he said.

Shortly before our arrival, a bus filled with Samoans had plunged over a cliff on to rocks by the sea. Although some way from the hospital, the evacuation was completed in two hours, and by the time Edgar had finished operating on the first case, all the others had been dressed and looked after by Samoan medical practitioners and Samoan nurses. Edgar said that however exasperating, lazy and unreliable they might be at their ordinary duties, in an emergency they were splendid. He thought that it was because of the system of Chiefs and of family discipline and respect, so that there was always someone to take command and others ready to obey without talk or comment.

We went off with Marie and Edgar to visit one of his far distant patients. One of the nurses at the hospital, Na Esse, came with us as we were invited also to visit her father, a "Talking Chief". A Talking Chief is the administrative officer of an island community, second in command to the High Chief or Chief. Na Esse brought a companion as a chaperone. "Not for her protection," Dr. Martin explained, "but for the protection of her reputation."

We passed many villages, most of them a combination of the Samoan "falés" and American clapboard houses. The former, on their raised platforms of coral and generally open but with screens to let down along the sides, appeared far cleaner, healthier, and more attractive than the others. In nearly every village there were one or more churches. "Look at them," Edgar said in indignation. "Because of rivalry between sects and the accursed Samoan pride, everyone must have a church, and, if possible, better than their neighbours. Because the missionaries are so dumb that they think God can only be worshipped in a house of stone, look at the monstrosities that they have built." Some of the monstrosities were of concrete and some of brick, but all were unfinished, awaiting funds. If you really wanted to rouse Edgar it was only necessary to mention a missionary. He was in charge of the T.B. control of the island. He told us that some of his patients, on being released from hospital after T.B. treatment, asked if it was now safe to have intercourse with their wives.

"It is all a matter of posture," he told them, "and before I give any advice I must know about posture."

"Well," they usually replied, "before the missionaries came there were all sorts of postures, but now there is only one."

At this moment Clio arrived and we never heard any more.

Before visiting Na Esse's father, Edgar explained how we were to comport ourselves. We had to sit with our backs to a post in the falé as soon as we arrived, while he gave a brief account of who we were and what we were doing. It was bad form to show too much enthusiasm, to laugh loudly, to be curious, to talk too much, or to speak in a language not understood by the host. This probably applies to any society except perhaps the North American one, where we naturally do all these things except speak in a language that our host does not understand. The admonition had a crushing effect on Beryl and I, who felt that all we could do now was to bow and smile without showing our teeth, like a church warden taking a late arrival to a pew.

After half an hour's desultory conversation with Na Esse interpreting, the Chief gave us a piece of dry kava root. Edgar explained that only Chiefs could own kava and this was a recognition of my chiefly status. The Chief rumbled again, and this time Na Esse interpreted. "The Chief says that in Samoa it is the habit to give and receive presents and now that he has given you the kava root you must give him something in return."

This was a desperate situation as, without actually undressing, all I had was a silk handkerchief round my neck given to me by Clio for my birthday. Disregarding all etiquette, Beryl and I hissed and gesticulated between ourselves and eventually decided to plead ignorance of their customs and to say that we had no worthy gift to return. The Chief appeared to accept this explanation a little doubtfully and took us in to a surprise spread of baked chicken, snails, breadfruit, yams, corned beef and tomato ketchup. We ate with our fingers.

We called at another Chief's house on the way back. Here we all sat within the falé with our backs to posts, while the kava was poured into a kava bowl from an old enamel wash jug. The Chief then clapped his hands and shouted in Samoan, "The kava is made and has been tasted. Let us drink." One of the attractive daughters of the house, dressed in a smart skirt and a jumper and on holiday from America, then brought us in turn half a coco-nut shell of kava dipped from the bowl. She bent one knee and offered it gracefully in both hands. It had to be drained, and it tasted rather like dishwater flavoured with red pepper.

All down the road on the way back, the people were leaving their houses for evening service, the girls in white dresses with plain little straw hats, the young men in white shirts and lavalavas and their broad low belts. In everyone's hand a Bible and a prayer book; in everyone's face a look of happiness at the idea of communal sing-song. At the gates of the unfinished churches, the missionaries waited with collecting boxes in their hands.

The following day Marie and Edgar took us to the village, where the shark and the turtle come to the edge of the breakers when the children call them. It is said that once, in a time of famine, fish were being distributed from a fisherman's meagre catch. A blind old woman and her granddaughter came down to collect her portion, but since she was an unpopular old shrew someone threw her a dead rat. She did not discover the deceit until she came to the tail when, in rage and mortification, she threw herself and her granddaughter over the cliff into the sea. The villagers were overcome with remorse and prayed at the cliff edge that they might be forgiven, until the dead returned in the form of a shark and a turtle and promised that as a sign of their forgiveness they would always come to the bottom of the cliff when the children sang the song that told their story from the cliff edge.

When we arrived at the village a cricket match was in progress. In almost every village that we passed through during our stay there had been a match going on; most villages had a concrete pitch and the batsmen used a three-cornered bat which looked more like a war club than a cricket bat. We were soon surrounded by children and told them that we had come to see the shark and the turtle. The children will not sing unless they are rewarded with sweets and we had come well equipped. As soon as they saw that we had something for them we set off along a path that led to the cliff edge.

There was a big sea rolling into the ragged little bay, rumbling and surging and sending great spouts of water up the cliff face. No sooner had the children started their song than the spray from a big breaker sent them flying away, but back they came, laughing and chattering, and started off again. It was obvious that no shark, and certainly no turtle, could come today into the broken water that swirled about the bay, but suddenly the song broke into a new and excited rhythm, and the children began to beckon to us with that open-handed over-arm motion that we knew so well from our days in the East.

There below, swimming near the surface and apparently keeping itself with difficulty from being dashed against the rocks, was a big shark. In my excitement I could not help pointing. A little girl knocked my hand down and scolded me. Pointing, she said, was the worst of bad manners and perhaps the turtle would not come. Marie, who translated, said that they almost always came together, but she thought that today was perhaps too rough. The shark swam around a little longer and then disappeared. That it should have come at all in such a turbulent sea seemed wonderfully strange.

Next day, children and parents were being collected from outlying islands in preparation for the celebration of Flag Day. We went to Auunu in a lighter which was to bring back a hundred and fifty children. As we arrived, several row boats, fully loaded, were waiting outside the reef. The beach was thronged with those awaiting embarkation and those who were staying behind. Up to his portly waist in water and directing operations was the local Talking Chief. The children were transferred to the lighter and numerous passages made through the gap in the reef by the smaller boats which worked a ferry service, without mishap and in a few minutes. Although everyone was talking and laughing, the whole operation was controlled by a strict, although not obvious, discipline.

No sooner had we set off in the lighter on the return journey than oranges and limes were pressed to brown noses to allay the pangs of seasickness. The village policeman hurried to comfort first one child and then another. For all their tradition, the Samoans seem to be very prone to seasickness.

In all, about five thousand visitors came into the little town of Pago Pago on the evening before the big day. There was no sign of rowdiness, no visible signs of exhilaration, no swash-buckling down the streets, no sudden eruptions from bar doors. Beryl and I wondered where they had all got to. A few more demure and happy couples, a few more groups of cheerful talkers, was all the difference to be seen that evening.

Early next morning, the children were being marshalled for the parade. The boys were wearing blue, red or yellow lava-lavas, or khaki trousers and blue shirts, while the girls were in white with red, green, or yellow sashes. They were in platoons and companies in all the side roads, squares and open places adjoining the town parade ground where the Governor was to take the salute. As any particular organisation marched into the forming-up area, the others would give them a round of spontaneous applause. We saw the Girls' Life-Saving Brigade of Valua halted and preening before marching in. Then, with two husky girl standard-bearers carrying the stars and stripes and the flag of the union in front, with a stout girl walking backwards carrying a drum, and a small girl walking forwards and beating a rub-a-dub-dub on it, they swung into their alloted position. So many brown legs stiff with *esprit de corps*, so many young faces radiant with pride and exaltation, so many bouncing youthful breasts. The boys of Lawaler High School gave them a round of subdued applause.

At eight o'clock the march past the Governor started; the formations wheeled past the starting point and round the green with military precision to the tap of kettle drums and the shouts of "One, two, three, four". It is difficult enough to get trained troops past a starting point at the right time, but the Samoan children, three thousand of them, did it with ease. The only policeman to be seen were running about and taking photographs.

After the parade there was a long programme of sports, dancing and song. Copra-cutting, basket-making, and fire-making were among the competitions and, apart from the histrionic efforts of five school children on "What can I do for Samoa", punctuated with uplifted fingers pointing at the U.S. flag, the day was full of life and colour. The songs and harmony and the dancing were enchanting, particularly by a large group of small girls who sat cross-legged and raised their knees up and down to the beat of the tune while undulating their arms and hands in dance rhythm. They looked like a lot of little frogs crammed into a pool.

After all these celebrations we felt that it was time to set off for Tonga, 350 miles away. *Tzu Hang* left from the side of the *Manua Tele* under sail and we managed to get out of the harbour on one tack, followed out by two Japanese tuna boats. One of these was flying two large red flags and her stern was stacked so high aft with fishing tackle, nets and buoys, that she looked like a medieval junk. She was an old and unkempt wooden boat no bigger than *Tzu Hang*, and so crowded that we wondered how she could have made the voyage; but there was a large, modern factory ship in the harbour. Years later, when we saw these small catchers leaving Japan for Samoa, they were of modern design and looked extremely efficient, although still crowded with men and tackle.

CHAPTER SEVENTEEN

To Tonga and New Zealand and on to Sydney

The passage from Fanning Island to Tutuila had been a fast one. Now, with only 350 miles to go, we had a desperately slow one. *Tzu Hang* managed to open the coast beyond the western lighthouse, and we were able to identify the bay of the turtle and the shark; but for all that night we lay becalmed and for all the next day we had the coast in sight. During the night a slight breeze from the south-west arrived and *Tzu Hang* sailed slowly south. It was not exactly where we wanted to go so that night we took down our sails and slept all night. Beryl had picked up a 'flu bug which was on the rampage in Samoa, but after a good sleep she was quite recovered.

For two more days we were becalmed. Clio was very busy with a plankton net which for most of the time hung vertically below the boat. She brought it up and discovered sand in it and announced that we must have touched bottom with it. According to my calculations, bottom should have been 2,100 fathoms below us. Beryl suggested that it might be the cat's sand that had been emptied over the stern, and I was relieved that we had not as yet had a meal of plankton, as Clio had intended.

On the evening of May 3, we were treated to a fantastic display of lightning in the south-west; the horizon and its frieze of cloud was continually aflame. The twin staysails were up, since we had had a light wind from the north-east, but now there was literally no wind at all. The booms, however, were so well guyed and the sails so taut that there was little wear and we hoped that the wind might come again. Several times during the night I got up to see how the storm was moving. At two we could see the lightning forking across the sky and spitting down into the sea, but it was still a long way away. At four we both awoke with a start to hear a wild hissing and the violent fluttering of the starboard staysail. We stampeded on deck and found one staysail hard aback and the other shaking madly. *Tzu Hang* answered to the helm, and as I turned down wind the port staysail filled with a resounding thump and we set off down-hill with a rush. It was a really violent wind and *Tzu Hang* flew; but it was in the wrong direction. Clio and Beryl got the headsails down but the log continued to spin and we were soon doing six knots without a sail set. The sea was surprisingly flat but it was building up quickly, the spray flying over the deck. The glass had been so low for the last three days that I felt alarmed. By breakfast it was all over, a fair wind blowing, and by evening we were thirty miles from our destination. We handed all sail two hours after darkness and set off again at four in the morning. As day came we saw Vavau on the port bow, a long, flat island rising to a five-hundred-foot cliff at the northern end.

As we rounded this end, the island exploded into numerous islets, flat-topped and with perpendicular limestone cliffs under-cut by the sea, so that they looked like large green mushrooms. Between these mushrooms a long passage led up to Neiafu. In a few places there were small beaches and there were any number of coco-nut trees. They stood like policemen containing a crowd, for they held back the jungle about them which in other places, hung by lianas and creepers, swooped in luxurious abandon to the sea.

Tzu Hang passed a sandy point on a small conical island with a red-roofed house on top, where Tongans were shouting and waving. Then the wharf appeared, backed by red roofs and white cottages. We saw the familiar masts and blue hull of *Trekka* moored against the quay.

As we came alongside, a crowd of men, women and children thronged the quay above. Brown hands and toes reached out to grasp our shrouds. Everyone was laughing and joking. Some of the sallies, which we could not understand, were greeted with guffaws. The port doctor was first on board, a young man of great weight, who made *Tzu Hang* stir as he put a foot on the rail. He squeezed through the hatch.

"Where is the customs officer?" I asked.

"He will come," replied the doctor, "but he is too fat. We cannot both come on board at the same time."

As the doctor left, the customs officer replaced him—a man of similar weight and equal geniality. We were cleared with the minimum amount of red tape, but I still had to see the harbour master, as all boats going to Neiafu which are subsequently going to Nukualofa must anchor a mile off shore on account of the rhinocerous beetle, which flies by night and has been known to make a test flight of almost this distance. The harbour master of the already-infected Neiafu did not insist on *Tzu Hang* obeying the letter of the law and allowed us to tie up to a buoy about 300 yards off shore. Great bundles of fruit and vegetables are transferred by boat between all the ports in the archipelago, and it is a wonder that Nukualofa has remained free of the pest.

As soon as we were on the buoy we saw a small motor-boat coming up the sound well down by the bow. The cause was obvious. John and an equally large Tongan were sitting on the foredeck. They had been down to see Mariner's Cave and the Cave of the Swallows; John's description of Mariner's Cave lost nothing in the telling. He had made a good trip from Apia, which he had enjoyed enormously, so we swapped Samoan stories far into the hot, still night.

"If you can dive ten feet and swim the length of *Tzu Hang* under water, you'll be able to make it," said John, referring to the entrance to Mariner's Cave. Next morning was spent in practising our underwater swimming, the length of *Tzu Hang* and below the level of her keel. Clio was not convinced that she could hold her breath for long enough. We also went ashore and wandered about the little village of wooden houses with red corrugated iron roofs. Its seedy appearance was mitigated by sudden splashes of colour, a blaze of scarlet Khannas, a wave of purple Bougainvillea, or a sudden view of the blue sound and the white yacht below.

The store was pure Somerset Maugham, dark, gloomy and cluttered. There were spades and axes, galvanised iron buckets, bush knives, rolls of cheap cloth, yams, sweet potatoes, and an all-pervading smell which reminded me of the brewery in Malton when I was a boy. It was not a pleasant smell. The store was presided over by a wrinkled white man who regarded us with disfavour when we went in and made no attempt to serve us while we were there.

We went on past one of the five churches of different denominations that serve Neiafu, along a grassy lane bordered by shrubs, to a small house on a hill where two boys were cutting the grass with long bush knives. This was a tapa factory and on the grass there was spread a long length of tapa on which an old lady was applying the brown and black pattern with which tapa is usually dyed. Inside the house weaving tapa, were a number of women whom the old lady chased outside with a sergeant major's scream so that Beryl could take a picture. The Polaroid camera was a great success, especially the over-exposure that gave them all a fair complexion.

On our way back to the boat we were intercepted by a tall, grey-haired woman, shielding herself from the sun with a black umbrella as is the custom of all Tongan women. She had a distinguished face and introduced herself as Tubon Fakatoufita, wife of the Chief of Ofu, an outlying island. She insisted that we all went to her tiny cottage by the beach and that Beryl and Clio should stay the night. The cottage had one room which was divided by a screen. She had two daughters; one, Fono, a tall, slim girl, came often to the boat during the rest of our stay, always wearing her mat, a ceremonial apron over her dress, and carrying her umbrella. In order to bathe from the boat she took off her mat, but otherwise, like all other Tongan girls, slid into the water fully clothed. They are continually in the water but, perhaps because of their clothes, they are extremely awkward swimmers. The other sister, Mrs. Fakatoufita explained, had just changed her religious denomination as she wanted to learn typing, which the Catholics taught and the Seventh Day Adventists did not.

The following day, when Beryl and Clio had returned, we set off in the small motor-boat in which we had seen John, leaving *Tzu Hang* on her mooring. John had decided to come with us to Mariner's Cave and then to sail on for the Bay of Islands in New Zealand. As there was no wind, he took a tow from us down the sound. Cecilia Faletau, the sturdy daughter of another chief, was coming with us, and we found her on board with her mother, and another Tongan woman, the wife of Lino Onesi, who owned the launch. Lino, being an enthusiastic sailor, had elected to travel on *Trekka*. Cecilia was wearing a lei of Frangipani, a rope of flowers and a grass skirt over her dress. Being triply chaperoned, she was free to roll her dark eyes at John who, alas, was on another boat.

It was stuffy and crowded under the cabin roof, so Beryl, Clio, and I made our way along the narrow strip of deck at the side of the cabin to the small foredeck. The launch was very tender and when Cecilia tried to follow, she (perhaps intentionally) slipped off into the water; there she floated on her back, like the maid of Shalot, surrounded by flowers and grass. John and Lino pulled her out and their combined weight with Cecilia in her water-logged condition must have been nearly eight hundred pounds. Beryl and I were astonished at how *Trekka* stood up to this with no undue heel.

To pick up our tow again, our helmsman circled and came up on *Trekka* from astern with the customary dash displayed by people who handle motor-boats. The Tongan crewman stood on the stern of the launch and took the line from John as we passed, travelling at four knots at least. He stood there grinning, holding the line in his hands and waiting for it to come taut. When it did, I have never seen a man fly through the air with such ease. For a moment his body was quite horizontal above the water before he fell into it. John picked him up, too, and we went on our way with Cecilia smiling contentedly as she dried off in *Trekka*'s cockpit.

There is, of course, a story about Mariner's Cave. It is said that a Tongan fisherman fell in love with a Chief's daughter, but since he was a commoner he was not allowed to marry her. One day the Chief's daughter disappeared and a great hue and cry ensued, but without result. It was seen, however, that the fisherman left his village every night, after hauling his boat up on the beach. One evening he was followed along devious paths to the edge of a cliff, where his dog was found waiting. An all-night watch was set, and in the morning the fisherman suddenly appeared in the sea below the cliff. He was taken before the Chief and confessed that the daughter was hidden in a cave reached by an underwater passage; the daughter was recaptured then she and her lover were put to death. I believe, however, that this is not a true story, but that they were forgiven and lived happily ever afterwards, catching and cooking many fish for the Chief's dinner. No doubt the ending as now told is a perversion of the truth, caused by the missionaries whom I also blame for the black umbrellas—why not gay sun-shades?—and the fact that Tongan girls bathe fully dressed.

We anchored off the cafe, whose dark and ominous entrance could be seen about nine feet under water. Then we put on fins and goggles, plucked up our courage and jumped in. A one-armed Tongan fisherman called Benny was our guide. He had once lit the fuse on a stick of dynamite and then become so interested in the movement of the fish he was after that he had forgotten to throw it. However, on this occasion he dived and we followed in turn, with the soles of his feet flapping close in front of our noses through a long dark tunnel. Knowing that I could not surface while in the tunnel made me more than usually conscious of my need for air and it was with great relief that I saw the feet turn upwards. A moment later I followed and broke the surface in a flash of blue flame.

He brought Clio through next, after a hesitant start, and then Beryl. John, who had already been through, came by himself.

The cave was about forty feet across and thirty feet high and we could climb up slippery rocks at the back to a rocky pulpit. From there we could see the distorted shapes of the swimmers as they came through before they surfaced in a splash of blue. The tunnel was the only source of light; every wave and splash shone with this sapphire light which illuminated the cave. Swimming in the pool, I felt like plum pudding surrounded by burning brandy. Whatever air that was in the cave had to come from the water, for there was no outlet. As the swells rolled against the cliff outside they increased the pressure in the cave, so that it could be felt in the ears and vision was momentarily distorted.

The last to arrive was a group of swimmers that seemed to fill the passage with strange shapes. It turned out to be Benny and Lino with the crew from the boat, all hauling Cecilia on her back, still dressed in gown, grass and flowers.

It was a cave of high spirits, partly because of its wonderful beauty, and partly because everyone was welcomed with shouts of delight and had to make some expression themselves at having overcome their dislike for the unnatural dive into Stygian gloom. Going out is easy; ahead is the bright light of day and the knowledge that you can make the passage. Going in is hard; the day is left behind and darkness lies ahead.

A few days after John had left for New Zealand, *Tzu Hang* sailed from Neiafu for Nukualofa, the capital of the Tongan Islands, on the island of Tongatapu. During the night Beryl awoke me. "Looks like a terrific squall coming down on us," she told me, but through the binoculars I discovered it to be the high crater of Kao, its top buried in cloud, which we were passing. Next we passed Tofua, seeing little of it, but smelling the sulphurous fumes from its crater that came to us through the night. This is the island on which Captain Bligh landed for water after being put off H.M.S. *Bounty* in the long boat, before making his four-thousand-mile voyage to Timor.

In the morning we passed Falcon Island, which, in a strange pulsation of the sea bottom, sometimes appears and then disappears. On its most recent appearance, Prince Tungi, now the King of Tonga, had landed and planted a Tongan flag, officially claiming it as Tongan territory. Its emergence had not lasted for long, and we could see no sign of it, nor even discoloured water, when we passed. We found the buoy marking the entrance to the main channel leading into the harbour at Nukualofa without difficulty and the passage through the reefs was well-marked.

For some reason, my engine was out of order again, but we were able to sail in and anchor in seven fathoms off the pier. The harbour master, who was also the quarantine officer and the postmaster, was a most unwelcoming Dutchman. He ordered us off and told us to anchor a mile off shore before dark. The light breeze that had brought us in had completely stopped, so I told him we would have to wait for the land breeze to take us out. In my subsequent years of sailing I have come to suspect harbour masters, quarantine officers and customs officers who combine their duty with that of postmaster; it seems to develop a paranoia. If I have anything to pass on to yachtsmen other than the advice not to lie a-hull in a really bad storm, it would be to treat such multipotent officials with distrust. Eventually we managed to persuade him to lend us his launch to tow *Tzu Hang* to an anchorage a mile away from the shore but still under the protection of the reef. There, *Tzu Hang* had to anchor in seventeen fathoms, and it took every inch of chain that we had on board to make her safe, and I wondered how we would ever get it all up again.

After an excellent night we rowed ashore, a long, long row; then walked down the waterfront and round behind the white wooden palace with its red roofs to the British Consul's house. As we passed the palace garden we hoped to see the old tortoise that Captain Cook had given to Queen Salote's ancestor; it was then alive, and perhaps would be alive still if he had not been caught in a grass fire a few years ago. He was not on view.

The Consul and his wife, Mr. and Mrs. Knott, insisted that we should spend a night with them and later Prince Tungi came out to see us on *Tzu Hang*. The kindness of the Knotts and the honour of Prince Tungi's visit eradicated the unwelcome feeling that the harbour master had given us. The Prince travelled, when not in his launch, in a London taxi, which, because of his princely size, he considered to be the most suitable vehicle for getting in and out. He was a charming and regal person to have on board and enthralled us with tales of his underwater diving, for he was a skilled skin-diver.

After fixing the cat and the dog with a suitable supply of available rations and leaving them on board, with *Tzu Hang* swinging at the end of her long anchor chain, we spent a night with the Knotts and drove next day to see the bay in which Captain Cook was said to have anchored. We also saw a large stone arch or doorway made of three huge stones, one across two uprights and morticed together like something from Stonehenge. No one knew their origin. There was really not much to see in Tongatapu and nothing to compare with Mariner's Cave, so having seen what we could we were eager to get off. The anchor came up with less trouble than we expected, with me hauling in the chain locker while Clio and Beryl were on the winch. *Tzu Hang* slid along the edge of the reef under her headsails, and as soon as the main and mizzen were set we sailed in to wave good-bye to the Knotts. There was a light breeze and *Tzu Hang*'s bow hissed through the calm lagoon. It was Sunday morning. All was silent in the bright little village except for the stupendous bellowing of the Tongans that came to us across the water as they sang a hymn at morning service. We did not know which particular sect was responsible, but no doubt others were already priming their lungs and pumping their organs for a retaliatory chorus. We gybed and with the wind right behind slid out through the darker blue of the channel, the reefs showing yellow and brown or bright aquamarine on each side. As soon as she had cleared the reef, *Tzu Hang* was close-hauled on the port tack, course west-south-west for Russel in the Bay of Islands, just over a thousand miles away.

Tzu Hang passed well to the west of Ata and on May 21 was east of Minerva Reef and making good progress; but for the following three days, she had only light head winds and there was every indication that we were running out of the trades. We had planned to visit the Kermadecs on our way if wind and weather permitted, although the best plan for a yacht is to make good her westing before she gets into the westerlies. On the night before we reached the Kermadecs I looked out of the hatch and saw that the full moon was almost totally eclipsed. I awoke Beryl and Clio, who were not especially impressed, and were asleep again before it was over. I had a primitive urge to beat drums and blow conches until it was back to normal again.

Meanwhile, the glass was falling, and presently a wind got up from the north-west. It was our first experience of the arrival of a depression in southern seas. Soon we were reefed down with the wind still freshening. We passed the Kermadecs, but I no longer felt inclined to stop, particularly as I was unsure whether the anchorage would be tenable or landing possible. Cruising is full of missed opportunities like this. Most islands can provide a sheltered side and depressions pass. It is unlikely now that Beryl and I will ever set foot on the Kermadecs.

All the next day we were close-hauled on the port tack, and on May 27 the wind was fresh from the south, cold and with clear skies. *Tzu Hang* crossed the date line and there was a lot of counting on the fingers to decide what day it was. We decided that it was Monday instead of Sunday, and time for lessons, at which there were howls of dismay. Somehow, Sunday at sea always felt like a Sunday, and Beryl always gave us something special to eat. We decided to have our Sunday and make the next day Tuesday.

On the 30th, *Tzu Hang* was becalmed in the morning, and in the evening there were a number of heavy squalls hanging round and a strange green light suffused the sky, almost as if we were under water. The glass was very low and I had a feeling that we were in for some cyclonic disturbance. A fresh wind came up from the north that night and by morning we were becalmed again with a very heavy and irregular swell from the north. The glass was still as low as I had ever seen it, and our glass was usually optimistic. There was nothing to do but to take down sail, when *Tzu Hang* rolled abominably and once fell off a swell to put her rail under; she scooped up a lot of water and emptied some of it down the hatch on to the cat. It was the only time that I ever knew her to do this, but then this was the only time that we were ever in such a windless and irregular sea. In the afternoon, the wind came from the south-west, clear and cold and, though the glass remained low, the oppressing feeling was gone of danger lurking somewhere not too far away.

The next day was glorious sailing. The sun was shining, white caps were all around, and our wake showed for half a cable behind us. For the first time we saw an albatross and soon we were escorted by several. Clio, down below, sounded as happy as a lark. She seemed almost a stranger, she had grown up so much on this trip. We had only 260 miles to go at noon, and the voyage for the time being seemed almost over. The following morning the glass was down again and the wind was from the north-west. Changing a jib in the afternoon, Beryl said to me, "Hello. There's Cape Brett." Somehow it didn't seem as exciting as other land-falls; but there it was, green and low, showing over a rough sea and below cloudy skies. We hove-to a few miles off the light and set off next day beating in to Russel. Whatever course I took, the wind headed me; it would have been much better if we had stayed out a little longer where we had spent the night. Nightfall found us almost back at the same place and it was not until the following morning that we were able to sail right in between the green hills and to find *Trekka* at anchor off the pier.

Starting in Hawaii, and from time to time in different anchor-ages, we had discussed with John the possibility of making a passage with *Tzu Hang* round Cape Horn. John told us that if we decided to do it, he would leave *Trekka* and make the passage with us. The correspondence course was not going well and we felt that it was time for Clio—poor Clio—to go to school again. Now it was decided. Clio was to go to school in England after we had reached Australia. John would ship with us and rejoin *Trekka* after the Cape Horn passage. While John shipped with us, Francis Arledge, the well-known marlin and shark fishing guide, offered to look after *Trekka* in Russel. In August he unbolted her keel on the beach and then floated her off on the next tide. She was taken to a berth ashore. *Tzu Hang* sailed down to the Bay of Plenty, when we had one night of high wind but otherwise lovely weather.

On the way back to Auckland we had a gale in the Gulf of Hauraki and cracked the main boom. We hove-to for an anxious night, feeling very land-girt, as I did not want to enter a strange port with a strong following wind in miserable visibility.

We came in next morning and tied on to a buoy off the yacht club. I took the dinghy in and put ashore a rather seasick passenger who had come with us from Tauranga. Then I wrote my name in the yacht club book and met various members. John was with me and I am sure remained silent while I, with that masterly under-statement that the British are supposed to be so practised in, left the impression that I was one hell of a sailor. Perhaps I was beginning to think that I was.

In fact, I was a sailor in that I both loved and feared the sea in all its moods; I was a good enough navigator, while I loved and had great confidence in *Tzu Hang*, whom I could handle well at sea. I could knot and splice and fulfil the normal duties of a seaman; but in handling *Tzu Hang* in close waters, which Beryl disliked, or in coming up to buoys, I was still somewhere near the novice class. I was also a thoroughly bad mechanic, although usually able to get the engine to go unless the batteries were dead.

The Vice-Commodore kindly suggested that I should bring *Tzu Hang* in to his mooring as his own yacht, with most of the other yachts, was still on the club hard. "You'll recognise it," he said. "It's a black buoy with a Vice-Commodore's pennant on it. You'll be much more comfortable there and nearer the shore; but make sure that you pick it up on your way down, as there is an underwater rock beyond it, and you will have the tide and wind behind you."

I thanked him, and John and I went off to make the transfer. Meanwhile, more members were arriving and migrating to the club verandah to see the British yacht come down to the mooring. Not only was the tide running strongly, but the wind, the relic of the night's gale, was still fresh in the channel. I was going to send John off with a coil of rope to make fast to the mooring, and then to row up to meet us well up-stream. With the end of a rope fast to the mooring, tide or no tide, I felt that we would be in control of the situation, and I did not want a foul-up in front of the club.

"You two have been out," Beryl said, "and I need some exercise. I'll go. What does the buoy look like?"

"You'll recognise it easily," I told her. "It's somewhere near that motor-boat. A black buoy with a black tin Vice-Commodore's pennant."

The engine was started and we were just going to move away when Beryl arrived back and I could see that she was angry. "I can't see the bloody Vice-Commodore's mooring," she said. When she is in this condition, fortunately a rare one, there is no point in arguing or explaining. "All right," I said. "You take *Tzu Hang* and I'll fix the buoy."

We made a rapid change and it was soon obvious why Beryl had not seen the mooring. The tide was running so strongly now that the buoys were under water and the pennants lying flat. I knew roughly where it was and the first ripple that I selected turned out to be the Vice-Commodore's mooring. I made fast to the chain and started rowing up to *Tzu Hang* and paying out the rope. All was going well, but I had forgotten that that very morning I had noticed that the nut had come off the bolt which attaches the gear lever fork to the gear box arm, and that, although I had intended to replace it, I had not done so.

Tzu Hang seemed to be coming down on me a little fast, helped by the wind and the tide. I could see her engine exhaust and expected Beryl to put her astern and slow down so that I might pass up the rope and come on board. Suddenly she seemed to be almost on me.

"Steady on!" I shouted. "Put her astern!"

Tzu Hang seemed to rush on inexorably.

"Astern!" I shouted. "Astern!"

The engine roared and *Tzu Hang* seemed to leap forward. I caught hold of the bobstay and the sudden drag pulled me out of the dinghy and capsized it, at which it disappeared under *Tzu Hang*, leaving me clinging to the bobstay. I cannot pretend that from this position I was any longer in command of *Tzu Hang*. Beryl switched off and stormed up the deck.

"He says, 'Astern'," cried John.

"I don't care what he says. I've done all I can," said Beryl.

A sixty-five-pound anchor flashed past my head and the chain rattled out and stopped. *Tzu Hang* swung like a polo pony, narrowly missing the motor cruiser, and brought up all standing, her anchor firmly hooked in the Vice-Commodore's chain. John dived below, leaving me to my fate. "One look at her face was enough," he explained later.

I discovered that Beryl had turned *Tzu Hang* and had come down at slow ahead. It must have been then that the bolt fell out and the gear lever became unattached to the gear box. When she put *Tzu Hang* astern there was no reaction, when she accelerated to stop her, the boat forged ahead. Fortunately Beryl had the presence of mind to switch off. Of course, we could not discuss these details for some time, and the members of the yacht club who had watched these extraordinary proceedings were good enough not to mention them. The dinghy was recovered later on, unhurt from the yacht club beach.

We spent a little longer than we had intended in Auckland, as John made us a new boom to replace the one cracked in the Gulf of Hauraki. Meanwhile, the yachts on the hard beside the club piped shrilly in their rigging. Their singing made me restless, as they told of winds to come, and I thought of the Tasman crossing ahead. I didn't like the waiting and wanted to be off.

After spending a few days exploring the lovely sounds and anchorages of Great Barrier Island, we set sail for Sydney, 1,350 miles away, on September 28. We passed Cape Brett next morning and then found a stiff breeze from the north-west. *Tzu Hang* was unable to make any westing, so continued to the north, hoping for less wind and easier seas. On October 3 the weather had improved and we were making north-westward, close-hauled and with the genoa up, 200 miles north of North Cape. *Tzu Hang* was sailing herself and it was time for supper, the light already failing. All of us were below, Beryl was in the galley, John and I sitting on the seats below the hatch, and Clio in the cabin. We watched Beryl, hawk-eyed, and mouths watering, while she got dinner ready.

Presently I stood up and looked aft. Close behind us was a big yacht in a sea that through four days had been empty except for albatrosses; there was something familiar about it. It was the *White Hart* that we had said we might meet in Fiji. She came up to us with her engine going. "Had a job to catch you!" Tony shouted. "We'll come on board."

It was far too rough to bring the yachts alongside each other. *Tzu Hang* hove-to while Tony and Bridget, leaving their ship and child in the care of a man they had sailing with them, came over to us in their dinghy. "Trust a west coast fisherman to launch a dinghy in this sea," I said to Beryl. They were soon on board.

"Where are you bound?"

"Sydney. Where are you bound?"

"Bay of Islands."

"We've still got lots of your salmon."

"And we have lots of your meat. How extraordinary to meet you!"

The sea might have been our village.

And so on. The questions and answers flew backwards and forwards, and it was long after dark, with a bottle finished, before they signalled with a lamp to the *White Hart* and she stopped a short way away.

We watched them pull over the dark waves until they were safely on board, then we freed our sheets, shouted, "Good sailing!" to the weaving mast light, and set off in one direction while the *White Hart* set off in the other. We have never seen them again, although we hear of them. The marriage broke up and both are married again, while their fine ship, in which they had had so many adventures, as if in despair caught fire and was destroyed.

On October 5 and 6 we were again struggling against strong head winds and making very poor progress sixty miles south of Norfolk Island. It was cheering to hear from the radio reports that North Island was catching it, with gale force winds and storm damage, while a large complex depression was stretching right across the Tasman. Two days of good sailing, and then we were becalmed in warm weather; but soon we were at it again with another three days of head winds. On the 12th we hove-to off Lord Howe Island, whose high peaks were lost in cloud, hoping that it would be fine enough to enter the lagoon next day, but next morning the surf on the small beach north-east of the island was too rough for landing. We sailed down the west side along the reef, but the landmarks were obscured by squalls and the low cloud made it difficult to pick out the shallows. It would have been foolhardy to attempt the entrance, which is narrow and difficult; the depths left little to spare, and also there was a wreck on the reef by the entrance. I decided to set off for Sydney and I don't think that anyone objected.

Five days later we sighted the Australian coast north of Sydney. There was no wind and an oily sea; dark, thirsty clouds groped ant-eater snouts towards the water, and beneath these questing noses the water whirled and rippled like shoals of frightened small fish. We did not actually see cloud link with water to form a waterspout; at times the disturbance on the water passed close to us, making the sails flop over, but apart from the rather eerie sensation of being below these groping, thirsty clouds, nothing alarming happened. Presently the welcome wind chased these strange clouds away and we set a course for Sydney. I failed to allow sufficiently for the south-setting current, and next morning we found ourselves becalmed off Botany Bay. Beryl and I bathed while John sat on the doghouse roof armed with my rifle, on the look-out for sharks. When I climbed out he gave it to me. I took out the magazine and snapped the trigger.

"But it wasn't loaded!" protested John.

"I don't think he had any great faith in your marksmanship," explained Beryl. If so, it was the only aspect of John in which I hadn't.

With a fresh wind we sailed in past the weather-worn heads that had watched so many ships sail in from afar. We had heard that the quarantine and customs officials in Australia were very objectionable. A big launch was soon alongside and two smartly uniformed officers boarded us.

"There's so much paper," they explained. "Suppose we go below and we'll fill in the forms for you."

"You don't want to stay here," said one. "Let's tow you up to Rushcutter's Bay. That's a nice place."

A large Italian liner was just docking. Now she blew on her horn.

"There's that emigrant ship ready for us," said the younger.

"Ah, she can wait," replied the other. "This is more interesting."

At anchor in Rushcutter's Bay when ready to go ashore and arrange for Clio's passage to England, I had a moment to think of the future. During my watch on the previous night, I had switched on the radio and heard a new tune. A girl was singing, "Qué sera sera, whatever will be will be". It became a theme tune for our stay in Australia, our subsequent voyage across the Southern Ocean, and our time in Chile. A writer reviewing the story of that journey said, "If only the cat had known of what was going to be, she'd have jumped ship in Melbourne."

"I wonder where we'll all be this time next year," said Clio, in a process of thought transference.

"Hopefully in England," Beryl replied, and so in the end we were—a little late and after various adventures—cat and dog and *Tzu Hang* all included.